Random Reflections

First Edition	2004
Reprint	2008
Reprint	2011
Reprint	2015
Reprint	**2019**

Random Reflections

Justice V.R. Krishna Iyer
Former Judge, Supreme Court of India

Universal
LexisNexis®

LexisNexis®

This book is a publication of **LexisNexis**®
(A Division of RELX India Pvt Ltd)
14th floor, Building No 10, Tower-B, DLF Cyber City, Phase-II,
Gurgaon-122002, Haryana, India.
Tel : + 91 124 4774444 Fax: + 91 124 4774100
Website : www.lexisnexis.co.in / E-mail : help.in@lexisnexis.com

---

Justice V.R. Krishna Iyer, *Random Reflections*

ISBN: 978-81-7534-400-6

Printed at Replika Press Pvt. Ltd.

CONTENTS

- A Special Note on Parole Jurisprudence and Narcotic Convicts 1
- Inhumanity on Adivasi and their Rehabilitative Strategy—A Kerala Fiasco 5
- Christian Personal Laws in Chaos 13
- College Campus Politics—Nocent or Innocent? 16
- Constitution of India—The Nation's Safety Valve 21
- Constitutional Amendments in India 27
- Indian Casualties as Substitutes for American Cadavers in Occupied Iraq? No 29
- Indian Policing—Some Social Dimensions 33
- Information Explosion—A Vision Statement 45
- Marad Massacre—A National Alarum 52
- Transnational Corporations and Piracy of Ayurvedic Heritage 57
- People's Commission on Perversion of our Patent Laws 61
- Some New Light on Constitutional Law—A Review 66
- The Marad Impasse—Omnious Portent 69
- Blanket Ban on Strikes by Labour—A Judicial Excess? 73
- Gujarat and Marad—Is Indian Secularism A Charade or A Soul under Siege 81
- Mata Amritanandamayi—A Votarist Salutation 92
- Two Constrasting Visionaries 94
- Random Reflections on our Ancient Cultural Treasury 107
- A Democratic Defeat without Personal Disappointment 117
- A National Judicial Commission—A Command for Reforms 131
- A Vibrant Vision and Militant Mission 141
- Numerological Nostrum for Pathological Procrastination of the Judicature 154
- Parliamentary Privileges, People's Freedoms and Judicial Invigilation 161
- The Jurisprudence of Constitutional Camaraderie among the Great Institutions 169

- A Case for National Prison Policy 182
- Animal Citizen 186
- Humanitarian Law—A Halting History of Global Evolution 201
- Humanitarian Jurisprudence within the Parameters of a Global Democratic Order 212
- *Wounded Nature* vs. *Human Future* 227
- Plachimada Patriotism—Toxicola Terrorism 260
- Rabindranath Tagore—The Assessment of A Visionary 268

A SPECIAL NOTE ON PAROLE JURISPRUDENCE AND NARCOTIC CONVICTS

The criminal justice system has moved away from its harsher Draconian days to the reformatory humanitarian present. The parole process has been conceived of as a progressive device to humanise prisoners and reward them for good institutional conduct by a conditional release subject to procedural safeguards and obligation to return to prison. Penological confusion used to prevail that parole was like suspension of sentence. But this is a fallacy as the Supreme Court of India has explained in *Dadu* (2000) 8 SCC 437. The court categorically states:

> *6. Parole is not a suspension of the sentence. The convict continues to be serving the sentence despite granting of parole under the statute, rules, jail manual or the Government Orders. "Parole" means the release of a prisoner temporarily for a special purpose before the expiry of a sentence, on the promise of good behaviour and return to jail. It is a release from jail, prison or other internment after actually being in jail serving part of sentence.*
>
> *7. Grant of parole is essentially an executive function to be exercised within the limits prescribed in that behalf. It would not be open to the court to reduce the period of detention by admitting a detenu or convict on parole. The court cannot substitute the period of detention either by abridging or enlarging it. Dealing with the concept of parole and its effect on period of detention in a preventive detention matter, this Court in Poonam Lata* v. *M.L. Wadhawan held: (SCC p.354, para 8)*
>
> *It is a provisional release from confinement but is* deemed to be a part of the imprisonment. *Release on parole is a wing of the* reformative process *and is expected to provide opportunity to the prisoner to transform himself into a useful citizen. Parole is thus a grant of partial liberty of lessening of restrictions to a convict prisoner, but release on parole does not*

change the status of the prisoner. Rules are framed providing supervision by parole authorities of the convicts released on parole and in case of failure to perform the promise, the convict released on parole is directed to surrender to custody.

Grant of parole is essentially on executive function Sethi, J. has clarified: 'parole has become an integral part of the English and American system of criminal justice intertwined with the evolution of changing attitude of the society towards crime and criminal'. The penal system now considered release on licence i.e., parole as an executive function.

In a Constitution Bench decision of the Supreme Court, the precise connotation in law of parole has been elucidated; 'parole ameliorates punishment by permitting convict to serve sentence outside the prison wall, but parole does not interrupt sentence'. During parole period there is no suspension of sentence, but the sentence is actually continuing to run during that period also".

Representations were made to the High Level Committee on Parole and Remission by certain aggrieved narcotics, praying for release on parole, notwithstanding section 32A of the Narcotic Drugs and Psychotropic Substances Act, 1985. They pointed out, and rightly, that they may be considered for release on parole since the Indian court 'in recent years made orders of release on parole on humanitarian condition'. In *Dadu*, after explaining the legal concept of parole as distinguished from bail or suspension of sentence the court, made an observation with lovely and lucent clarity.

> *It is thus clear that* parole did not amount to the suspension, *remission or commutation of sentences* which could be withheld under the garb of Section 32A of the Act. *Notwithstanding the provisions of the offending section,* a convict is entitled to parole, *subject however, to the conditions governing the grant of it under the statue, if any, or the jail manual or the government instructions. (2000) 8 SCCP-444 Para 11)*

Narcotic sentencees cannot, therefore, be denied parole since the court has stated, with specific reference to section 32A of the Act, 'notwithstanding the provision of the offending section, a convict is *entitled to parole,* subject, however, to relevant conditions governing the grant of it under the statute, if any, in the jail manual or Government instruction. One thing that follows from this crucial dictum of the court is that a narcotic convict has an equal title to parole which is a compassionate consideration. There is no specific statutory provision forbidding *parole* to narcotics.

The present 32A of the Act had ostensibly persuaded the Kerala Government to deny parole to narcotic prisoners. The rule is obviously the offshoot of the Act. Now that the Supreme Court has gone to the extent of striking down that part of 32A, which deprives judicial power to grant bail and *a fortiori* the grant of parole is an *entitlement*, subject to other conditions, the jail manual must be read down and the ban on parole to narcotic convicts deemed non est. With the tree falls the branch. In the light of the court ruling, denial of parole on the score that the prisoner is a sentencee under the Narcotic Act no longer holds good. The humanitarian philosophy of parole equally applies to this category of prisoners, especially after Dadu. If there be doubt, its benefit belongs to Freedom as parole, as a process is geared to a reformative goal.

Rule 452 BB (vi) deserves to be deleted now that the Supreme Court has spoken and the survival of the negation of parole to narcotic convicts is no longer sustainable. We recommend to Government repeal or deletion of that sub-rule and act as if the bar has been dropped. However, the other conditions regarding emergency leave and regular parole require compliance since the guidelines prescribed for grant of parole are just, fair and reasonable. There is a measure of discretion, within the parameters of the parole rules, vested in the executive; but arbitrariness on the part of the executive is allergy to the Constitution. Therefore care must be taken to comply with the remaining conditions that apply to all parolees most apply to narcotic convicts. It is unjust and arbitrary to reject parole *solely* because he is a narcotic convict. Since reformation is the object of parole there is no reason to differentiate between a narcotic convict and other criminal convicts. Articles 14 and 21 make it just, fair and reasonable to obliterate the narcotic invidiousness *vis a vis* parole decision.

Criteria for granting or denying parole and the terms of parole have been indicated in *Maru Ram's* case and in the extant jail rules as of now. This point needs emphasise because, among the various points in the criminal justice process, no point offered more opportunity for abuse and arbitrary exercise than parole release decisions. The courts do not take a "hands off" attitude towards such executive decision as is evident from the recent ruling of the recent Kerala High Court leading to the setting up of the High-level Committee.

Even in the United States, since the early 1970's; there has been an explosion in case-law on the parole release decisions with potential promise far greater accountability in this process. Sufficiency of reasons or frivolous reasons or absence of reasons has been the subject of judicial scrutiny. Sheldon Krantz, in his classic work **Corrections and Prisoner's Rights** (P-299), writes thus:

The court determined that the reason was insufficient after applying this test:

> *Can such a reason be so meaningful that a reviewing court can determine whether the Board has adopted and followed criteria that are appropriate, rational and consistent, and does it protect the inmate against arbitrary and*

capricious decisions or actions based upon impermissible considerations? 389 F.Supp. at 409.

Thus, it appears that the giving of reasons requires both explicit criteria and facts indicating why the criteria were applied in a given way. This area obviously is in need of further development, however. It is clear that the giving of very general or abstract reasons would result in Childs amounting to a meaningless victory.

In sum, the notion that parole is grace of the Executive has been eroded by decisions of the Supreme Court of the U.S., and the *constitutional right of the parolee,* when it touches his freedom, attracts procedural due process. Finally, the State always must remember that parole is a kind quasi-imprisonment geared to the ultimate object of humanization and socialization of a person under incarceration. Here the narcotic stands in the same footing as any other convict.

INHUMANITY ON ADIVASI AND THEIR REHABILITATIVE STRATEGY—A KERALA FIASCO

The adivasi humanity of Kerala, as elsewhere, humble in numbers, homeless have-nots in status with negligible political clout and live in landless despair. The rule of law blinks at them and politicians of all parties betray them. This micro-community a little over one per cent. of the Kerala population, is victim of social deprivation, dubious promises and dishonourable existence. Are they Indians? Yes. Are they forest dwellers from ancient days? Yes. What is their distressing status today? *De facto* dishonoured by the State and *de jure* proffered jungle slices which do not exist these tribal communities are refugees without territory, not even a trace of what once belonged to them. The law plays hide and seek with these 'specially favoured' children of the Constitution. Driven by despair these less miserables have began to dare to demand rights. This militant mood may explode justly every day heedless of Khaki fury unless the adivasi land question is settled with justice, equity and good conscience weaving a jurisprudence which treats tribals as humans with title to survival. Kerala is an advanced State and if their destiny is terrorised travail, their lot in other parts of the country must be more pathetic. From a pan-Indian angle the current Kerala tribal crisis is an event and portent.

Adivasis are mostly *vanavasis*, forest-dwellers. They live in jungles, collect forest produce and own small cultivable lands, the green woods being their habitats. Their unlettered way of life, their naivete and artless ethos make them easy prey to exploitation by cunning settlers from the plains who rob the tribal proletariat of their patches, leaving these hoodwinked humans victims sans basic human rights, without which their survival is in conditions of shock and shame. The endemic social disease of alienation of adivasi holdings became an extermination operation too unconscionable for the State to tolerate without legislative intervention. So in action ceased to be an option.

In 1975 the Kerala legislature unanimously enacted The Kerala Scheduled Tribes (Restriction of Transfer of Lands and Restoration of Alienated Lands) Act. The legislation had a mission—the redemption of dispossessed, destitute tribals in distress. Had this Act been implemented with the social passion which drove the House into salvationary locomotion the tribal revolt which has now escalated into a mass upheaval could never have happened. Alas, this legislative manoeuver proved to be a dastardly double deception. It was the commission of a grave guilt, the corrupt culpability having tainted every political party. The tribal innocents were stabbed in the back by deliberate default in not notifying the law for years after being doped and duped by a statutory pretense of restoration of their gullibly alienated humble holdings. The people of the State who sympathised with the tribal proletariat were left with an illusion of land legislation which was allowed to slumber. The neo-settlers meanwhile developed the lands, defying the legislation and silencing Governments in turn by Fronts of *'radicals'* and *'democrats.'* In politics, nomenclature is Orwellian diction meaning the opposite of what it seems to say. Every party professed support, to adivasis; every party had opportunity to enforce the law while it was in office but not one did put back an acre of alienated land. The non-tribals settled on these lands, encroached on more neighbourhoods; and the forest-dwellers were disowned by the forests. To recover lost land from aliens and encroachers Government had to implement the law with passion for the cause, compassion for the powerless. The settlers, mostly Christian, had the Church with them. By their political numbers, well-organized under political flags, they could not be dislodged. The scattered adivasis, with a stillborn law in the statute book, had but futility and mockery. Imagine the seriousness of a Government which has been ruled by two rival Fronts, treating the law as all but dead. The rules were framed more than a decade later, and giving effect to them from January 1982 was mere jugglery with the calendar. The law was not implemented on the ground and so the adivasis wandered in the jungle with not a cent to claim as their own. Then came one Dr. P.Nallaambi Thera who filed O.P. No.8879/88 before the High Court seeking implementation of the Act. It is unfortunate that even the Marxist party-led government was guilty of insouciance. There were 8088 cases pending under the Act for restoration and yet orders were passed only in 1201 cases and alas, only in 3 cases actual restoration took place. The grossest contempt for the adivasi law and the adivasi right is thus loud and clear. Today the Left Front is violently vitriolic against the Congress government, but their performance while in power is a shameful chapter.

The High Court was more radical than the noisy political parties and directed Government to dispose off all pending restoration applications within a period of six months from 15-10-1993. The vocal socialism of all the parties, judged by their performance *vis a vis* the adivasi proletariat had lost the cosmetic crimson in practice. Despite the High Court directive, Government dawdled, delayed and deprived the tribals of their dues. Ultimately, the High Court ordered peremptory compliance. The lack of sincerity of the Left Front in power became manifest when instead of giving land under the 1975 Act as ordered by the High Court, a legislation largely scuttling the original Act was brought under guise of Amendment in 1996. The teasing illusion and promise of unreality held out to the adivasi ended with this Amendment. But a contradiction in history took place. The Marxist Bill was withheld assent by the President who was advised by the Congress Cabinet to do so. A student of dialectical materialism has much to explore in this curious anti-climax. The bankruptcy of socialist sympathy for the landless adivasi is evident from the fact that Government moved the High Court, time after time, to gain an opportunity to fulfill the obligations under the Act. Finally, the High Court granted time for Government to give right and justice to the tribal proletarian by 5-1-1999. Meanwhile, the dubious policy of the Government became apparent and a new bill, namely, the Kerala Restriction on Transfer by and Restoration of Land to Scheduled Tribes Bill 1999 was introduced before the Assembly. The tribals are political trivia, the settlers and the church and others who had seized adivasi land had tremendous political clout. Inevitably, the new bill of 1999 was enacted and the progressive bill of 1975 was repealed. The Meanwhile, litigative anfractuosities followed by petition in the High Court and the Supreme Court. Contempt proceedings were also instituted and the legal destiny of these proceedings depends on the final verdict of the appeal now pending in the Supreme Court.

A new chapter of nonviable commitments by the Chief Minister Antony of the UDF was made on 16th October, 2001 at a conference where Janu, a lady leader of the adivasis, took militant part. Five acres of land for every adivasi family as far as possible was the basic understanding. Wynad District is where the adivasis are hard hit in landless destitution. But Wynad Region is where under the 1971 Act vast extents of private forests were vested in the State compensation free. An affirmation was made that lands from these vested forests may be identified and allotted to landless adivasi folk, of course, after securing Central Government approval. The deplorable fact remains that most of the S.Ts are duped. The Kerala Private Forest Vesting and Assignment Act, 1971 was upheld as a measure of *agrarian reform.* Section ten of the Act obligate the State to assign vested forest land to property less tribals. In breach of the promise by the Chief Minister, and mindless of the constitutional urgency of land allotment after a procrastinated game of hide and seek, the State Government sought an option in inaction infuriating the tribal starvelings. Perhaps, the alibi was that a Central Forest Conservation Act was brought into force in 1980 and any assignment of forestland needed approval from the Central Government. Had the 1975 Act been implemented the 1980 unborn Central Act could hardly have been a hindrance. The problem now is to secure large extents of land to settle the landless wandering forest dwellers. The apparent impasse is not a deadlock, which cannot be surmounted, given the political will. Some measures which obviously occur may be considered in the context of the grave crisis which looms large over the whole State worked up with the confrontational fury of the adivasis escalating after the battle of Muthanga between the tribal intransigents and the police.

Who deprived the land of the tribals in yesteryears? The settlers from the plains mostly Travancoreans from the Christian belt. It is true they sold away their belongings at home and settled in large numbers dispossessing the tribal population by petty allurement and tricky operations. Gaining foothold, they expanded by encroachment. Of course, arriving with their culture and working hard on the hilly terrain they made improvements, cultivated crops, built homesteads, constructed schools and established churches. This civilising mission eclipsed the adivasi flock and the uprooted chunk of humanity became alien in their own land, desperate for source of survival and slaving for rightless existence. Historic justice may well warrant redistribution of lost land and rehabilitation of the rootless diaspora. The moral foundation of the 1975 Act is the re-taking from the aliens the alienated land for re-settlement but the intervening period of development where the settlers had, with blood and toil, added to the value of the land and created a new homeland became a reality which could not be wished away. At the same time the forlorn aboriginals ware a poignant territorial truth and morally and legally deserved re-instatement.

The obvious source of land for re-settling them was, therefore, re-taking reasonable slice from the plains people. Perhaps exceptions may have to be made to exclude from resumption church buildings, schools, essential community centers, and the like. Where there has been expansionist encroachment of adivasi land there is clear justification for evicting the occupants from such excess. There will be resistance, especially because the occupational community is politically powerful. Indeed the inexcusable delay of the State in implementing the 1975 Act and the legislative and the litigative strategies to undo the 1975 Act prove beyond reasonable doubt the culpable operations of the settlers over the goofy aboriginals. Today, when a crisis is brewing, the mood has to change, the mind- set has to become sterner and the commitment to restorative justice uncompromising. If this new locomotive of land redistribution were adopted without hanky-panky a substantial portion of land can be given back to the landless tribals.

Government can, on a warfooting, survey the encroachments, discover and recover the extra-land so occupied and, on just terms of compensation, give it back to the adivasi. Fifty committees spread all over Malabar *with adivasi representatives* and technical services of land surveyors can implement this operation in a few months time. Immediate orders must be passed vesting in the local tribals the encroached land. Will the Government, what with its commitment and legislative backing, undertake a blitz operation?

A brief chronicle of the tribal kinsman, with special reference to their habitant, may help understand the land grab victimisation and homeless helplessness which lead to adivasi desperation. Conditions became so distressing that in the 1950s the Dhebar Commission was appointed to go into the traumatic tribal situation. A land-mark report recommended legislation for prevention of alienation of tribal lands and restoration of alienated land back to the tribal. The states were dragging their feet because tribals were politically lightweight nitwits. However, during the Emergency, the Kerala Legislature enacted the 1975 Act a salvationary legislation which was a casualty in its implementation. However, the 'bio-diversity' charade was used as a new alibi to throw the tribals out of their natural habitats. Vested interests operate blowing up 'environment' to gain strangle-hold over forest land-eliminating aboriginals who have all along contributed as friends of the woods and integral part of forest preservation ethos. Indeed, the tribal human is part of bio-diversity and is its sentinel rather than its hostile. Based on this fundamental the Forest Policy Statement of 1988 was formulated, propounding the philosophy of 'symbiosis of tribal and forest', harmonising this duality. This ecological confluence of aboriginal and his forest milieu, if applied to Kerala adivasis and their arboreal haven, will happily resolve the present confrontation and clashes. The Forest Conservation Act, 1980 which is held out as a legislative taboo for the entry of tribals is an exaggerated hermeneutic distortion of the law rather than an embargo on user of forest as tribal habitat. There is an elitist antipathy in this interpretation. The welfare and survival of the tribal community resident in forests from ancient times is not considered by forest bureaucrats to be a 'forest purpose' under the 1980 Act, although construction of quarters, destruction of trees for provision of facility for comfortable official living, road and other amenities for the forest boses and echotourism are considered 'forest purpose'. To my mind, having read the 1980 Act and the explanation regarding forest purpose, I see no semantic sense in excluding the bare occupation of aboriginal in the wilds with an obligation to protect the trees, prevent braking up of the land and otherwise damaging the forest qua forest. The tribals can take the forest produce, live and watch against poachers and be the natural instrument of forest preservation. Joint committees with forest officials, tribal members and departmental watchdogs can be constituted in every forest to oversee forestry. The adivasi families may innocently live there, take natural forest produce and make a living without injury to the arboreal integrity. *No ownership* of forest may be given to the tribal, but the right to live there by leave and license, the right to take the customary forest produce and be on duty to see that wild animals do not destroy the forest and poachers do not trespass. Jaundiced environmentalism, which is allergic to tribal presence but is at home with game-hunters and personnel of Forest Departments, fussy environmentalists, professional photographers of wild life, and affluent holidayers in tours conducted by liberally staffed contingents of officials, agents and other hangers on Forest and Tourism Development Departments. Humanise your arboreal vision and viably operate the philosophy featured prominently in the 1988 Forest policy statement of *Symbiosis of Tribal and Forest*—do this creatively, and the adivasi is part of bio-diversity. Imagination is lacking in the bureaucrats when he reaches the definition of *'non-forest use'* in the 1980 Act with an uppish prejudice. In my humble submission, all the stranded adivasis of Kerala can be accommodated by adopting the above formula and constituting *joint management committees* with tribals and officials sitting together to guard our forests.

Large extents of forest were once private lands of Malabar landlords but were vested in the State by virtue of the Kerala Private Forests Vesting and Assignment Act, 1971. No compensation was provided and the High Court struck down the law as *ultra vires*. But the Supreme Court reversed the High Court, upheld the vesting on the score that it was an *agrarian reform measure.* Significantly the Supreme Court directed redistribution and assignment of half the vested lands to be assigned to landless tribal people, or exclusively to them in areas where they formed a substantial population. The court had cautioned that this re-distributive process should not remain a teasing illusion. If only this desideratum had been carried and diligently before the 1980 Forest Conversation Act there would have been no adivasi problem at all. This culpable failure has deprived the major stakeholder, namely the tribal, of his homeland. On the contrary, through various guidelines the State Government has declared these forests as reserved forests and sanctuaries for wild life preservation. Indeed, while driving out the tribals Government did not put into operation any massive afforestation programme. In recent times, there has been an explosive episode of land hungry adivasis trying to occupy whatever crumbs of land they could get but here the might of the State threw them out.

T. Madhava Menon, I.A.S., who had worked intimately among forest dwellers has narrated the chronicle of one police operation *vis a vis* the tribal population.

2.6.1. Kerala case. A glaring example of arbitrariness is seen in the Muthanga Forest, recently the scene of the violence against tribal people who had occupied portions of it. When the Nilgiri Biosphere Reserve was constituted, several forests falling within a pre-determined compass were included in it. In Muthanga, areas that had been clear-felled for planting eucalyptus for supply at subsidized prices to the defunct Gwalior Rayons Factory at Mavur near Calicut have also been included. This enterprise of planting eucalyptus failed and the area did not regenerate successfully with other species. It has been subject to annual fires, and is covered with Eupatorium and other weeds. But for administrative convenience, and for geographic contiguity, it has been included in the Reserve. It was this area that the tribal people occupied; they did so deliberately so that their occupation would cause the minimum ecological consequences, but the Government thought it was the unforgivable sin, and turned all their organized violence against the hapless tribal folk.

2.6.2. A larger significance. Nothing illustrates the validity of the thesis of symbiosis between tribal people and the forests better than the Muthanga case. The Forest Department had thoughtlessly clearfelled the area and planted eucalyptus there, an enterprise that failed. It had been unable to prevent annual fires, so that the natural vegetation could not re-establish itself. Even bamboo regeneration was not possible. The area became overrun with weeds. Obviously, it provided no forage or habitat suitable for a viable wild life population, except as a portion of migratory paths. The tribal people intuitively recognized the tract as one that required human presence and intervention for regeneration. Their occupation would inhibit wild life migration through the tract, and thus enable regeneration of some species that would otherwise invite browsing. The upper soil, hardened by repeated fires, could be broken up by human labour. The stage was set for the symbiosis of a human community capable of a technology of mild intervention so that the bio-productivity of the tract would be stored, if not to what was its original composition, to at least one of better value for humans and wild life than its present condition.

(Report on Tribal Land Rights)

The crying need of the hour is to give creative shape to tribal and forest in such manner that rehabilitation becomes a reality. One concrete proposal which I wish to place before the State legislature is to enact a Tribal Resettlement Act. This will have to be a case of carving out of vested forest under the 1971 Act necessary lands for providing tribal habitat. Forest is a subject in the Concurrent List of 7th Schedule of the Constitution. Therefore the State is well within its powers to legislate subject to Central assent. There is a good case to make. The Kerala State acquired vested forests under a statutory blitz which survived the Supreme Court scrutiny. In that very judgement the court had addressed itself to assignment of land to tribals. Secondly, there are Muthangas which are formally 'reserved forests or sanctuaries' but are woodless areas available for dwelling by adivasis. The best forests can be left intact but the marginal ones may be made available. Here again, my proposal is not to spare the neo-settlers and the Church who have grabbed lands in defiance of the 1975 Act. To evict them is a statutory duty that may not satisfy the entire needs of the tribals. That is why we must fall back on alternative resources of vested forests by special legislation. Humanism and compassion, history and geography, once seen in proper setting, will persuade the Central Government to the necessary constitutional assent. In the special project by way of legislation, sufficient conditions can be imposed to protect forest trees and to regenerate the fictitious forests, to inhibit damage to forests by wild animals and defend forests against poachers may also be Adivasi Rehabilitation Project. I would urge once again that Muthanga is more a message and a sign-post rather than an adivasi invasionary occupation as it is prejudicially presented. Operation Muthanga has a salvationary dimension.

Government must not lose a sense of priority in regard to land ownership. The first charge on land for sheer survival belongs to the aboriginal, the last claim, viewed from a value base, belongs to huge corporations. In Kerala, large (excessive) forest land for alleged plantation and other purposes are with Big Business like the Tatas, the Gwalior Rayons etcetara. Those lands must instantly be taken over by the State and made over for adivasi occupation. This will relieve the scarcity situation a great deal without tears. All that is needed is for Government and the people to decide on whose side they are—with the needy tribal or the greedy corporation.

CHRISTIAN PERSONAL LAWS IN CHAOS

Legislative colonialism dies hard in India. For instance, fifty five years after the bells of Independence tolled Indian Christian are still ruled largely by laws made in Great Briton in the nineteenth century. Thanks to the insouciant indolence of Parliament which finds time for 'parliamendemonium', if I may respectfully express my exasperation. In proof of my criticism of such inaction, I quote what the author Prasada Rao has said in his preface to his three-volume work titled Law Applicable To Christians in India:

> ***As far as Christians are concerned, the law relating to solemnization*** *of marriages is contained in the Indian Christian Marriage Act, 1872 and the Cochin Christian Civil Marriages Act, 1095; and the law relating to matrimonial causes is contained in the Converts' Marriage Dissolution Act, 1866 and the Indian Divorce Act, 1869, the latter being renamed as "the Divorce Act, 1969" in 2001.*
>
> *The Indian Christian Marriage Act, 1872 extends to the whole of India except the territories which comprise the State of Manipur and the State of Travancore and the former State of Cochin; and the Cochin Christian Civil Marriages Act, 1095 has been in force in the territories which comprised the former State of Cochin.*
>
> *There is no substantive law in the Indian Christian Marriage Act. It deals only with the form of solemnization of marriage and the substantive law relating to solemnization of marriages in respect of Christians is yet to be legislated.*
>
> *The provisions of the Indian Divorce Act were exact copies of the English Matrimonial Causes Act, 1857. The English law was amended in 1923 and 1937. But the corresponding amendments were not made in the Indian Divorce Act. (Vol.I)*

The Christian community is a small minority where consensus is not a difficult process and yet the Law Commission Reports which led to the Christian Marriage and Matrimonial Causes Bill, 1962 was allowed to lapse. The Christian community proffered a proposal for revision commanding consensus. The Ministry of Law prepared a bill *viz.* the Christian Marriage Bill, 2000, but nothing came out of it. The Indian Divorce (Amendment) Bill, 2000, a marginal measure, was enacted as the Indian Divorce (Amendment) Act, 2001. But there were several defects in that enactment, which remain unremedied even today. The author points out, "the law in the Indian Divorce Act goes back to its position in 1869". So in substantial measure, the British of old days still govern post-Independence-Indian Christian community. The author urges that the law relating to marriage be revised in such manner that it is at least as progressive as the Hindu Marriage Act and the Special Marriage Act.

Kande Prasada Rao, a Christian, has produced three tomes which are heavy in volume, but weighty in wisdom. The research that has gone into these prolix pages deserves commendation of a high order, especially because Mr. Rao is not a jurist by profession but has excelled jurisprudents by the massive work of which he can be proud. In the laudatory words of Justice Jeevan Reddy:

> *The author has also given texts of numerous judgments of different High Courts and the Supreme Court which have pointed out the defects in the Indian Divorce Act, exhorting the State to take necessary steps for the revision of the said Act.*
>
> *The most important part of this book is the proposals for revision in the form of two draft Bills, one for the solemnization of marriages and the other for the law relating to matrimonial causes.*

The daring publisher, Universal Law Publishing Company, among the foremost in the law publishing field and progressive in venturing to bring out rare legal literature of *avant garde* character has rightly enriched the *corpus juris* of India by his pioneering Prasad Rao volumes.

It used to be said of George Bernard Shaw that his pen produced a pennyworth of *play* and a poundworth of *preface*. Indeed, his luminous, lashing and acidly incisive prefaces excelled his powerful, socially surgical plays which were classics too high for praise. In the same strain, if I may say so with pardonable adaptation but without pejorative implication, the three-volume marvel of Prasad Rao has for its Foreword a superbly informative and creatively critical contribution by Justice K.T.Thomas which, in itself, is an excellent piece in Christian legal literature. Justice Thomas is at his lucent best in his indignant assessment of the failure of the Parliament in retaining on the statute book, Christian Family Law which 'survives after death'. Perhaps, it is fair that I allow the learned judge to speak his thoughts in his own words:

The Indian Divorce Act should have been revised soon after the enactment of the Hindu Marriage Act in 1955. But that was not done. The Marriage Laws (Amendment) Act, 1976 which revised the Hindu Marriage Act and the Special Marriage Act did not touch the law applicable to Christians. The Indian Divorce Act was not revised along with the Parsi law when the latter was revised in 1988. Consequently, the law relating to matrimonial causes in respect of Christians remains as it was enacted in 1869, in spite of thorough revisions made in the law applicable to the other religious communities.

The Supreme Court of India and Full Benches of different High Courts held, on different occasions, that some of the provisions in the Indian Divorce Act violate the Fundamental Rights ensured in Articles 14, 15 and 21 of the Constitution of India and directed that the Union of India should take immediate necessary action for the revision of the law in the Indian Divorce Act to bring it in tune with the law in the Hindu Marriage Act and the Special Marriage Act, and reminded of the directive in Article 44 of the Constitution of India that the State shall endeavour to enact a Uniform Civil Code for all the citizens of India. Yet the attempts made in that line remained where they started at.

Erudite and instructive messages from four judges of the Supreme Court (three retired and one still on the bench) adds to the value of the volumes. Sri. Soli Sorabjee, that liberal battler for human rights, has called Prasad Rao's work as "monumental" and he is right and justified in his statement. The Universal Law Publishing Company with its unique success in merited publicity, will surely reach the books widely so as to find a place for them in every library, especially in the personal libraries of those who are concerned with family laws. I wish the adventurous and industrious Prasad Rao, a lucubrative dalit scholar, a lasting name in Indian jurisprudence.

COLLEGE CAMPUS POLITICS—NOCENT OR INNOCENT?

The academic discipline which describes and analyses the operations of the Government, the State and other political organisations and any other factors which influence their behaviour, such as social and economic, in short, a study as to *how* power is exercised, and *by whom* (and for whose benefit), through the administration of public power, of people's affairs may perhaps be described as politics, a great concern of every intelligent member of society. Albert Einstein has observed: "It is the duty of every citizen according to his best capacity to give validity to his conviction in political affairs". The ignorance of politics among the masses of a country paves the way for the rise of tyranny and the fall of democracy. The right to govern belongs to every citizen and so political science can never be alienated from the concern of the community which ultimately secures for the citizenry justice, liberty, equality, dignity of the individual and the integrity of the nation. It is a grave default, therefore, to deny to the population at any level the right and, indeed, the duty to acquire a basic knowledge of local, national and global political forces. It is a gravamen of injustice and goofy understanding of public affairs to command that political science shall be anathema in a college campus since, in the last analysis, such allergy amounts to an advocacy of political illiteracy, social insensitivity and cultural philistinism. The grammar of politics, in an enlightened sense, is the birthright of every member of our polity which is a sovereign, socialist, secular, democratic, republic as India is and shall be. The great guardian of the rights of the people in a Republic is an enlightened youth educated in the various dimensions and instruments of political science such as the legislature and the judicature. Indeed, the right to vote vested in everyone *at an age of eighteen* becomes a meaningful operation if only the exercise of franchise is an expression of political wisdom. In the finest sense of the word, politics must be obligatorily a subject of learning inside every college campus which owes allegiance to the Constitution and its Preambular Pledge. 'We, the People of India'—the first five words of our Constitution—have made a revolutionary resolution to defend the politics of the Constitution. Winston Churchill once defined and defended the ballot process which every judge and administrator must constantly remember: "A little man, walking into a little booth, with a little pencil, making a little cross on a little bit of paper—no amount of rhetoric or discussion can possibly diminish the overwhelming importance of the point". Be politically educated at age eighteen or be damned as dumb-driven cattle in a dying democracy.

There is a judicial impression among the robed brethren in India that politics is a vice like alcoholism or drug addiction and therefore be banned or ostracized as a mischief or menace, pathologically spreading as a dangerous syndrome in our institutions of higher learning. A division bench of the Kerala High Court, gave a ruling which through the media was popularly interpreted as a toxic tendency of student politics in college campuses which has to be curbed or tabooed for salvation of education. Professor J.A.G. Griffith in his powerful book The Politics of the Judiciary has argued: 'judges are human with human prejudice.........some are more human than others' and considered right wing opinion as an occupational bias of the *British* judicial profession. Surely, the Indian judiciary of which I had been a member for some years, is made of more liberal staff, more democratic ethos, more progressive eidos.

The Kerala judges in the Sojan Francis case held against the nineteen year old undergraduate, a member of the SFI, on the ground of inadequate number of days of attendance necessary as a qualification for taking the examination. This would have disposed off the matter. But the court, on the score of political importance, launched on a long discussion about the constitutionality of prohibiting political activity altogether within the college campuses. The college concerned, St. Thomas College, Palai, has certain guidelines regarding general discipline. One of them with which the court was concerned directly states that political activism is strictly banned in the campus and that 'students are forbidden to organise or attend meetings other than the official ones'. Strikes are prohibited within the campus, and the challenge of the student was that such forbiddance was violative of Article 19(i)(a) & (c) of the Constitution. Since this question is of 'considerable general importance', the court felt the urgency of the issue as one of adjudicatory moment.

The prohibitive clause which has been upheld by the court, if scrutinised with a little care reveals that organisation of or attendance at meetings which are *official* ones are permitted (even if they be of the character of political activism). So much so there is a discriminatory dimension underlying the ban which, in fairness, means that meetings which finds favour with the management fall within the permissible category. Communal managements of educational institutions are the bane of the Kerala educational establishment. It is full of politics, survives by politics, propagates political perspectives and controls the State educational establishment through its political clout. Therefore, officially permitted political meetings, often dangerous to the progressive development of the State and the Nation, enjoy open sesame or free access. Now that the controversial clause has received judicial sanction the ruling allows the Principal to spread within the campus his brand of politics and make every other political study through meetings and campaigns *bete noire*. Reactionary politics of private managements thus finds a haven inside colleges and all *avant-garde* political thought and action is frowned upon. This is arbitrary and unconstitutional. Indeed there is no rationale or logical basis of classification as the foundation for the forbiddance. There is no rational differentia indicated in the clause which will make a meeting *official* just, fair and reasonable. It is vague and can be capricious, depending on the management's will to give free rein to the partisan politics of a management. If clear guidelines comporting with the values of our Constitution *vis a vis*, political education and action, are transparently stated as governing the management's power to prohibit, it is a different matter. Absent such directive, liberal discussion becomes suppressed or hidebound and the cause of free thought fails as violative of Article 19, 20 and 21—Article 14 because the classification is not based on a rational differentia related to a constitutionally acceptable objective. The *ipse dixit* of the Principal calling it *official* does not make the meeting lose its vice of inequality before the law. Article 19 is violated because freedom of expression involves freedom of action, information and communication of ideas to deny which the college authorities can stamp a kind of activity as not *officially* acceptable. It is violative of Article 21 because the 'right to life' includes the right to moral, social and cultural development which, in turn, involves a free opportunity for uninhibited political education and it is contradicted by the clause which vests a ukase in the management. College education is improved through college debates and free speech. To control this collegiate freedom is to permit manufacture of young minds conditioned by the management politics. To swear by what is officially ordered as sound political activity and to swear at every other political process to which the Principal is allergic is to create conditioned minds which is the negation of political pluralism, democratic diversity and developmental autonomy. Our Republic will suffer from robotism if the creative vitality of the young generation at college is ordered about by the official church, communal management and mindless establishments which run schools of higher education. This is a new menace which benumbs the intellectual potential of the Nation.

Apparently, even the judiciary is not sufficiently alerted about this ominous portent. Citing Supreme Court decisions about the political calamity of student wings of Parties in campuses misses the great tragedy of petrifying human originality. Every young mind passing through Colleges must be trained to be sensitive to the constitutional pledge of justice, social, economic and political, liberty of thought and expression and the dignity of the individual in relation to the nation's integrity. Platitudes and claptraps about student politics and Party allurements misses the oxygen of socialism, secularism and democracy which are nothing but politics but are the quintessences of our constitutional culture.

The Principal is the head of the institution but functions under the management and its political philosophy. It is right to prevent hostile groups of students battling within the campus or creating babel or bedlam making the process of learning impossible. Peace, health, morality and like vital values constitute discipline and must be preserved by the Principal. College premises cannot become scenes of sound and fury obstructing classes, but these important control measures of discipline do not justify taboo of political discussions, political magazines, political association and political seminars inside the premises save with the permission of the Principal as if to avoid law and order problems.

It is unfortunate to compare Government servants and their rules of conduct with student's code of conduct. The difference is too obvious to need explanation. Students study and learning has several processes. Teachers, government servants and other employees in public institutions certainly can have their political views but cannot resort to conduct or membership which will distract from or interfere with the neutrality needed for functional efficiency. It is confusion to mix up this category with the student community; of course, disturbing demonstration, obstructive strike, ragging and other operations which make classes difficult to be conducted or people's study menaced by turbulence—these can always be prevented, because they have a nexus to the goals of a student in college to equip himself with knowledge.

To banish politics for a student of eighteen years of age is to deny him the fundamental opportunity of becoming a good citizen to vote. It is anti-democratic to refuse a student a campus opportunity to talk politics, to read politics, to discuss politics in an association, to argue politics with his fellow students, subject, of course, to a peaceful atmosphere, disciplined behaviour and obedience to public health and morality. That orderly political activity by a student community governed by democratic decency and academic dignity will cause chaos in the campus is a fashionable fallacy and dubious diagnosis and I humbly believe will never be a judicial illusion. Educational pharmacopoeia, I agree, must cure the anarchic pathology of party-politicking, *even if officially backed by*

Management—disguised policy, which often is subversive of radical constitutional activism. Blanket ban on campus political activity, save official ones, has a fascist flavour.

Politics is a social science and its study through organized movements, if peacefully pursued, even if a wee-bit restively and passionately, deserves no veto. Heeding the protests against a blanket ban, maybe, the Court has agreed to a review and, as a democratic gesture, invited everyone interested to present his/her submission. I pay a tribute to the judges for this judicious measure. I remember that while on the Supreme Court, presiding over a bench, I was hearing a case involving the parameters of death sentence I orally announced that any member of the bar interested in the cause would be heard, since the question was of life and death moment. A review is a remedy for the judges themselves to correct an error if a flaw has vitiated the judgement already delivered. No one, not even the wisest judge, is above a commission or omission which needs correction. Way back in 1980 in one judgement the court reviewed and reversed itself. There I wrote:

> *Horace Wrote "But if Homer, who is good, nods for a moment, I think it a shame". We, in the Supreme Court, do 'nod' despite great care to be correct, and once a clear error in our judgment is revealed, no sense of shame or infallibility complex obsesses us or dissuades this court from the anxiety to be ultimately right, not consistently wrong. The present petition for review is one such and we have listened, at unusual length, to counsel's oral submissions having felt that an error in the judgment under review, likely to injure and unsettle, needed to be mended.* (AIR 1980 SC 1187)

I am convinced; and by this I once again pay a tribute to the judges concerned, that the case will be reheard with a conviction that infallibility is not a judicial inviolability.

CONSTITUTION OF INDIA—THE NATION'S SAFETY VALVE

The Indian Constitution is the cornerstone of a liberated nation. It lays the grand foundation of a great people's political edifice of governance. It projects the socio-economic vision of a generation emerging from a feudal culture, colonial domination and federal negation. It spells out the fundamental rights and socialistic aspirations of the vast masses long inhibited by an imperialist ethos. It creates a trinity of democratic instrumentalities with checks and balances, parliamentary in structure, quasi-federal in character. Endowed with adult franchise, empowered with periodic elections, provided with plural Parties, equipped with a unitive justice system with a uniquely supreme judicature at the apex which gives access to every citizen against injustice, the political stricture of the billion-strong Indian humanity is a paradigm of secular, socialist, democratic Republic.

An independent judiciary, an accountable Parliament at the Centre and like legislatures at the State level, a powerful Election Commission and fearless, critical Comptroller and Auditor General provide a paramountcy of democracy, at once responsible and responsive. Judicial review of State action, public finance auditable by a constitutional authority, obligation to seek fresh mandate through general elections with adult franchise, accountability, direct and indirect, to the people in several ways,—these are fundamental in the governance of the country. The people, though free, have fundamental duties mandated by Art.51A of the Constitution to exercise which, as in cases of environmental and ecological preservation, compassion for living creatures, protection of the value of *composite* culture, the authority of judicial writ power may be moved in aid. In the words of Dr. Ambedkar, winding up his speech moving the passage of the Draft Constitution, "I feel that it (the Constitution) is workable, it is flexible and it is strong enough to hold the country together both in peace time and in war time. Indeed, if I may say so, if things go wrong under the new Constitution the reason will not be that we had a bad Constitution. What we will have to say is, that Man was vile".

Stability does not mean immutability. Times change. Social conditions are altered by various factors. Each generation may differ in values from a previous generation. Therefore, realism dictates flexibility which implies amendability. Therefore, our Constitution (Art. 368) vests power in parliament to amend the Constitution but with more rigorous procedures than in passing ordinary legislation. Indeed, amendment of the Constitution, necessary in certain circumstances, has been provided for, blending pragmatism with special safeguards, avoiding rigidity, but facilitating flexibility. At this point it must be remembered that a mere majority cannot be allowed to tamper with the Constitution. Why? There are certain great values, which our founding fathers have regarded as paramount and inviolable. If those values can be jettisoned by a majority of Parliament a fanatical majority or absolutist party commanding huge numbers in the House may destroy democracy, secularity, independence of the judiciary and the rule of law itself. All constitutional safeguards and safety valves may become ephemeral, unless basic values are put beyond parliament's power to truncate. So it is that we have, as settled constitutional law, re-enforced by *Kesavananda Bharathi, Minerva Mills, Indira Nehru Gandhi, Bommai* and other cases, the doctrine of basic structure of the Constitution which is beyond mutation by the plenary power of Parliament. Thus the great fundamentals are immunised; at the same time variable values can be given validity by appropriate amendments. Indeed, the Constitution has undergone around seventy-eight effective amendments. What are the basic features of the Constitution which are outside the pale of amendment? The Rule of Law, for instance is one; equality before the law is another; secularism is a third; judicial review is a fourth. Even federalism and supreme sovereignty are substantially inviolable.

India is a pluralist society with a huge Hindu majority with subsidiary caste minorities, and a number of religious minorities with separate identity. To preserve our democracy and the confidence of the minorities, safeguards need to be incorporated and wisely therefore, protection and reservation for minorities, autonomy for religious communities and freedom for linguistic groups find a haven in the Constitution. Dr. Ambedkar, in the Constituent Assembly, has defended the provision of reservations and other safeguards. "To diehards who have developed a kind of fanaticism against minority protection I would like to say......one is that minorities are an explosive force which, if it erupts can blow up the whole fabric of the State." Therefore, he argued for a tolerant majority with respect for minority rights.

He quoted Grote, the historian of Greece:

> *The diffusion of constitutional morality, not merely among the majority of any community but through out the whole, is the indispensible condition of a Government at once free and peaceable; since even any powerful and obstinate minority may render the working of a free institution impracticable, without being strong enough to conquer ascendency for themselves.*
>
> *By constitutional morality Grote meant—a paramount reverence for the forms of the constitution, enforcing obedience to authority acting under and within these forms yet combined with the habit of open speech, of action, subject only to definite legal control, and unrestrained censure of those very authorities as to all their public acts combined too with a perfect confidence in the bosom of every citizen amidst the bitterness of party contest that the forms of the constitution will not be less sacred in the eyes of his opponents than in his own. (The Framing of India's Constitution-Vol-IV P-428)*

A great safety value of Human Rights, constitutionally inscribed, is the power of judicial review even to the extent of correcting and invalidating executive and legislative excesses by binding writs Articles 13, 132, 226, 136, 141, 142 are some of the vital provisions which grant access to the people to move the court and seek redressal against injustice. Be you ever so high, the law is above you. This proposition must be read with the power of the independent judiciary, *viz.*, the law is what the judges say it is. Since judicial review is a basic feature of the Constitution, the citizen has inalienable power to defend himself. Of course, what are "basic features" depends on the pronouncements of the judiciary in their wisdom. Judicial independence is itself a basic feature of the Constitution.

Two questions remain before us. Who appoints judges? Who will correct judicial misconduct? Equally relevantly, the question arises, as Prof. Griffith (The Politics of Judiciary) points out, the social and political position, the class bias and communal influences of judges themselves may colour their objectivity and their social vision. A National Judicial Commission may perhaps be a partial answer. What should be the composition of such a Commission?

> *The concern on the issue is very succinctly expressed in a Private Member Constitution (Amendment) Bill, 1996 to amend articles 124, 217 etc. by Mr. V.N. Gadgil, Member of Parliament in Rajya Sabha on December 18, 1998. The salient points made in Mr. Gadgil's Bill are as under:*
>
> *i. The Constituent Assembly while providing for appointment of High Court and Supreme Court Judges in the Constitution did not intend that consent of the Chief Justice of India should be obtained. What was envisaged was only consultation with him. Dr. B.R. Ambedkar clearly expressed himself against a provision requiring concurrence of the*

President since according to him, Chief Justice after all "is a man with all his feelings, all the sentiments and all the prejudices which we, the common people have."

ii. The judgment of the Apex Court is based on distrust of Parliament and the Executive.

iii. Nowhere in the world there is a system where Judges themselves decide as to who will be the next Judge. One cannot be Judge in one's own cause. No Parliament should accept such a proposition.

iv. In the United States, selection of Judges is a political process and Chief Justice or other Judges of the Supreme Court are neither informed nor consulted in the matter. In Britain, the proposal is made by the Lord Chancellor who is head of the judiciary but also Minister of the Crown. In Canada too, the power to appoint judges vests in the executive.

v. Independence of Judges is a myth. All judgments are not objective as Judges' own views do get reflected in the judgments.

A Judicial Commission which will have a mix of representative from the judiciary, executive and others has been advocated from time to time by many including the Law Commission of India (see 121st report) with a view to ensuring that judicial appointments at the level of High Court and Supreme Court Judges are made with the collective wisdom of a representative body rather than leaving the same to absolute or sole power of one wing of the State.

(The Constitution of India—Select issues and perceptions by Subhash Jain P-5/6)

In our democratic system, the strongest safety valve to protect our freedom is the exercise of adult franchise whereby every person, above age eighteen has the right to cast his vote at a general election held obligatorily by an independent Election Commission. This power of the people is the ultimate sanction to control the Executive and the Legislature. In Churchill's famous words:

At the bottom of all tributes paid to democracy is the little man, walking into a little booth, with a little pencil, making a little cross on a little bit of paper—no amount of rhetoric or voluminous discussion can possibly diminish the overwhelming importance of the point.

In our cabinet system the council of ministers must command a majority in the House. This sanction is a protection against authoritarian regime. The historic Indira Gandhi debacle, after the Emergency span, demonstrates how effective elections are as a safety valve.

Freedom of expression, which covers freedom of the media, is a constitutional guarantee which properly exercised, will empower, as the

Fourth Estate, the political opposition in the country and make Part III of the Constitution (Fundamental Rights) a living reality. Parties play a vital role in the operation of the democratic order. Even if a plurality of parties form Coalitions or Fronts they are answerable to the House and the House itself, functionally powerful, is a sentinel of people's liberty and an incorruptible responsive and responsible Government. The pity is that our legislatures are not functioning meaningfully and are often lost in 'sound and fury signifying nothing'.

The rule of law is a great principle which gives access to every aggrieved person to seek justice before an independent judiciary. However, litigation is expensive, backlogs colossal and final pronouncement of judgement so delayed that judicial justice becomes a mirage. Here again, judicial reform is a necessary measure which cannot wait longer because the situation is already nearing breakdown point.

The Constitution is a social document and economic instrument. Secularism is a guarantee and socialism is an imperative of our Republic. In this context, part IV and IV-A which deal with Directive Principles fundamental in the governance of the country as well as the provisions regarding Fundamental Duties, if taken seriously, will ensure life, liberty and the pursuit of happiness of every Indian a basic birthright. Above all is the judicial process, but it is in a lamentable crisis currently, so much so; we have miles to go before claiming that social justice is an enforceable, realizable credential of citizenship.

The salvation of Swaraj—every Indian human's right to dignity, development and democratic voice—depends on the creative, sensitive, sarvodaya spirit of our constitutional order.

> *It is well to remember the oft repeated passage from the last speech of Dr. B.R. Ambedkar in the Constituent Assembly on November 25, 1949 to the following effect:*
>
> *"....I feel, however good a Constitution may be, it is sure to turn out bad because those who are called to work it, happen to be a bad lot. However bad a Constitution may be, it may turn out to be good if those who are called to work it, happen to be a good lot. The working of the Constitution does not depend wholly upon the nature of the Constitution."*
>
> *Dr. Ambedkar further added:*
>
> *"The Constitution can provide only the organs of State such as the legislature, the executive and the judiciary. The factors on which the working of those organs of State depends are people and the political parties they will set up as their instruments to carry out their wishes and their politics. Who can say how the people of India and their parties will behave? Will they uphold constitutional methods of achieving their purposes...."*

(The Constitution of India—Select issues and perceptions by Subhash Jain P-12)

The ultimate Safety Valve of our Republic rests, vests, in the last analysis, in the practical wisdom, social active and collective comity of "We the People of India".

CONSTITUTIONAL AMENDMENTS IN INDIA

Dr. M.V. Pylee is among the notable scholars in the field of Indian constitutional law. His book manifests rare erudition and will readily find a place in every legal library. On federalism he is an authority and his collection of the constitutions of the world is a prized possession for any jurist, researcher or law teacher. His present book covers a wide spectrum and each of his works has a unique feature. M.V. Pylee's Constitutions of the World, for instance, spans thirty-nine countries from Albania to the United States of America. The Constitution of India is reputed to be the longest whereas that of the United State of America is the shortest. The book under review "Constitutional Amendments in India", has special features which makes its possession a necessary companion where Indian legal literature is the primary focus. Universal Law Publishing Company, which is the creditable publisher in this case, is a usual, among the foremost in the country's law publishers.

The Constitution of India is our paramount legal parchment, our national charter, our fundamental law, our legal wonder with prolixity unlimited. We are a billion people, diverse in a hundred ways, at once federal and unitary, socialist and democratic and operationally so vibrant and up-to-date that it has undergone at least eightysix amendments with more in store.

This massive Constitution is beyond a jurist's easy comprehension unless he is ably aided by a large and learned work which tells you the story of the Indian people's constitutional development, the making of the Constitution and its philosophy, the basic principles which form its foundation and the plurality of amendments, their object and historical perspective. For everyone of these problems Pylee, in his wisdom, gives answer in his book which is heavy of course and weighty to boot. I salute you Dr. Pylee for your extraordinary energy and sensitive study resulting in a volume which amazes me as I peruse the pages.

What is a Constitution and why is the Indian Constitution so bulky? Dr. Pylee suggests the answer in the opening pages. How was the Constituent Assembly constituted? What was the democratic procedure adopted? Who were the great members of the drafting committee? Dr. Pylee tells you all about this with necessary brevity.

There are many other dimensions of information about the basic principles and social philosophy which make our Constitution great. Dr. Pylee has devoted two chapters on these subjects.

Truly, Constitutional amendments in India is a magnum opus. Why? Because every amendment—and there are so many, which beat counting—is dealt with separately, its objects and reasons stated for easy reference, its legislative history briefly set out and its text given in fine print. Each amendment has received separate treatment. Imagine the labour involved in assembling these details relating to eightysix such provisions. Appropriately, the entire Constitution, with the twelve schedules, also finds a prominent place. India has Jammu & Kashmir with a separate Constitution. That document too has undergone amendments. There is so much debate about Jammu & Kashmir and every serious student must naturally be inclined to learn about the Constitution of Jammu & Kashmir and the amendments wrought into it. Dr. Pylee has given us this precious information in his voluminous book. There are informative charts which researchers find useful. On the whole, this great work is more than its price because it contains a wealth of information, knowledge and wisdom which, together in one book, is rare. Dear publisher, you too deserve some praise for making Dr.Pylee write this book.

INDIAN CASUALTIES AS SUBSTITUTES FOR AMERICAN CADAVERS IN OCCUPIED IRAQ? NO

Never shall India recover her culture of non-negotiable swaraj, her stature as a leader of Non-Aligned Nations and her post-Independence credence as defender of International Law once it surrenders to the pressure of an armed conqueror in continued military occupation but exposed to the exasperated daily guerilla terrorism of the Iraqi people who say 'no' to dictator Saddam and 'get out' to imperious Bush. Indian battalions as colonial cannon fodder to Iraqi resistance forces is a betrayal of our tryst with the Free World. This militant nationalism is the dominant opinion of Indian humanity regardless of class, community, region or religion, whatever opportunist politicians in dubious diplomatic diction may articulate for Washington consumption. Would the White House have dared or deigned to hint to Pandit Nehru or Indira Gandhi, Morarji or V.P.Singh to deploy a single Indian soldier to foreign territory to offer submissive support to illegal American occupation? To send Indian troops to occupied Iraq is to abet the arrogant invasion of a sovereign country sans United Nations sanction in defiance of world opinion and as an act in violation of *Art. 51 of our Constitution.* It would be a traducive travesty and brazen breach of the said provision which mandates that our nation shall *promote* international peace and security, *foster respect for international law* and maintain *just and honourable relations between nations.*

How did the U.S. ignore the U.N., uttered notorious falsehood globally about tyrant Saddam's horrible Weapons of Mass Destruction (W.M.D.) and, in gross violation of international law, invaded Iraq, incessantly showered bombs on Baghdad, destroyed a Mesopotamian museum, massacred an innocent population by trying out recklessly its arsenal of weaponry and, after conquest, occupied by brute force, as an extension of the Bush empire, sovereign Iraq? President Bush is in no mood to quit, audaciously aware there is none to challenge the imperial guilt and robbery of oil resources.

On October 7th 2002, President Bush told the American people that Saddam was targeting U.S. to disperse chemical and biological weapons across broad areas. Han Bliz, the U.N. Chief Weapons Inspector, openly called the bluff of the Bush campaign based on non-existent W.M.D. Before the war, through the war and after the war, the Bush Administration totally failed to prove its concocted case. On the subject of evidence of W.M.D., U.S. Defence Secretary, Donald Rumsfield argued like a pettifogger that 'absence of evidence is not the evidence of absence'. In short, the preemptive aggression by the sole super-power had no legitimacy whatsoever, except that Might is Right and Unlaw is Law, whatever the U.N. or its Secretary General may shout in impotence. In a recent article in the Hindu, N.S.Jagannathan has quoted Richard Cohen of the Washington Post calling Bush a liar. But "he doth bestride the narrow world like a Colossus" (Shakespeare-Julius Caesar). Global anger, including within the U.S., vociferously against the Bush administration's macro mendacity, contemptuous indifference to the U.N. and hell-bent intent to colonise Iraq, gain control over its rich oil wealth, deny its people basic democracy and establish a haven for profiteering by U.S. giant contractors to "reconstruct" what U.S. itself bombarded and blasted.

The Indian Opposition (?) and people in their millions were aghast at all these reprehensible operations. The Indian Government had initially opposed the unilateral invasion by the unipolar U.S., by-passing ineffectual World Body. Several leaders in Parliament recently criticised any talks by Government with the U.S., regarding despatch of troops to Iraq, a move contrary to Parliament's unanimous resolution on April 9 2003, which, *inter alia*, called upon the U.N. to protect the sovereignty of Iraq and ensure that the reconstruction of Iraq is done under the auspices of the U.N.

Until now, the U.S. administration has refused to had over Iraq for reconstruction and humanitarian aid to the U.N. and its agencies. Obviously, sending Indian troops to face Iraqi firing line, to shoot and be shot, "will amount to total subservience to U.S. military interest which the people of India will never accept"—so sums up a joint press statement released on June 24th, presumably by the several opposition parties. The Opposition leaders went on to demand that the Government should "forthwith declare that in the country's national interest and prestige, it will never be part of the US occupation or police force in Iraq and that the Central Government should not enter into any negotiation with the Pentagon officials, whose very presence in our capital is being resented by the patriotic and freedom loving people of this country." Releasing the statement this evening, CPM MP Nilopal Basu said the Opposition would raise the issue in the monsoon session of Parliament.

India and Iraq have been on friendly terms although Saddam Hussain was a despot. We have sent pharmaceuticals and have received oil. We have no reason to supplement the American Terror Rule in Iraq by sending our Army to serve under Pentagon Command; What a fall my countrymen, if it does happen. Why should we go to the aid of a rule by the American gun denying democracy to a broken people? Why this dependencia syndrome, vainly hoping that Bush & Company will back us on Kashmir, a prospect as distant as the moon, what with Mushraff and his militarist Pakistan wooing and winning White House favours. In the final analysis, never be under any illusion about yankee yen for the Indian cause, having known U.S role in the earlier wars with Pakistan and American armed aid to that country. History teaches sanity and Indian humanity will not forgive its rulers for giving humiliating military aid against Iraqi people who hunger for democracy, not yankee raj, now that the dictator is gone.

Baghdad is nowhere near self-government. The occupying forces are no longer on a liberating mission but are operators of the opposite objective to facilitate exploitation of Iraqi oil, keeping the people suppressed. It is unprincipled to send Indian soldiers to die of Iraqi terrorism. To get the Indian Big Business sub-contracts for reconstruction of Iraq and, in exchange, send our army is unscrupulous and betrayal of India's moral authority in the comity of nations. Contract for Indian tycoons can never be a bribe to barter away our international prestige. As I.K. Gujral has pointed out in a recent article in the Hindu: 'in any case, there is something unIndian and undignified in becoming a sub-contractor to the Pentagon in order to become a sub-contractor to American multinationals. Our decision must never smack of mercenaryism". I agree with Gujral that even if there is a pretense of U.N. cover, our armed forces will all the same be under the authority of the occupying powers. What a shame and shock, disgraceful and crawling for the Indian General to take orders from an American Commander! Indeed, such a role, if we accept, is an active participation in U.S. imperialism.

What has made me sensitively distressed nights is the pensive thought that *Indian soldiers* should lose their lives in Iraq not to defend their own country's freedom but to replace U.S. soldiers who would otherwise die of Iraq's desperate 'do or die' groups who represent their country's wish 'America go back'. Every day American and British soldiers are dying of guerilla suicide squads. If the Indian troops land, American troops will withdraw pro tanto. Indian casualties will replace American cadavers. The American soldier, when he dies, defends American occupation. The Indian soldier, when he is killed, dies for whom? Every martyr has a cause to die for. But the Indian corporal has no honourable cause but only a cursed fate if he fights for Americans to keep Iraqi freedom down. The

Indian army has a great tradition of patriotic obedience to orders. It is for the Supreme Commander of the Defense Forces of the Union, the President of India, to advise his cabinet as to what is right and great in the circumstances of the case. The statesman in the Prime Minister, the swaraj spirit of the Cabinet, the final accountability to the people will say *no* to the White House overture to suppress a free people and assist, under foreign command, a foreign domination. This shall not be. Not that I admire the great American people less but that I uphold my great countrymen and their patriotic tradition more.

INDIAN POLICING— SOME SOCIAL DIMENSIONS

The criminal justice system is the conscience and foundation of the social order and, in turn, the basic structure of this system has two fundamental components. Of course, paramountcy belongs to the Judiciary. Why? Because, as St.Augustine put it, Justice being taken away then, what are Kingdoms but great robberies? For what are robberies themselves, but little kingdoms? (The City of God) Next to the judicature, probably more vital in certain respects, the police establishment plays a cardinal role on which hinges people's life, liberty and the pursuit of happiness in peace and security. Policing, like justicing, has therefore to be at the service of the people commanding the credibility of the community at large without fear or favour, affection or ill-will. Independence and accountability with commitment to the rule of law, are as much the non-negotiable qualities of the invigilating, investigating police force as of the 'robed brethren' on the bench. If the investigative process fails, if the police presence to guard law and order is not functionally successful, the adjudicatory apparatus collapses and our adversarial system of justice becomes dysfunctional. The safety of society, sans police integrity, accountability, transparency and efficiency, suffers illusion and unreality. Once we accept this critical proposition of the police process in people's protection, orderly development and creative participation in people's right to justice, we have to focus on the systemic flaws, performance failures and room for reform of the uniformed cadres and higher echelons so that the police paradigm may present a transformation rid of the evils which now beset the establishment. Police reform is too grave to neglect, too urgent to delay, too serious to be left to self-corrective strategies.

Chronic indifference to progressive reform may make police presence as good as absent. This will certainly fuel increase in social conflict and encourage crime, mafia operation, terrorist activity and vigilantism; and inhibit good governance and economic development. The whole criminal justice system is, with exceptions, currently obese, obsolescent, obscurantist and obnoxious. Overhauling is overdue but holistic measures and comprehensive correctives cannot be an excuse for not implementing feasible reforms to the immediate extent possible.

Initiatives from the Centre to catalyse police reform is a good beginning. There are many valuable reports of valiant Commissions at the national and State levels which slumber and gather dust because, apart from cosmetic changes, Governments rarely bother to undertake radical mutations. It is unpleasant to implement reforms because the political Governments with power appetite do not take kindly to the constitutional fundamental of insulating the police establishment from illegitimate political control and external interference. To be a Minister is to be able to manipulate police power and therefore this corrupt proclivity inhibits self-restraint and autonomy of the police service. It is necessary to stress without mincing words that the police are indeed accountable only to law and must be beyond clout or threat from any other oblique quarter. However, the present system has created such a deep subversion of the concept of independence and accountability that it requires a radical reorientation in the philosophy of police control and management. The political will to reform the police is presently beyond visibility. It must be created through public pressure, political campaign and judicial mandate.

A diagnostic approach to the present pathology of the police system is a good beginning. I have had experience of conducting many tough criminal cases while at the bar and have known the vices and weaknesses, the moral deviances and inhuman violations the police have indulged in during normal duties, investigative operations and stages of prosecution. The institution, as such, has great potential, as I have discovered while I was Home Minister in the Kerala State for a brief while (1957-59). I know the deterioration and excellence of that Establishment and, as judge, I have pronounced on the performance of the Police *a la* Nandini Satpathy case (AIR 1978 SC 1025) *et al.*

The police have their own problems and difficult situations without realising which criticism will be unjust. For instance, 'a policeman called to the scene of a crime must make an instant decision on what action he must take, then take it. A judge may be presented with the same set of facts a month later. He can take all the time he needs in deciding what to do about it. But not the policeman. He has to act and act now. (Bill Schipp) (Readers Digest Oct 1962 P-112). This does not mean that the police can be a law unto themselves under guise of urgency. However, as Roger J Traynor has lucidly expressed 'The great advantage of police compliance with the law is that it helps create an atmosphere conducive to a community in respect for officers of the law that in turn serve to promote their enforcement of the law. Once they set an example of lawful conduct they are in a position to set up lines of communication and to gain its support'. Police performance is thus a community asset promotive of the rule of law. At present, custodial abuse is often at the door of the police and investigative infallibility is rarely regarded as an attainment of the police. On the contrary, political interference, corrupt practices, third degree methods and fabrications of evidence are imputed to the police. Maybe, there are black sheep, but to generalise is to forget the presence of great policemen at every level. There are inadequacies in police equipment, training and culture. Commission after commission has pointed out the peculiar predicament of the police service caught in a dilemma between political bossism and legal obligation. Those who are generous to the finer police patriots will agree that—to borrow Churchill—'never in the field of human conflict was so much owed by so many to so few'. Crimes are escalating; society is deteriorating, politicians are interfering; power abuse is becoming a growing syndrome. At the same time, policing intelligence is on the wane; police violence is on the rise. A new sense of dignity and reverence for institutional reputation must develop from within the police establishment. Technology is rapidly advancing and canny criminals corner them, making the methods of crime technologically superior to police strategy. The integrity of the police establishment must also become unassailable and its credibility invincible so that court may not dismiss police processes unworthy of *prima facie* acceptance. All these and other matters of concern make it imperative that *avant garde,* progressive metamorphoses in police functionalism are the challenge of the time.

The ethos of the police must change. So too its eidos. Do remember that the police organisation in India was established after the Indian mutiny in 1857 to curb dissent, to enforce obedience and make loyalty for the foreign ruler the basic objective. Inevitably, this systemic cult engendered a pro-ruler, anti people culture. Since Independence, nothing radical has been done to infuse a progressive dynamism, a people-oriented democratisation and a versatile measure of professional excellence geared to national values. Commissions have been appointed, Reports submitted but not implemented. True, some initiatives have been taken like the National Police Commission of 1979-81, but the central issues and recommendations which the report emphasised remain slumbering far too long and the Police Act of 1861 needs to be replaced and modernised with ideological changes incorporated, so that the system may be in tune with the constitutional teleology and technological advances. The Rebeiro Committee and the Padmanabaiah Committee have made valuable proposals for reform. The late Inderjit Gupta (CPI leader), as Union Home Minister, took the initiative in 1997 to exhort the States to introduce police reform on the lines of the N.P.C. Indeed, all these are part of history and the police *modus operandi* is basically left without ideological or methodological modifications of a cardinal nature. The price of lethargy is that expectations from the police remain a frustration in practice. There is so much mistrust of the police among the people that an iron curtain has descended between the two Reforms cannot tarry.

Speaking generally, people regard the police as an inevitable evil, a ubiquitous need, a physical power whose proximity is desiderated for prestige and pomp. Sans police activism, chaos in the cosmos will be the grave risk. Crimes will be committed recklessly, absent the deterrent mobility of the State's armed might. If police intelligence does not detect and arrest criminal gangs and omnipresent mafia, if the investigative machinery does not bring to justice anti-social offenders with celerity, the syndrome of turbulence, social clashes and even terrorism well shock society into anarchy. Therefore, the police is people's inseparable friend. Then why mistrust him, malign him and condemn him as if khaki uniform is a sartorial virus or toxic professional disease. No, not at all. They are part of us, share our problems and will be our source of strength *once a progressive Police Reform Agenda becomes operational.*

Critical to our millennial march is the defense of human rights which are vulnerable to violations from many angles and we fall back on the sensitized police personnel for protection and preventive action.

What are the ground realities *vis a vis* the police in their conventional activities? Some hard evidence reads horrendous. ACHRI publication reports:

In 1999 alone, over 74322 complaints were received from the public against police personnel in the country. (Crime in India 1999)

> *In 1999-2000 the National Human Rights Commission received reports of 177 deaths in police custody, 1157 illegal detention and arrest', 1647 'false implication' and 5783 'other police excesses'. (NHRC Annual Report 2000)*
>
> *In addition, there are the recent incidents of what happened in Gujarat. There is strong evidence to show that the police force not only failed to handle the disturbances efficiently but showed partiality in dealing with the rioters. They were not merely indifferent but complicity involved in several incidents of violence targeted against the minority community in the state. Besides the loss of lives and property of the riot victims, the state has suffered an economic loss of over Rs. 3,000 crore.*

Although repetitively, let me emphasize the fundamentals with some supplementary thoughts.

The social order in a civilized society needs a Force to maintain public order and prevention of crime plus bringing the criminals, by prompt prosecution, to condign punishment. To ensure this process we need an organized body sensitive to human rights, beyond purchase or pressure and totally committed to a crime-free-society. Towards this end, the State must empower the police echelons and cadres, from top to bottom, to take preventive action, investigate crimes, impart confidence in the people about their security and, apart from defending the victim, to take punitive measures according to law. In this larger sense, the police represents the collective interests of the community *vis a vis* life; liberty and the pursuit of happiness. The functional fulfillment of the police duty requires non-interference by those in political authority, extraneous clout or coercion or even impractical, ill-informed and unwarranted judicial commands. Indeed, the measure of a society's stability depends on the autonomy, integrity and fearless performance of duty by the police hierarchy. Of course, broad parameters for the fulfillment of the objectives of the constitutional system will be laid down by legislation and general directives, consistently with constitutional imperatives and the laws. These may rightly be issued by the political government, which is ultimately answerable to the people who are the final political custodians of power and beneficiaries of the Welfare State. Within these boundaries, autonomy is enjoyed by the police force with its own internal discipline, control and command. Of course, judicial review is a constitutional corrective, which binds and guides and pronounces upon police action. Thus there is a controllerate to keep the police within bounds and a sanction for operation by the police of its duties and commitments. In this sense, the police is not merely the friend, philosopher and guide of the citizenry but also a stern engineer of the laws necessary for peace and security.

> *Just as the character and the quality of a country's police forces provide a touch-stone of spirit and quality of its government and civil administration, the 'police' provides a touch-stone of the quality and conduct of the people themselves. In short, a student of the political institution of any country desirous of understanding the 'ethos' of any country's Government can hardly do better than to make a close study of its police system, which will provide him with a good measuring rod of the actual extent to which its government is free or authoritarian.*
>
> *(Coatman, John (1959)*

The inevitable interrogation posed from ancient times is "who will police the police?" Generally speaking, there is an organisational pyramid and the Ministry at the top – which keeps the police in leash and guides its powers promotive of the welfare of the people and their peaceful life. It must always be remembered that the Constitution which is paramount vests in the Court the power of judicial review which is a basic feature of our Constitution. But judicial review is not teasing tinkering; and forensic excess harms successful investigation. Judicial oversight, with becoming restraint, comports with police dignity, autonomy and accountability.

Centres of research, hi-tech equipments which will beat the criminal's tricks and enable squads in uniform or in mufti to chase and trap the criminals, are necessary for efficiency. White Collar crimes, economic offences and dangerous proliferation of the underground criminal world compel the State to train a police force with ultra-modern machinery, methodology and manpower so that the most sophisticated and cunning of criminals cannot escape the coils of the police net. Most embarrassing situations arise when an Executive Boss or political heavy weight is himself the doer of crimes and, very rarely though, even a robed brother on the Bench plays truant and is a hidden abettor of criminals.

The police officers have to deal with crimes, which are too intricate unless trained adequately in specialised fields. He may have to interrogate, hypnotise, subject persons to psychic examination, dig up unsuspected places, enter and seize seemingly sacred spots and seek the assistance, during investigation, of medical specialties and call in aid experts in technology and even dogs with sixth sense or olfactory sharpness. Indeed, even prevention of crimes or identification of criminals summon versatile forms of training and know-how, without use of third degree methods, which is the current coin of the third world constabulary. Torture has to be avoided, molestation of women and children should be mercilessly rooted out and yet results must be produced so that the confidence of people in the police will be kept high even as the morale of the police is sustained.

A fundamentally different aspect deserves serious consideration. The police whose sacred task is search for truth is sometimes perverted into victimizing people on account of corrupt motives, outside pressures, pornomania and sadistic sex and torture. The result is that the credibility in the police is at stake. When the police become criminal the violence that they inflict escape punitive proceedings. So much so, it is essential to have a Vigilance Commission or other ombudsman to act immediately when police delinquency or criminality is brought to its notice. So it is important that apart from the long-winded judicial proceedings we must have an instant instrumentality, outside the police department, which will blitz into action when reports about the police violation come to its notice. Torture and rape, custodial molestation, illegal detention, unwarranted shadowing violative of basic privacy and roping in of innocent people in grave crimes are not uncommon. Even children are made to suffer mayhem and dalits are subjected to humiliation. Whenever peasants and workers organize strikes and demand rights, it happens the police are used to break strikes and deprive the tenants of their claims because mangements and landlords influence the police. So, certain guidelines are necessary to forbid such unjust police interference under guise of anticipated violence. Similarly the police connive at smuggling, blink at alcohol-based crimes and wink at like anti-social offences. Rackets by the mafia have often links with the police at various levels. In short, the role of the police is reversed and complicity in crimes by the police escalates since offenders are rich underground operators who buy up and grave crimes go undetected. If hawalawalas and their allies and bribe-givers and their go-betweens bribe the police and make them limpets and manipulate investigations, courts acquit and people are perplexed. Political pressure on the police thwarts straightforward investigation and the aggrieved are helpless and voiceless. Sometimes police documents are fabricated or tampered with. In all these cases there is need for an organization to guard the guards, to try offences by the police by an independent agency *a la* Vittal (and his web site) and insist upon compliance with constitutional guarantees. In *Nandini Satpathy* case, referred to earlier, many directions were given regarding the accused's right to counsel and forbidding excessive and torturesome interrogation of women in police stations. Hand-cuffing by the police, insultingly inflicting indignity on the victim is violation of human rights. These and other matters deserve special attention when reforms are under consideration.

A two-volume report by a Committee appointed by the H.R.D. Ministry, and chaired by me, on custodial justice to women contains concrete steps and practical recommendations but governments have paid no heed to those suggestions. The National Police Commission Report contains exhaustive recommendation but we are still governed by the British Indian vintage Police Act which is more than a century old. The Indian Republic and the Constitution's Preamble can promote a just social order only if there is radical reenactment of a progressive police code where women and children will receive special attention and the police force will undergo special courses in human rights and keep pace with updated judicial pronouncements. In this sense, a courier between the police and the judicairy is a systemic necessity. To dismiss the police with contempt or cynicism is irresponsible. To bring in a new spirit of humanism and constitutional responsibility in every police person, man or woman, is the task of the legislatures. Democracy is stable only if the police are conscientised, trained and treated, not as a gang of uniformed musclemen but as State functionaries mandated to maintain peace by legal means.

Victimology is burgeoning into an important branch of criminal jurisprudence. The present system which is adversarial and of Anglo-Saxon vintage, deals with a criminal case as a battle between a person accused of crime and the state which impersonally represents the people. The individual victim, the community which has suffered in a riot or clash, the relatives and other concerned persons who are affected by the occurrence are ignored. The police take charge of investigation. The victim has no voice, as of right, to compel the police to take evidence or to move the court to be heard through his prosecutor. The community, as such, though vitally affected in the public peace that is violated has no *locus standi* before the police or the judge nor is a claim for compensation maintainable at the instance of the victims save in an action in *tort*. Even after sentence is imposed, when parole is granted or suspension or reduction of sentence by way of commutation ordered, the victim is not heard as of right. This leads to gross injustice at times. We therefore need a developed system of victimological jurisprudence and legislation in that behalf. Police policy must make it obligatory to involve the victim community in the investigative and prosecutory operations.

Today, we live in an era of human rights in a wider sense than the individual aggrieved person. The police functionary has crime-free community responsibility far beyond particular crimes. Law and order, 'in widest commonalty spread', becomes his concern. Simmering disturbances, underground activities, foreign presence insidiously active, become the duty of the police person to discover before the explosion occurs. Intelligence, these days, is a highly specialised operation and demands skills, technologies and strategies sometimes too complex for lay persons to discern. Here is a field of specialisation for the police. Likewise, a course in human rights, what it means and how to resist their violation must be a compulsory course from the constabulary upwards. Third degree methods cannot be eliminated by more judicial rhetoric. A new culture has to be evolved, a new ethos has to be woven and a new drill has to become an exercise so that the policemen and police women by a humanised chemical change, truly become the collective defender of the social order.

Accountability of the Police

A basic feature of democracy is transparency coupled with accountability. Secrecy of operation and refusal to be accountable to the public amount to negation of the rule of law and respect for human rights.

All policing has to be brought in line with the requirements of democratic functioning and must take into account the fact that Indian citizens have constitutionally mandated fundamental rights and all instrumentalities of government must be accountable to the people.

The Victorian vintage Indian Police Act does not speak of the role of the police beyond law enforcement and does not recognize the need and responsibility of the Government to establish an effective and efficient system of democratic policing. State Police Acts passed after Independence are mostly modelled on the 1861 Police Act and there is little to distinguish them from colonial legislation. By contrast, the police Acts of UK, British Columbia and several other Commonwealth countries, make it a statutory responsibility of the government to set out objectives and performance targets for the police and clearly lay down how these responsibilities are to be discharged through a process of consultation. Similar provisions are found in the Police Act of South Africa and, in fact, the Constitution of South Africa envisions such responsibility on the state.

The presence of a lawyer when an accused is questioned or arrested promotes accountability because an advocate corrects police excess on the spot, prevents third degree and makes the uniformed authority answerable to legality. It must be remembered that the police, as a law enforcement agency, command far more physical power than any other public service agency and therefore the mechanism for accountability is all the more necessary. The weaponry the police carries, the large powers the police possesses under the Prevention of Terrorism Act, the Gunda Act and similar State laws demand a greater level of accountability from and invigilation of the police as a force. This sense of accountability has to be visible if it is to carry confidence with the public. That is why the presence of an advocate is a great safeguard. True, the advocate cannot be obstructive of interrogation or negative road blocks in the investigative discovery of truth.

Another dimension of accountability in the evaluation of police performance needs mention. The statistical test of number of conviction leads to distortion. Apart from the fact that the conviction rate is discreditably low as an efficient instrument, there is a tendency not to register cases, extract forced confessions. Facile use of third degree methods and other undesirable practices for detection escalate as easy methods of procuring conviction. Accountability, so long as this para terrorist process prevail, takes a long holiday. Therefore, more scientific and continuous assessment of police performance is to be formed to evaluate individual and collective performance. The National Police Commission has suggested independent directorates of police evaluation in every State. Another commission which deals with justice to women in custody (of which I was the Chairman) recommended the empowerment of responsible non-official organisations to enter and inspect places of police custody. There is no reason why representatives of the people and responsible agencies of the public with acceptable credentials should not be allowed to meet and ask for information, including the right to see persons in custody. This will largely promote openness and considerably let it down police abuse. Indeed, police-people interaction, public participation in crime prevention, common operation in situations of distress or commotion will bring the community into closer relations with the police and consequential elimination of extra-legal methods habitual with the police.

A major area of public dissatisfaction with the police arises from the inability of the public to follow the progress of reported crime and victims' complaints to police. At present, police feel themselves under no obligation to provide information to a victim or complainant about how the investigation is progressing. It should be made mandatory in law for the police to inform the complainant about the progress of the investigation. This will not only enhance accountability to the complainant as far as investigation is concerned, but also progressively build confidence that will bring in more willing public participation into policing.

The police process must possess a democratic culture if the Republic is to bear true faith and allegiance to the Constitution. Today, the situation is different, because police-public relations are soured by hostility and allergy. It would appear that in 1999-2000 the National Human Rights Commission received reports of 177 deaths in police custody. 1157 illegal detentions and arrests, 1646 false implications and 5783 other police exercises. These facts illustrate the current estrangement between the police and the people and stresses the need for healthier constructive police-community inter-action. Today there is lack of communication and accessibility between the police and the citizen and a new functional nexus must remove the mists of misunderstanding.

The basic premise of community policing, as Dr. Doel Mukerjee put it, lies in allowing the community to collaborate with the police force to perform various duties. These could include maintenance of peace and security, safety of citizens, law enforcement, crime control and orderly flow of traffic. If these functions are taken care of, it will leave ample time for the police to execute their remaining duties such as investigation of cases.

International experiments have also proven the viability of the community policing idea. In the UK, the new Police Act, it is claimed, gave a fresh image and responsibility to the beat constable making the bobby a household person in hamlets, in the back alleys and the big cities. More recently, the Police Act and the recent UK Police Reforms Bill, 2002, further entrenches the idea by requiring community consultation and providing scope for induction of Community Support Officers and Community Accreditation Schemes. In addition, the Reform Bill allows the Chief of Police in the UK to liaise with the business community of an area to supervise their employees in carrying out certain community safety functions.

Police liaison committee celebration of Annual Police Day, participation of police officers in community welfare activity and other pre bono operations are promotive of better relations and elimination of mistrust. It has been suggested that citizens' boards may be set up which may include advocates, business people, women's associations and retired judges who may work in close association with law enforcement agencies and keep a crime database. Meeting and discussing together issues of common concern may bridge the gap between the police and the people. What is needed is an attitudinal change on both sides, so that a creative camaraderie between the people and the constable may become a *modus vivendi.* Perhaps, statutory support may lend strength to this dynamic concept. After all, in our days of terrorism and crime explosion people-police activism is of socially therapeutic value.

CODA

What should be the nature of the structure which will bring together the public and the police? An advisory body with sentinel status in every district may do liaison service. Here, again, the presence of a retired judge to help such a committee of police public relation may be welcome. Similarly, a retired senior police officer on the committee may be salutory since he/she will bring the needed knowhow about police public problems. While the local MLA and MP may properly figure as people's representatives great care should be taken to exclude political, communal and other undesirable influences to sap or convert the credibility, integrity and impartiality of the committee. Surely, the committee's discussions should be frank and fair and fearless criticism of the police will enhance the work of the committee in ventilating general grievances and felt necessities bearing upon policing proper. The police too get an opportunity to communicate with the public. The party in power, or for that matter, any other powerful political group should not utilise the committee to shape the course of particular cases. Nor, indeed, should the committee have any power to pronounce on or steer the course of any individual case. The selection of the members of the committee may probably be made by the District Collector in active consultation with the seniormost judicial officer locally available and also the District Panchayat President.

The authority and responsibility of the Government *vis a vis* the police force must be regulated by statutory process, so that nothing lawless, dubious, arbitrary or oblique is done under guise of oral or written instruction, secretly making the police a political instrumentality or amenable to extraneous pressures and partiality.

Periodic professional courses in Human Rights and social justice must be imparted at every level of the police hierarchy by competent and seasoned organisations like the National Law School or Judicial Training Institute. The course must be based upon an agenda for community policing and the play of human rights in the daily dealings, involving the people and the police.

I suggest, with respect, that non-official bodies or highly respected personalities be given legal access to police officers to obtain information about matters of public concern *vis a vis* police operations. Another suggestion, which I found in Madison (USA), may be adapted so as to promote openness and reduce shady or secret methodology. Final year law students or those who are doing doctoral thesis in criminology may be given access, guided by a senior professor of the law school to visit police stations and offices at higher levels and acquaint themselves with the happenings inside. Not that confidential matters should be made available to the injury of investigations but that police offices be open to the public and nothing secretive, canny or dubious takes place. In short, such a procedure may strengthen the confidence of the people in police probity and processual rectitude.

The National Police Commission has recommended a draft Police Bill for consideration. That may have to be updated and brought in tune with the fundamental freedoms of the citizen and the victimological obligations of current jurisprudence. Today, the police is a suspect body. It need not be. Today, the police is regarded as an *armed force* not a *public service.* It need not be. Finally, policing must be given a high functional status, considerable technological training and constant subjection to invigilatory oversight by a statutory functionary with power to inquire and, in turn, submit public reports like any other public authority amenable to the rule of law. The Police are trustees of public peace and are under on fiduciary duty to the people.

Let me conclude with a sober quote:

> *Much about the moral fiber of a society can be learned from the way it deals with crime. It is not enough to treat criminals with as much compassion as we can, especially when this liberal spirit is carried to the excess of interfering with crime prevention as the courts have done. It's about time society showed a little moral strength by acknowledging that victims, real people, are hurt by crime and that it is to them that criminals owe their debt.*
>
> *—Editorial, "Making Criminals Pay," The Wall Street Journal.*

INFORMATION EXPLOSION—A VISION STATEMENT

We live in an age of technological revolution a fallout of which is the information explosion. The inconceivable speed and global reach of information communication marvel makes the world shrink and humanity an intimate family. Our media age, with the extraordinary volume and wonder of transmission, has diminished distance and facilitated instant informational delivery. If only this great potential could be operated in a just and fair manner promotive of peace, equality, just relations and human rights, this phenomenon would midwife a better World Order. Such a glorious prospect would catalyze stability, peace and universal happiness. Such a tremendous transformation would be a fulfillment of a dream too dazzling to believe and too paradasiac to be a reality. Why? In an unequal world, with disproportionate distribution of power to deliver motivated information, control over the dissemination of news and views to their best advantage by the State or the Proprietariat may lead to manufacture of public opinion to advance the interests of giant corporations and gargantuan institutions. The poor of the world will suffer, because suffocation of information which will tell the truth about the suppression and oppression of the weaker sections will deny them freedom of expression and destroy their democratic right to gain equal space in the minds of mankind, mould world opinion and win social justice. In this view, the basic question is *for whom* does the information revolution prove a blessing, *who* operates the communication process, *what* is the content of the facts fed into the circulation system and *whom* does it target.

In a globally brain-washed society, the management of power and the manipulation of minds are operated through pliable institutions and profit-promoting technologies. Corporations are the macro-institutions readying to capture markets and putting to unscrupulous use the processes of information technology. Indoctrination through suitably designed information processing is their expertise. Calvin Coolidge, long ago President of America, once told the world that 'the business of America is business'. Bush Senior and Bush the Younger, recent and current Presidents of the U.S.; assuming universal jurisdiction, hold Big Business interests as *their business* and use explosive information technology to expropriate the world's resources. The invasion of Iraq, with no U.N. sanction or other legal or moral justification as an urgent necessity to defend the American people and the world from Saddam Hussain's *Weapons of Mass Destruction* was, by a preposterous perversion of propaganda, criticised by many as *Weapons of Mass Deception.* Baghdad is the most heavily bombed city in the world in history and yet, by media mendacity and informational unveracity, a crime against humanity was projected as liberation of Iraq. Truth loses its language and speaks the way the information controllerate orders it to perform.

When we glorify information revolution we must investigate the hidden agendas of Corporate Power and the victimisation of the voiceless Unpeople of the Earth. John Pilger trenchantly observes in his brilliant book Hidden Agendas:

> *The children of Iraq are Unpeople. So, too, are the half a million children who, according to UNICEF, die beneath the burden of unrepayable debt owed by their governments to the West. One Filipino child is said to die every hour, in a country where more than half the national budget is given over to paying just the interest on World Bank and IMF loans. These facts are not allowed to interrupt the cosy British ritual of Red Nose Day, when the money raised for 'the poor of the world' is but a fraction of that paid by the governments of the poor to Western banks on the same day. Britain, which has an 'ethical' foreign policy, demands levels of debt repayment that far outweigh new loans or aid; only the United States has a longer record of taking more money from the developing world than it gives out. It was not until the government of Mexico threatened to repudiate its debt, an action that might have brought down the Western banking system, that the wider issue was retrieved from media oblivion. (Page 3)*

The developed world drapes its exploitative devices in attractive informational apparel making disaster of developing countries look like blessing in disguise, making a colonised state appear as salvaged democracy, making every country under American military dependency a free nation. Informational exaggeration and communication manipulation project globalisation, liberalisation and privatisation as the dawn of a golden era, a myth, while, in truth, it is ambitious, aggressive, global economic occupation, market conquest for Multi-nationals and subjugation of cultural pluralism by imperial, consumerist mono-culture.

Whenever events have occurred which affect vast masses of humble humans, little space and time is given to the fair communication of information or to the quality of their presentation or the style of their projection. Coco Cola advertisement claims more importance than T.V news of mass starvation or disease. Indeed, 'infortainment' and 'infoadvertising' programmes flow seamlessly into commercials with little time for poverty news or facts which concern the underprivileged. Britain and the BBC are not far behind in the ever diminishing importance to the little men of the world. Multi-nationals control the media taking the cue from the media baron Rugert Murdoch who set his role in the communication revolution as a Colossus. In Britain, on what is still lauded as 'the best television service in the world', only 3 per cent of peak-time programmes feature anything about the majority of humanity, and almost all of that is confined to the 'minority' channels, if you exclude Clive James laughing at the Japanese. In the media's 'global village', other nations do not exist unless they are useful to 'us'.

> *Regardless of the BBC's enduring façade of 'impartiality' and 'standards', news is now openly ideological and uniform, as the demands of the 'market' supercult are met. When slow news is included, it is more than likely dressed in a political and social vocabulary that ensures the truth is lost. Thus, in Britain, as in the United States (and Australia), the systematic impoverishment of a quarter of the population is routinely filed under 'underclass', an American term describing a corrupting, anti-social group outside society. The solution to poverty, which is the return of vast wealth taken from the poor by the rich, is seldom given a public airing. The 'new' system of capitalism for the powerless and socialism for the powerful, under which the former are persecuted and the latter are given billions in public subsidies, is rarely identified as such. Terms like 'modernisation' are preferred.*

Information becomes disinformation and misinformation when interests of powerful nations are involved. For instance 'The Gulf War in 1991 was reported as a technological wonder, an event of bloodless science in which, rejoiced one editorial writer, there were 'miraculously few casualties'. It was one of the most covered wars in history, yet few journalists reported the truth, still widely unknown, that a quarter of a million Iraqis were wantonly slaughtered or died unnecessary deaths. The bloodfest, the fate of the children of Iraq has been the slowest of news. Who knows that at least half a million children have died as a direct result of economic sanctions imposed by the Western Powers? Who understands that the sanctions are aimed not at bringing down Saddam Hussain, or deterring him from building some mythical nuclear bomb, but at presenting the 'market' capture of Iraq oil for forcing down the price of oil produced by Saudi Arabia, the West's most important Middle Eastern proxy.

By the art of suppressio veri and suggestio falsi, facts can be made to tell flexibly the opposite of the truth by making the worse appear the better reason. The Vietnamese war where America shocked the world by raining weapon to wipe out a people, with no legal or moral justification, is one of the mega-instances where Himalayan lies and Niagara of motivated views were poured forth to make out the all- out American assault on the Vietnamese people as a noble cause. The defeat of America, after inflicting a tragedy on Vietnam, was not a triumph of information but a tragedy of truth until M. Namara confessed that he was guilty of waging the war.

John Pilger, in his great book the 'Hidden Agendas', has sharply observed:

> *A Freedom of Information Act unfettered by 'exemptions', the establishment of a public body to provide start-up funds for newspapers, journals and broadcasters independent of the monopolists, a new Broadcasting Act that stops the richest and biggest swallowing the smallest and requires an unfettered commitment to original drama and independent factual programmes—these would begin to win the second battle for the freedom of the press.*
>
> *It is a freedom we are in danger of losing without even knowing it. For when there is no longer anyone speaking out, who will be the last voice? (P-546)*

Indeed, lies are spread as information invented, not merely for purposes of war but also for purposes of cultural occupation of minds of people, so that global economic exploitation may be concealed and ideologically projected as world-wide benefaction. This syndrome of terminological travesty as credible verity through information channels is what Vandana Shiva, the Indian Social Scientist, challenges as the western-imposed mono-culture of the mind and has called for an 'insurrection of subjugated knowledge' against the 'dominant knowledge of capitalism. She wrote '90% of the dominant knowledge could be stopped without any risk of human deprivation'. Alas! Media technology has become a wondrous communication tournament. The speed at which pictures, voices and the printed word can be transmitted ought to invest in news gathering a socially responsible obligation so that what is now terminological terrorism in the hands of political, military and economic power may be tamed into a socially beneficiant instrument for the good of humanity. Otherwise, as brought out with a sting in the book 'Food First', world hunger will be a harmless profit-making process of Big Business, World Control of Water will become the thirst-relieving business of Big Business and the agricultural revolution in developing countries, now propagandised as a boon, will be a bane, a ruse to expand the business of multinational and rob the cultivation of Third World countries of their land's fertility and counter land reform. Farmers in these countries will gradually become the 'new slaves' of exploitative technology. Banana republics, Cucumber republics, Cocoa republics and like other victimised agricultural republics demonstrate the power of information manipulation as a mammoth weapon of Mammon.

Information Technology, by greatly promoting the power of multinational corporations, holds the South as ransom and brings down employment. Post-modern technology needs no manpower and thrives without a large number of people at work. But this vastly increases unemployment of the masses, accompanied by the 'affluenza' of the classes, is cited as a sign of progress. There will be more cars in the streets, more fast-food shops in the bazaars and more sky scrappers for the rich to occupy. But there will be more hunger and disease, more illiteracy and suicides, more infant mortalities and less hospitals (except fivestar hospitals for the wealth). This dimension of social reality is hidden as non-information which the electronic and print media do not reveal.

A brief deviation here is instructive about the corporate game of suppression and manipulation of technological information. One dimension of corporate control over information unlimited is the 'knowledge monopoly' they possess and use to their advantage. Illustratively, I may make a parting reference to the use of chemicals in agriculture. Pest management and the propagation of pesticides is a danger zone. The authors of Food First point out that while agribusiness corporations are trying to promote 'blind', scheduled spraying in underdeveloped countries such as India, farmers in the United States have found that on top of environmental and health damage they were being just plain swindled. The painful truth is that chemical companies dominate research institutions to promote their brands of pesticides which are injurious but produce profit to the chemical companies. Pesticide alternatives are prevented from coming into the field by pressure tactics of these monopolies. The real threat is that pesticides technology is in the hands of a few corporations that will profit only if they can continue to make farmers and 'concerned people' everywhere believe that our very survival depends on the indiscriminate use of their products.

The threat is ever more ominous since some supposedly impartial bodies that could form a counter force to the power of multinational agribusinesses have become, instead, their agents Organizations such as the F.A.O., far from developing and disseminating suitable alternatives or even the knowledge of the appropriate use of pesticides, are becoming partners in promotion for chemical corporations.

We live in an era of GATTS domination and TRIPS regulation. In consequence, ownership of intellectual property rights, patents for news-views innovation and invention and processes and products, other trade secrets are now monopolised by patent-holding and like MNCs. Information is thus the property of Big Business and 'new knowledge' is blocked and barred by broad-based patentisation and similar legal throttles. Information revolution is now a controlled commodity available to affordable sections at fancy prices fixed by world corporates. News slavery is the 'new slavery'. An occupation army of hired researchers helps MNCs hold the Third World in intellectual colonialism.

Such can be the tragedy of twisted Information Revolution. It is a reversal of the values inscribed in the International Convention on the Freedom of Information which emphasises the right of the people to be *fully* and *reliably informed* through reportage of honest information and opinion and elimination of the scourge of war. If human rights are to be a pervasive reality in the world, a people-oriented freedom of information jurisprudence must be on the statute book of every country.

Information is light and absence of it is darkness. If democracy is to be luminous, access to information in the custody of any public functionary, with appropriate infrastructure, must be available at every level of the State and on every matter of public concern. Transparency in public affairs, if denied, totalitarian governance will deprive the people of their great rights. That is why, a comprehensive Freedom of Information Act, covering every range of exercise of authority, must be a feasible reality. An apology of Freedom of Information Act has been provided by Parliament by enacting Freedom of Information Act, 2002 (Act V of 2003). The creation of a Public Information Officer notwithstanding, the statute is a poor substitute for a peremptory power to acquire every class of information which is of concern or interest to every person in the polity. A detailed discussion of the insufficiencies of the Indian Act V of 2003 is a worthwhile adventure but beyond the range of this essay.

Governmental secrets are a negation of the citizens' *right to know.* Most often, the ruling class manages to hide inconvenient truth and even where there is a law compelling disclosure, it is too expensive, procedurally complicated, in practice dilatory, and as a nett result the right becomes ineffectual. The appointment of judges, for instance, is a secret process, altogether beyond the reach of the common man. The judiciary has vast powers. Therefore, candidates for appointment to these high offices must be publicly known, their assets and relationships publicly known and their past activities and social perspectives must be publicly known. Regrettably, the Indian judges, and everything about them including the manner and criteria of their appointment are a closed book. These observations apply equally to all other public functionaries. There should be a law compelling publicity about these aspects of the judiciary and other categories. Currently, their misdoings are kept a guarded secret.

There is a code of conduct and ethics for judges now said to exist, but unknown to the public and with no legal backing.

The assets of candidates, who seek to become legislators and ministers and local bodies members must be revealed to the public. The people who are governed by these representatives, if elected, must have an opportunity to gain full information about their standing, their wealth, their commitments, their communal association and their social philosophy. Similarly the fate of files pending before the Government, the source of dockets pending before the court, the fate of resources of voluntary agencies in the public field, must be an open book. Indeed, if democracy is Government *by the people,* public authority must be obliged to live in transparency. Corruption in public life, undue delay in disposal of litigation, including delivery of judgements, concealment of police investigation and secret surveillance, income tax evasion and huge bank deposits and defaults can no longer be immune from people's right to know. The modern corporations are the engine of economic operations. They are mindless juggernauts hell-bent on high profits and big rackets. They can do harm to the consumer public and in that sense corporate activities cannot enjoy deleterious confidentiality. In all these cases, freedom of information must enjoy priority status. The professions, medical, legal and other, are practitioners of power. Their functionalism must come under social audit. This is possible only if the law of freedom of information provides open sesame to their work and wealth. Of course, these general statements are subject to exceptions, privacy and confidentiality being necessary in public interest in special cases. Military secrets, cabinet secrets, mutual judicial deliberations and even domestic secrets may enjoy privileges of privacy. The broad proposition is, as the old Roman adage runs, 'whatever touches all should be decided by all'. But Decision is preceded by knowledge and knowledge by information. Thus freedom of information has a high democratic status. Consumers of justice, of good medical treatment, of sound administrative policies and in public corporate managements *are the people*—if they are to fulfill their functions as citizens it is fundamental that the freedom guaranteed under the Constitution must become viable, not illusory, pragmatic not merely philosophic.

MARAD MASSACRE—A NATIONAL ALARUM

The Marad beach, a fisher folk's small colony a few miles off Calicut, has lovely sands and salubrious breeze, the Arabian Sea making the ambience of the place so soothing that people, not putting out to sea, are tempted at sunset to sit and gossip until yawning hours of night. Two communities, Hindu and Muslim, live in proximity and seeming amity and their hefty oarsmen's occupation is coastal fishing. There is a temple nearby and so too a mosque. Speaking generally, no overt communal rivalry marred the peace of the locality nor was there provocative pugnacity between the Arayas (Hindu fishing community) and their Muslim counterpart. But there did break out in January 2002 a sudden breach of the peace which had no antecedent communal tension on the surface; but five people died, three Muslim and two Hindu and it was a Hindu-Muslim scrimmage too violently planned to be dismissed as a spontaneous eruption. The methodology suggested the presence of outside elements in the perpetration of the crime. There was a terrible outcry about this communal carnage. Many, including me, visited the scene and measures to mollify, grant relief and restore peaceful coexistence were undertaken. Apparent calm came to prevail although only a small police outpost and some relief measures in separate centres made symbolic State presence. The indolent investigation where a clash and carnage with grave portents gored the locality, did not result in a charge-sheet till *May next year.* Who will police the police? Remember, if the culprits are not brought to book with blitz speed reprisals and bitter fall-outs will breed revenge. No alibi avails the State in procrastination of investigation and inaction in intensification of invigilation. Anyway, for well over a year the fishermen's boats were busy occupationally and the people of Kerala slumbered assuming that life was normal. Terrorism dies hard and eternal vigilance is the desideratum of communal pacifism. The embers burn beneath, the surface quietude deceives. When external forces have access, ad hoc exercises are self-delusive. Deeper probes, more fundamental therapies, more perennial fraternization alone can counter Hindu-Muslim alienation, which may look local, but the groups hardly bury the hatchet. A hard look at the etiology of underground strategies of communal extremists reveals that mere monetary compensation to victims and formation of all-party conciliation committees are short-run anodynes while subterranean sinister indoctrination and invisible infiltration of fundamentalist operators remain undetected. Trained police intelligence capable of gathering light about subversive planning is a professional job of which the clumsy lathi-happy swaggering police force, easy at violence and facile with third degree crudities, are innocent.

It was Friday, 2nd May; the breeze was cool, the white sands, with a lovely view of the waves foamy blowing, were a refreshing rendezvous to relax and gossip in the evening. A group of simple Araya fishermen slipped and sat in the cushioned sand dunes and enjoyed idle conversation with the crimson sun beautifying the sky in the distance. The temple on the other side, at lamp-lighting time, found a few devotees around and otherwise Nature was calm, women were inside their humble homes and the scenic beach was brimful of rustic delight. And then swooped on the Araya innocents a savage brood of Islamic extremists with sharp weapons like swords or long curved knives with blood-thirsty blitz to unloose murder most foul, most treacherous, most barbaric. From more than one direction rushed this rabid rascal gang, with lethal arms and killer plan, stabbed the defenseless Araya gossip group, a devotee returning from the temple and a neighbouring petty tea shop dealer and spread terror by throwing bombs which did not explode. Had they burst, the number of the dead would have multiplied. Eight lost their lives and many more were wounded. One Muslim from the attacking raiders was hit by accident (?) and died in the melee. The glorious Marad sunset scene, in a few horrendous minutes, was drenched in blood and rent in cries and tears, with the police arriving after the savage carnage was committed and the terrorist felons had fled. Mobile phones were in action, the murders were perfectly organized, the villains made good their escape in vehicles waiting to operate the quick exit. A large cache of swords and knives were stored in the neighbouring masjid and the unholy heap of dastardly weapons were later siezed by the police. Beneath the heavy sands were hidden a large sabre stock ready as a reserve for a mass massacre. And the holy mosque, as a culpable custodian of weapons artful and asylum of assailants, betrayed an organised plot for a macro-scale gory *modus operandi*. The armed aggressors were not necessarily local Islamic hostiles retaliating the earlier year-old brutal battle—what is often referred to as Marad I. Maybe that too was a malignant motivation. Extraneous extremist infiltration and preparation, if true, make Marad II a darkly dangerous portent, not a mere coastal clash of Arayas and Mohallah fishing rivals. There is deeper ideological militancy, graver fundamentalist extremism, terribly more astute strategy and monetary investment; and Project Extermination outwitted Police Intelligence, political information and people's suspicion. Marad, with a little police outpost and no professional criminal intelligence mechanism, reveals the disastrous flop and tragic inefficiency of State and society in the preservation of secularity and security. If this happens in Kerala, the paradigm of political alertness, media ubiquity and communal harmony, what is the prospect of Indian humanity as a fraternity? *The Marad syndrome sounds a national alarum.* Beware!

Last week, in the company of leading social activists, I visited this coastal suburb, was enchanted by the charming azure expanse and wafting winds but as we entered the tiny homesteads where the Hindu victims of the killer villains had lived, cries of the bereaved changed our mood. What solace can you offer when the bread-winner of the family in the very flower of youth is brutally stabbed dead while sitting in the sunny sands relaxing and guilelessly gossiping? My eyes were wet and I was speechless as I heard the women sobbing and narrating. Grief from cottage to cottage! But yet the pity of it—O, the pity of it! In helpless silence we listened and each widow added a new dimension to dastardly death. Then we heard the Araya Samaj President and Secretary who were tense and yet sombrely sober as they demanded from us not sympathy but justice. Sympathy is easy sentiment but justice is made of sterner stuff. Secular progressives merely condemn, in general neutrality, communal chauvinism. Hindu communalists, as majority communalists, are trenchantly stigmatized. But, but the Araya leaders challengingly urged us why Islamic communalists who shoot and hate are not denounced harshly. They have a point, as I explained at an evening dialogue that day. They argued with agony that the mosque was the sanctuary of Islamic terrorists and nidus of weapons for Hindu slaughter. Then why should they not be taken over by the District Magistrate for the sake of law and order? Was not the Golden Temple, where Bindranwala sought refuge, the subject of Blue Star operation? Was not Sivagiri, sacred shrine of Narayana Guru glory, taken over by the District Magistrate? True, mosques or other shrines cannot be operational shelters of religious extremists for violent incitement or surprise siege? These issues are of national relevance, especially since sacerdotal bigotry, all religions included, has no territorial barrier. Blandly describing communal disturbances as obnoxious is different from zeroing-in on communal terrorism which is diabolic treachery. Deadly divisiveness is assuming apartheid dimensions. In Marad, the Araya Samaj told us, with burning rage, that the Muslim game plan is to drive out the Arayas from the entire Malabar sea coast to monopolise sea fishing for their community. This territorial terrorism is dangerous, if true, because this would lead to massive battles all along the West Coast and may spread to the East

Coast. The pharmacopoeia of human solidarity must discover dynamic panacean processes if Indian democracy is to survive. No serendipitous recipe is ready in the political repertoire. "We, the People of India" *as a dialectical reality and cultural fundamentality,* is dearer than party politics and regional or religious devotion. This is the first axiom of patriotism and the last testament of Hind Swaraj. A passionate nationalism, with paramountcy over party loyalty or paroctual obduracy, is high on the agenda of Indian integrity. Let us begin with this *mandate of Marad.* Who lives if India dies? That solemn summons, not one-up-manship in power-crazy politics, is the *yuga dharma* from classrooms to Houses of the Legislature and every public office in our native land. Kilkenny cat communalism can be conquered only by a profound, pervasive swaraj commitment in action and a tearing and raging campaign for an indivisible unity as the warp and woof of Indian humanity. All else comes next. Statesmen, do you listen?

The Marad massacre, as the victim families reminded us, proves that minority Islamic communalism, is as militantly blood-thirsty as majority communalism 'red in tooth and claw' as Hindutva extremism is—a la Gujarat. The voice of secularism cannot be soft towards either.

State action in countering communal explosion, tension and underground operation has been an exercise in futility all over the country, with political 'sound and fury signifying nothing'. Look at Marad—and there are Marads in every State—with a background of communal slaughter, and yet a mere police outpost! After the event, khaki uniforms and guns everywhere! I found the same dismal neglect in other communally explosive areas like Nadapuram. A new police road map is an urgent desideratum. Location of fully equipped police stations where simmering violence may burst aflame any moment, more technology and mobility, more special training and intelligence wings, more vigilance personnel and nocturnal rounds with focus sod attention on shrines, festivals and secret hide-outs, more scrutiny over religious classes and drills—these are 'more honoured in the breach than the observance'.

Epilogue—The Lessons of Marad

The first battle of Marad, a broad daylight lightning attack with bleeding communal consequences, took fifteen months for the police to issue charge sheet giving dubious excuses. True Marad II, (by Islamic extremists) produced a better account of alert police operation. They rushed in numbers, searched and siezed from the sands and the Masjid huge quantities of arms and incriminatory articles, took into custody many suspects and got on to the trail of the culprits, although some of the key planners and cunning perpetrators are still to be tracked down. The Crime branch has done a good job despite the political—communal imbroglio and the complete discovery is yet distances away. Why?

Terrorism, be it in Kashmir or Kerala, Assam or Tripura, often outwits the State machine in technology, strategy mobility and celerity. Police reforms with creative cadres, talented and trained personnel, updated familiarity with technology, sociology and criminology to match the enemy, is a 'consummation devoutly to be wished'. A *miscellany* of policemen on traffic duty and V.I.P. duty, on intelligence gathering and investigative functionalism plus plus can never be equal to the challenge of specialisation in each department sans which police efficiency is sure to be a uniformed futility and authoritarian illusion.

One final plea

Divided Marad is divided Bharat. Homogenise or perish! Therefore, the two communities in dynamic comity, with distinct identity but neighbourhood fraternity, must come together in moral and spiritual fellowship and material camaraderie. A tearing and raging campaign to extirpate violent extremism and terrorist godism is the only means of promoting civil society solidarity and preserving pluralist democracy. Rehabilitation of refugees, regardless of religion, by a process of communal symbiosis, organised as a non-discriminatory, people-oriented unitive project, is the beginning of a dynamic *modus vivendi*. That is the message and mandate of Marad.

I do not lend any credence whatever to the displacement bogey contrary to the fundamental freedom of residence for any Indian anywhere in the territory of India. Propagandist gambits, scary rumour and intimidatory stratagems must be dismissed as mischievous myth to unnerve the weaker Arayas by the local Mahal majority or as exaggerated imaginary communal concoctions by vicious vested interests. But rumours may inflame and spread and claim harmony as casualty unless timely joint vigilant action convincingly extinguishes the alarm.

TRANSNATIONAL CORPORATIONS AND PIRACY OF AYURVEDIC HERITAGE

Introductory

The General Agreement on Trade and Tariffs (GATT) was launched in 1948 with the creative objective of promoting fair international trade relations and tariff reduction so that the goal of global justice in commerce and business may be achieved among member nations the world over. However, the leopard cannot change its spots nor super-capitalist powers miss opportunities to exploit the developing nations shedding their imperialist appetites.

The treaties of TRIPS, TRIMS and TRIS eventually led to the creation of the WTO which is the international instrumentality now in force. This organization and its North-biased operation have made it clear that the South is in the grip of Gattastrophe and neo-colonialism. From Seattle to Doha to Cancun it has become plain that the developing countries have to face victimization from the developed countries. That apart, multinational corporations are proving a menace to the wealth of the South in other ways. India, in particular, has to safeguard its vast, unique and world-famous pharmaceutical wealth by appropriate strategies.

Defense of Ayurveda against Piracy and Patency

The Uruguay Round of GATT Negotiations concluded in 1993 and the World Trade Organization (WTO) came into being in 1995. This global legal authority, with its imperial slant, controls the commercial destiny of East and West, North and South. Its jurisdiction is international in operation and its jurisprudence subjugates the South to benefit the North with an apparent veneer of judicial neutrality. The agreement on Trade Related Intellectual Property Rights (TRIPs) governs all types of Intellectual Property Rights (IPR) including grant of patents.

Conquest of markets everywhere through technologies as well as by capturing product patents is a master-strategy of Multi-National

Corporations (MNCs). Indian intellectual property, in the ancient field of ayurveda, may come under the skullduggery of MNCs using the dubious device of piracy and patenting of ayurvedic pharmaceuticals. Our pliable Central Government may repeatedly amend the 1970 Act and Indian ayurveda may well become an exotic MNC pharmacopoeia. The accessibility and affordability and authenticity of ayurvedic medicines will be adversely affected if the patent laws are so changed by the cunning and clout of MNCs to bring them in line with their interests. In this context, we must remember our *constitutionally* mandated *fundamental duty*, under Art. 51A(f) to 'value and *preserve* the rich heritage of our composite culture'. Our medicinal legacy, a few thousand years old, is ayurveda, derived from the Maharshis and supplemented by tribal medicals and other plural systems native to the soil. It will be a betrayal of fundamental right to life (Art.21) and duty if we allow insidious invasion by macro-corporates committing piracy of our ancient formulations and drug wonders, with a view to practise 'golden deer' packagery, and thereby alienate Indian producers of ayurvedic pharmaceuticals from their own country. This is not a theoretical apprehension but an operative misappropriation against which sovereign India, as the defender of its people's health, must take preemptive steps. Swaraj jurisprudence, with sensitive nationalism and concern for the health of the people, must use parliamentary legislation and WTO litigation, to defend our unique system of medicine from conquest by patent—a peril to ignore which is to jettison our priceless pharmacopeial asset well known globally for its curative glory. In this context, the nation must conscientize itself so that patents cannot be granted of any ayurvedic or tribal medicine since it *involves no invention* but belongs to India's widely known indigenous materia medica. Insidious foreign invasion and stealthy transmission of our drug wonders can never be novelty, invention or creative innovation, a sine qua non of patent claim.

We may note at this point that neither TRIPS nor other international agreements will bind the Indian people unless national legislation is made in implementation. It is useful to note that the U.S. law specifically stipulates that no provision of the WTO, inconsistent with any law of the United States, shall have effect. In the U.K., treaties are not accepted until given effect to by Parliament. It is thus open to the Indian Parliament to make a comprehensive legislation protecting ayurveda and other native systems of medicine from inroads by foreign countries. The indigenous medical knowledge of India must be insulated from piracy and patents. Of course, India will be under increasing pressure from U.S. and Europe to further amend its patent laws not to exclude ayurvedic drugs. Demands for green medicines, instead of synthetic products, are escalating in the western world. Sales of plant based drugs rose from $4.5 billion in 1980 to $15.5 billion in 1990. Similar increases in other countries are noticeable. 50% of the world's estimated plant species are in tropical rain forests and India is world's richest bio-diversity hotspot and is now a prey of bio-quarry and bio-piracy. In the interest of our country it is basic nationalism to make effective legislation against injury to ayurvedic system of medicines. Our vast bio-diversity and well-developed indigenous medicine system developed through generations shall not be bartered away thoughtlessly as if we are a colony and the North is an imperial power.

Independently of this argument, our national leaders must remember that *health for all is an international commitment by India* and that guarantee must override any other international agreements advocated by powerful corporations hungry for markets. The right to medical care for the humblest human is integral to the Alma Ata Declaration (1979) in which India, among 134 nations, pledged urgent action. A recent session in August 2000 of the sub-commission of U.N. Commission on human rights has concluded that the TRIPS agreement constitutes contravention of international human rights law. The implementation of the TRIPS does not adequately reflect concern for the *right to health of the people.* Parliament has a solemn obligation to protect the fundamental right to life under Article 21, of every Indian. Western medicine, now that product patents are included by amendment in the Patent law, will rise in price sky high. In this view it is just, fair and reasonable and consistent with international human rights law to legislatively defend the native systems of medicine against piracy and patentisation.

Already Germany and other countries are committing covert robbery of our herbal therapy and bio-diversity. They are taking patents in their country on the view that patents in their country, because of TRIPS provisions, will bind our country. India must, with all emphatic opposition, resist the application in our country or elsewhere the validity of patents of ayurvedic drugs. Even under the existing patents law, no patent can be granted unless there is a clear *case of invention* claimed by the patentee. It is outrageous that any German can claim any *invention* of an ayurvedic drug. So also of herbal medicines popular all over India. What we have to do is to drive home the point that ayurveda, siddha, unani and tribal medicines are not secret therapies, never German serendipities, but public property available to anyone who reads the relevant texts and meets any medical practitioner of the system. A data base, comprehensive in scope, plenary in planned presentation, collected with painstaking investigation and made available with appropriate sources and references to anyone interested, will defeat the pretense of any foreigner who urges a phoney plea of *discovery*.

Apart from drugs and medicinal herbs, there are a wealth of medical treatments by way of oil massage, eye exercises and yoga practices which are fantastic in their curative benefits. Kerala has a glorious tradition in these therapeutic procedures. Tamil Nadu has an excellent native orthopaedic system with special oils and ointments. So too Kerala. These cannot be smuggled and patented. To claim that our life-saving indigenous drugs now open to numbers of native physicians as inventions is a therapeutic outrage. Glittering packaging and minor manipulations do not sustain a patent claim.

Our pharmacology is part of our sovereignty and it is public property beyond the pale of patent jurisprudence. Our case against such patentisation must be fought before the W.T.O. The recent controversy of patent for cotton seeds, turmeric powder, neem extract, basmati rice and others, and securing of patent by M.N.Cs. for common place items like dosai, idli, pullao, curry etc has brought out the fact that we have foreign foes who will fight even for frivolous and fraudulent patents. Indigenous therapeutics, herbalist heritage and publicly owned treasure house of medical knowledge, now in peril of deprivation, must awaken Parliament into nationalist legislation. To exclude patents based on traditional/ indigenous knowledge and essentially derived products and processes from such knowledge, has been the stand of the Government of India *vis a vis* Article 273(b) of TRIPs agreement Parliament must hasten with adequate legislation to make this claim a legal reality.

Coda

Negative hostility to foreign surreptitious operations and patentisation is not enough. Our Governments and native pharmacologists, vaidyas and custodians of ancient Indian therapeutics orally transmitted from generation to generation must collect all these processes and products, document them, popularize their use and modernize their qualitative and quantitative availability in capsules and bottles and other traditional containers and market them attractively. Our pharmacology is a rare treasure house which can benefit humanity if preserved, pooled together presentably and protected from adulteration and pilferage and betrayal for a few pieces of silver or dollars.

Maharshi Mahesh Yogi is making ayurveda internationally known as a great gift of India to humanity. There is an Ayurvedic University in London founded and run by Dr. Varier (belonging to Kerala). There are a few distinguished ayurvedic treatment centers in India, particularly Kerala, where scrupulous attention is paid to authentic herbal medicine and massage methodology. But the new menace of foreign invasion, money-oriented and packaging glitter, may have to be resisted by appropriate national legislation.

Swaraj has a pharmacopic dimension derived from sages and tribals and enriched by ages of practice and progressive changes but emphatically insisting on purity of drugs and methodologies.

PEOPLE'S COMMISSION ON PERVERSION OF OUR PATENT LAWS

When the economic history of Independent India comes to be written with the vision and passion of the Founding Fathers of our Constitution, the perversion of our excellent Patents Act 1970 and the subversion of our national interests through GATT treaties will be condemned as brazen betrayal of people's concerns committing the country to global corporate commands. This humiliating syndrome has been called GATTastrophe and Operation Recolonisation. The Report of the People's Commission on Patent Law for India, which is the book under review, exposes, stage by stage, the shameful story of the Government of India's unfortunate surrender and political cover-up landing the nation in a situation where people's battles for winning back Patent Swaraj, inside parliament and through campaigns outside, are necessitous.

Patents are monopolies and monopolies are evil unless regulated by law designed to serve social justice, national interests and pragmatic considerations. Patents have come to stay the world over and India inherited a colonial system which was overthrown by a fine piece of legislation—the Indian Patents Act, 1970—based on the brilliant, balanced Ayyangar Commission Report. Public interest was in the forefront but foreign patent holders also had a fair deal. The Americans held the largest number of patents under the 1970 Act. The philosophy of the Indian legislation is that patents are granted to promote inventions to be worked in this country on a commercial scale without undue delay. Only *process* patents, not *product* patents for food, medicine and agro-chemicals. No profit from pain and suffering and no patents for living matter and other vital items of national concern. Public interest mechanisms like compulsory licensing, licenses of right and revocation, these and other pro bono provisions made the Indian Act a glory that benefited the people, stimulated native pharmaceuticals and saved the health of the nation from the grab rapacity of foreign corporate operators. Says Keayla, who has a life-long record of study of Indian pharmaceutical jurisprudence and commitment to Indian humanity, has authoritatively stressed, with facts and figures, how our benign law kept prices down *vis a vis* Pakistan, UK, USA *et al.* It is because of our patent system that the price differential is so favourable for us.

Had not the 1970 Act arrested prices of medicines and given incentives for phenomenal pharmaceutical development India would have been in a crisis instead of being the lowest in relation to the glaring differences in product patent regimes. Likewise the availability of new products and medicines from indigenous sources would have been hard had our dependence on imports been the main source. The truth is that the finest hour of pharmaceutical jurisprudence arrived with the 1970 Act but the decline and fall of health for all began with the Uruguay Round of GATT and the Dunkel Draft Text. The right to medical care for the humblest human is integral to the Alma Ata Declaration (1979) in which India, among 134 nations, pledged urgent action and the resolution of the 38th World Health Assembly gave this promise practical shape.

Nevertheless, American pressure mounted, Uruguay Round negotiations made September 1986 the beginning of the end of the great days of Indian Patent Law. GATTastrophe, if one may express the Patent Law tragedy graphically, found the Indian Government a *soft State.* Indeed, Government was playing hide and seek with Parliament and pretended to be resistant to the retaliatory threat of the U.S. Trade Act (Super 301 and Special 301). This was evasive comedy and contradictory. There was public opinion mounting against Government's surrender to the Dunkel Draft. Indeed, in between, the Gujral Departmental Related Parliamentary Standing Committee on Commerce in its Third Report (1993-94) was critical of Government's ambivalence.

Alas, at Marrakesh (1994) without parliamentary approval the Central Executive signed away India's commercial independence. The deed was done, the WTO treaty was signed—sans serious parliamentary debate. Government ratified the Final Act of GATT and the 'fifth act' of the tragedy was completed. Any important international treaty innocent of parliamentary ratification is guilty of sabotage of democracy—a fundamental flaw overlooked by our Founding Fathers while framing the Constitution. The Constitution Review Committee headed by Justice Venkitachaliah has drawn attention to this basic blemish. Anyway, the Marrakesh signature of 1994 obligated India to implement TRIPS, trade related Intellectual Property Rights (IPR) Agreement. Thus the nationwide opposition to TRIPS became futile and the struggle was to salvage people's rights as much as possible out of the traumatic TRIPS patent system. Government went ahead with The Patent Amendment

Ordinance, 1994. The bill to replace the ordinance was opposed but passed in the Lok Sabha where the Government had a majority. However, in the Rajya Sabha, Government had no majority and so the bill was referred to a Select Committee of the House. Meanwhile political events, consequent on the dissolution of the Lok Sabha in May 1996, led to the lapse of the bill. During the budget session of Parliament in March 1999 a bill was passed varying the provisions Act of 1970. A subsequent parliamentary committee of both houses submitted a report and a fresh bill as revised was finally passed in May 2002, with 64 amendments. The discussion in parliament was powerful and voiced on the floor of the House the importance of affordability, accessibility, and availability of drugs to all sections of society. Vain words!

The passage of the bill is not the last word on the law and the life of the people. Creative criticism cannot be silenced until Patents Jurisprudence comes to human terms with social justice. Murassoli Maran at Doha demanded deep concern for the welfare of the Indian people while interpreting and applying the TRIPS agreement. We must begin the battle for change. Parliament must speak for US, not for the U.S. The present People's Commission is an expression of this desideratum. Headed by Sri I.K. Gujral this eminent collective of intellectuals is a powerful mission capable of informing public opinion and illumining parliamentary cerebration. Look at the composition. Gujral's great experience, Dr. Yusuf Hamied's specialisation par excellence, Rajiv Dhavan's superlative juristic expertise and the distinguished participation of Muchkund Dubey, Ashok Parthasarathy and Yash Pal command compelling attention. The wisdom of the commission has resulted in positive recommendations of an extensive nature and I am sure the whole problem of patents may have to be subjected to luminous re-examination.

Dr. Yusuf Hamied, Managing Director, CIPLA is a pharmaceutical celebrity and humanist researcher whose universally recognised contribution to the curative dimension of AIDS deserves tribute. Each member of the People's Commission is an excellent choice. Let us listen to them.

One weighty view of the Commission needs emphatic mention.

> *India is a vast and poor country. Our Constitution in its Preamble provides that India is a Sovereign Socialist Secular Democratic Republic. It is thus obligatory on the part of the government that the people of the country are directly or indirectly apprised of the major economic issues. The people of the country have to be taken into confidence and there should be no question of maintaining any secrecy about the handling of WTO issues. A system has to be devised whereby people are able to debate and also there is debate in parliament to ensure arriving at national consensus on such issues.*
>
> *(Report of the Peoples' Commission Patent Laws for India, P-110)*

Articles 73 and 253 (the relevant treaty provisions) have to be so exercised by the Union Government as to bring the treaty *under the Constitution, not over it.* You cannot barter away the sovereignty of People of India by entering into a treaty making the country a vassal or colony of another. Such a treaty would be repugnant to the basic features of the Constitution.

Eventhough, the Patent (Second Amendment) Act, 2002 has been passed into law in May 2002, the plenary power of Parliament is not exhausted and the Supreme Court power to pronounce any provision of the treaty violative of the basic structure of the Constitution may still be exercised.

It must be remembered, as the commission reminds us:

> *TRIPs itself leaves open many matters for future consideration. Secondly, more importantly, treaties evolve and change over time in response to exigent needs. Before 1994, the international patent regime was very different from that which emerged under the aegis of the WTO treaty. A decade is a long time in such matters, India needs to approach the WTO and TRIPs with wide angled lenses so that the long term perspective is as much as they affect India's national interest and the interest of other nations is also not overlooked. (Report of the Peoples' Commission Patent Laws for India, P-92)*

The scope of patentability is a core issue. Article 27 of the TRIPS agreement covers not merely an inventive step but capability of industrial application. The Indian parliament can read down the meaning of 'invention' in such manner that it serves national interest. India is passing through a scenario of transition from process to product patent which has great relevance to pharma industry. All our ayurvedic wealth, herbal medicines and tribal recipes involve no novelty to an Indian and should not be available for patentisation under the western illusion of glittering packages and trivial tampering, to produce a seeming dilution and claiming the right to a patent.

Compulsory licensing system is extremely important to ensure the role of domestic enterprises to provide adequate availability of patented products. India's provision of licensing of right under the 1970 Act helped a great deal. The pharma industry has prices lowest in the world. The Commission has made flexible recommendations in formulating its compulsory licencing system.

The term of patents for twenty years is too long, taking the practical view that products become obsolete sooner. Therefore, we must insist on a shorter period suggested by realism. Pricing of patented products is very relevant for a country like India. Therefore, prices of patented products need to be regulated to safeguard the interests of the poor. Already seventy per cent. of the population cannot reach medicines. Therefore, affordable prices should be our slogan, so that the vast masses are not priced out of the market. Other recommendations of the Commission need expert examination. The Minister of Commerce and Industry has indicated that there will be another bill *viz.* the Patent (3rd Amendment) Bill which will be introduced before 1-1-2005. This is an occasion when a comprehensive study of the lacunae in the existing system and the necessity for flexibility in various provisions may be considered closely. Indian legislation must serve Indian reality *vis a vis* health resources and access, especially in times of emergencies.

> *8.31 The Doha Ministerial Declaration of November 2001 has already laid down a comprehensive work programme. Based on our past experience of Uruguay Round of GATT negotiations it would be in fitness of things if the new issues are first debated in Parliament. The government can prepare approach papers on various issues and then the same could be presented for debate in Parliament and if need be also in the State Legislative Assemblies. The constitutional provision is extremely important for the democratic system to survive in this country. Report of the Peoples' Commission on Patent Laws for India, P-112)*

The right to life of billion-strong Indian humanity—We, the People of India—is the ultimate accountability of our Indian Democratic Republic. People first, TRIPS next.

SOME NEW LIGHT ON CONSTITUTIONAL LAW—A REVIEW

Great books are rarely written by secretaries to Government, whatever the department. Subhash C. Jain is an exception, and as an author is a wonder of legal erudition. In his book—The Constitution of India—Select Issues and Perceptions—we have an instructive introduction reading which I have gained new knowledge, new dimensions of constitutional law and new angles from which difficult and disputed aspects of law could be luminously viewed. A bonus which one gets by buying Subhash Jain's book is a lovely, lucent foreword notable for its precise presentation of points with brevity and originality, coming, as it does, from the pen of my dear friend Justice Jeevan Reddy. Indeed, Jeevan's foreword deals with a few intricate issues of constitutional law with a facility and felicity which adds to the value of the book.

The Indian Constitution, is the cornerstone of the nation's governance. One of the longest in the world's national constitutions, our Paramount Parchment contains challenging issues which demand fuller exploration and more daring research than have been undertaken in the past; although we have a vast constitutional literature encyclopedic in value and lucubrative in volume. The handy work of Subhash Jain is packed with scholarship but is only five hundred pages in length. Delicate issues, embarrassing problems and ambiguous propositions find the author at his best, because without fear or favour, Jain brings to bear on the subject courageous analysis and recondite scholarship. For instance, he refers to the Westminster pattern we have adopted, which means that the President has to act on the aid and advice of the Cabinet with little discretion left; but is he a glorified ciphere? No! Here Subhash Jain wonders whether there is any scope for the President to play a positive role when the Lower House has been dissolved and, consequently, there is only a Government but no controlling Lok Sabha. One may agree with his view or not, but one must appreciate the fact that he has discussed the subject with discernment sans.

There are a number of disturbing issues which ordinary books on constitutional law ignore, but Jain has done justice to these abstruse questions. The rainbow range covered by the book is remarkable. It is not a commentary on the Constitution, article by article. Nor is it a series of chapters, comprehensively covering the whole constitution. On the contrary, Subhash C. Jain has handpicked select issues and presented his perceptions thereon elevating the discussion to a higher level with historical background, controversial viewpoint and his own insights. For instance the question of appointment of judges is a debatable issue. The elite brethren of the higher courts are against a National Judicial Commission while the rest of the world is for it. Here is Subhash presenting his view:

> *The concern on the issue is very succinctly expressed in a Private Member Constitution (Amendment) Bill, 1996 to amend articles 124, 217 etc. by Mr. V.N. Gadgil, Member of Parliament in Rajya Sabha on December 18, 1998. The salient points made in Mr.Gadgil's Bill are as under:*
>
> *(i) The Constituent Assembly while providing for appointment of High Court and Supreme Court Judges in the Constitution did not intend that consent of the Chief Justice in the Constitution did not intend that consent of the Chief Justice of India should be obtained. What was envisaged was only consultation with him. Dr. B.R. Ambedkar clearly expressed himself against a provision requiring concurrence of the President since according to him, Chief Justice after all "is a man with all his failings, all the sentiments and all the prejudices which we, the common people have."*
>
> *(ii) The judgment of the Apex Court is based on distrust of Parliament and the Executive.*
>
> *(iii) Nowhere in the world there is a system where Judges themselves decide as to who will be the next Judge. One cannot be Judge in one's own cause. No Parliament should accept such a proposition.*
>
> *(iv) In the United States, selection of Judges is a political process and Chief Justice or other Judges of the Supreme Court are neither informed nor consulted in the matter. In Britain, the proposal is made by the Lord Chancellor who is head of the judiciary but also Minister of the Crown. In Canada too, the power to appoint judges vests in the executive.*
>
> *(v) Independence of Judges is a myth. All judgments are not objective as Judges' own views do get reflected in the judgements.*
>
> *A Judicial Commission which will have a mix of representative from the judiciary, executive and others has been advocated from time to time by*

many including the Law Commission of India (see 121st Report) with a view to ensuring that judicial appointments at the level of High Court and Supreme Court Judges are made with the collective wisdom of a representative body rather than leaving the same to absolute or sole power of one wing of the State. (Page 5-6)

The definition of the words 'secular' and 'socialist' in the Preamble is usually avoided by conventional authors. But Subhash deals with them. The power of the President to grant pardon and petitions by *foreigners* is one obscure issue the author takes up for discussion. More importantly, he considers the problems of Caretaker Governments pending election, President's competence to remove a Union Minister without consulting the Cabinet, President's assent to bills passed by Parliament and a catena of constitutional questions which cover luminous pages. The follow-up of the forlorn Sarkaria Commission recommendations, the revival of a legislative assembly, the doctrine of separation of powers, the conflict between judiciary and legislature are matters of great moment on which light is thrown by Subhash Jain. National Government, former President Venkataraman's favourite demand, is also considered in a whole chapter. I do not agree with Subhash Jain or Jeevan Reddy in their support for a constitutional provision to promote small family norms. What is biologically difficult cannot be constitutionally feasible, what is a source of human resource, wisely developed, need not be a national hindrance. Indeed, gifting a condom to every adult male making obligatory to use it, making vasectomy, tubectomy, abortion, sterilisation a compulsory obligation after two children are born may be a better popular campaign than a constitutional provision which is but printed futility. Financial inducement by the State and educational-informational-agitational propagation with fanatical insistence may go a long political way in achieving the objective *with which I wholly agree.* I am for family control.

The Constitution of India—Select issues and Perceptions by Subhash Jain is a commendable book which will be a valuable addition to every law library.

THE MARAD IMPASSE—OMINOUS PORTENT

Marad, is a beautiful beach by the side of which, Hindu and Muslim fisherfolk live in proximity but separately. The Marad carnage, where several Hindus were murdered brutally by a gory group of Muslims, has convulsed the Kerala State into a communal division of public opinion. The criminal episode is under police investigation by the State police. Terrible bitterness on the part of the Arya Samaj (Hindus) has escalated, thanks to obvious groups within the 'hindutva' fold. The Muslim fisher families have fled the place and there is a police contingent guarding the peace of the area. At the present moment, tension prevails and Araya allergy to Muslim entry to their old residences has created a great crisis. How can a community be violently resisted from occupying their residential locality in the light of the constitutional right of every Indian 'to reside in any part of the territory of India'? Acid anger and biting hate together fertilise the Upas tree under whose shade reason fails and justice dies. This explosive syndrome deadens communal harmony so vital for tranquility and progress.

This crisis baffles solution, but if the fundamental duty under Article 51A to 'promote harmony and the spirit of common brotherhood among all the people of India transcending religious diversities is to be a human reality, violently enforced apartheid has no place in our national scheme of life. The bleeding Araya indignation against the lethal treachery of their mopla neighbours is the motivation behind their anti-muslim ire. But we must never allow our Kerala culture of communal amity to be a criminal casualty. Tagodias and their ilk may bully or browbeat but their animosity cannot be allowed to stab inter-religious cordiality. This is not merely a governmental responsibility, but a sacred societal concern and commitment. Not police presence but Hindu-Muslim fraternity is the pharmacopoeia of peace. We must seek a remedy for the malady of deep estrangement.

True, the issues are complex. Platitudinous political appeals by parties are placebo, not recipe. The deceased families must be generously recompensed for the loss of life and Government employment given to one member at least to each bereaved family. This is a minimal State obligation, to be carried out with spontaneous compassion. A major demand, uncompromisingly urged, is for condign criminal justice with blitz speed preceded by instant, fearless, favour-free police investigation. The C.B.I. (Central Bureau of Investigation) fills the bill to investigate this pre-planned communal crime of diabolic magnitude. We must recognise that a large section of people are behind this demand, especially because the Muslim League is a big partner in the State Cabinet and the State police may blink at important criminals allegedly involved in the large conspiracy resulting in the terrorist attack, because they allegedly have close association with those in power through the Muslim League. This may be a baseless suspicion about independent State police whose integrity is beyond purchase. The State police has arrested a large number of Muslims, siezed considerable weaponry from the nearby mosque and buried in the sands and are proceeding with collecting evidence on a large scale. But the impression among the *arayas* and many in the 'Hindutva' fold is that powerful elements linked with the Muslim League are *participes criminis* and will escape the culpable net if an outside agency with nationally accepted renown is not put into operation. The Chief Minister, who is the Home Minister, is justly disinclined to bring in the C.B.I., casting a reflection on his upright police department. This attitude is a response to Muslim League pressure, according to those motivated elements who demand C.B.I. intervention. The Muslim League lobby is supportive of the Chief Minister's stand for obvious reasons.

The short question is how to get round this stalemate. There is inflexible insistence from either side and there is something to be said in favour of each side. True, police investigation, like judicial justice, must *appear* to be above board. However, a great deal of material has been gathered and an outside agency, like the C.B.I. registering a case and beginning investigation *de novo* without familiarity of the locality and the background to the crime, may cause delay, contradictory statements and even language problem. But those who swear by the C.B.I. also have a point, although it is not an infallible instrumentality. A *modus vivendi* has to be evolved so that a deadlock may end, credibility restored and the investigation conducted impartially. Pragmatism blended with principle, if acceptable, may offer a way out.

The following proposal may be given serious consideration by the State Chief Minister. He can address the Home Minister at the Centre to lend the services of a very senior C.B.I. officer to supervise and invigilate the State police investigation done so far, to continue the investigation under his monitoring direction, to supplement the investigation with fresh perceptions and no preconceptions, take a larger perspective in which the obviously well planned and master-minded offense was perpetrated and use, if need be, the services of a few more C.B.I. officials to assist him in the process. This would mean the guarantee of an independent investigation. This would also mean that the case continues as one registered by the State police. All the evidence collected till now will be available for the court. Considerable new material brought in by the C.B.I. deputy with a wider vision, uninhibited intelligence and freedom to infuse into the case further investigative input, will generate public confidence. But the State police remains the investigator primarily. It is not taken over by the C.B.I. *as a fresh case.* This procedure is not without precedent, as I gathered from a senior former additional director of the C.B.I. The Chief Minister must agree, *not* to ask for a C.B.I. investigation, *but* for a senior C.B.I. officer on deputation to fortify the investigative mechanism. Both sides may thus be satisfied and the only persons who will be nervous are those who seek shelter under the illusion of State police favour.

There are in Kerala many well-meaning voluntary bodies non-communal in texture and secular in their soul. They must lobby with both sides so that the impasse may be overcome. This must be possible, what with our rich heritage of peaceful religious co-existence and the command of national survival through secular solidarity. In that event the Muslim community must be freely allowed to occupy their former residences, burying the hatchet and restoring the lost harmony. Marad divided is Kerala divided, and Hindu-Muslim unity is an inalienable value. We want *not rabidity but sanity, not hostility but humanity* if Kerala is to win back its historic glory of Hindu soul, Christian heart and Islamic body, if I may adapt a Vivekananda message of May 1898.

Post Script

Two matters need better understanding to throw light on the Marad imbroglio. Some sections of the public demand that the Marad Mosque where explosives and long knives were kept should be released although it is now under the Magisterial custody of the Collector. Legally speaking, the building has been taken over appreciating the situation of tension by the District Magistrate under the Kerala Police Act. It was siezed not under Government orders and so government has no control over the order of seizure which is done statutorily under magisterial discretion. The Second point that needs noting is that Marad communal carnage is a disturbing and potentially expanding explosion which may spread across the West Coast with families of women and children in distress. Therefore, Madam Poornima Advani informed me about her deep concern and readiness to visit Marad. So too, Swami Agnivesh, whose spiritual appeal for religious comity has won countrywide acclaim. He too telephoned me, wanted to come and campaign to extinguish the fires of hatred in Marad. This means that what is at stake is not a village feud with communal fuel, but a grave omen of Muslim alienation from the coastal belt with a sinister portent of more clashes erupting pervasively. Alas, how appalling, if it happens!

BLANKET BAN ON STRIKES BY LABOUR— A JUDICIAL EXCESS?

A serendipitous pronouncement by a Division Bench of the Supreme Court declaring is as it does, regarded by critics as a curial aberration, a broad-spectrum ban on Labour's right to strike without investigating the grave grievances of the employees over a hundred thousand strong, which the State Government, in alleged intransigence, ignored, leading to the menacingly militant lightning strike. The Court, in its wisdom, disposed of the matter without discharging its adjudicatory function of examining the central issue under challenge viz. the vires of the bizarre, blitz Ordinance dismissing into the streets, with Draconian severity and stunning celerity, the lakh and odd staff members, sans enquiry under Article 311, sans chance to make representations. The Court, however, was eloquent about the disruptive, illegal, iniquitous, anti-social and unconstitutional dimensions of strikes generally which, the Bench felt, held the public to ransom. In an impassioned purple passage, the learned judges observed:

> *Strike as a weapon is mostly misused which results in chaos and total maladministration. Strike affects the society as a whole and particularly when two lakhs employees go on strike enmasse, the entire administration comes to a grinding halt. In the case of strike by a teacher, entire educational system suffers; many students are prevented from appearing in their exams which ultimately affect their whole career. In case of strike by Doctors, Innocent patients suffer, in case of strike by employees of transport services, entire movement of the society comes to a stand still; business is adversely affected and number of persons find it difficult to attend to their work, to move from one place to another or one city to another. On occasions, public properties are destroyed or damaged and finally this creates bitterness among public against those who are on strike.*

This is powerful prose but is it legal hermeneutics or jural exegetics carrying judicial authority, or hardly anything more than an emphatic expression of chaos and distress caused by strikes, a view which many may share because of the indiscriminate infliction of social disruption by negligible, irresponsible and disorderly elements unaccountable to anyone and measured by the anarchy they generate. Indeed, the irrational frequency and impertinent frivolity of intimidatory strikes are self-defeating operations which sound trade unionism never sponsors. But are all strikes illegal, immoral, unjust or liable to be suppressed by State authoritarianism, employer reprisal or judicial allergy by angry negation of writ relief? My personal regard for the two judges on the *Rangarajan Bench* and the institutional reverence for the Supreme Court, the hallowed home of the human rights guarantee, social justice, jurisprudential creativity and curial remediation (of which I was a humble member long ago) persuades me to critique respectfully but ratiocinatively the *Rangarajan ruling* which *seems* to hold all strikes as productive of havoc in a democratic society and *bete noire* and menace to public interest. To critique is not to carp but to correctively comment in good faith. Trade unions are a legitimate, lawful instrument of the working class and strikes, under necessitous circumstances, are a strategic weapon which has legal sanction under just conditions.

Lord Atkin, in one of his classic judgments, observed what every member of the judiciary in the Commonwealth and elsewhere will do well to remember:

> *Whether the authority and position of an individual judge, or the due administration of justice, is concerned, no wrong is committed by any member of the public who exercise the ordinary right of criticizing, in good faith, in private or public, the public act done in the seat of justice. The path of criticism is a public way; the wrong-headed are permitted to err therein; provided that members of the public abstain from imputing improper motives to those taking part in the administration of justice, and are genuinely exercising a right of criticism, and not acting in malice or attempting to impair the administration of justice, they are immune. Justice is not a cloistered virtue; she must be allowed to suffer the scrutiny and respectful, even though outspoken, comments of ordinary men.*
>
> *(Judges P-114)*

After all Judge Jerome Frank of the U.S. Court of Appeal sensibly explained:

> *In a democracy, it can ever be unwise to acquaint the public with the truth about the workings of any branch of government. It is wholly undemocratic to treat the public as children who are unable to accept the inescapable shortcomings of man-made institutions.... The best way to bring about the elimination of those shortcomings of our judicial system which are capable*

of being eliminated is to have all our citizens informed as to how that system now functions. It is a mistake, therefore, to try to establish and maintain, through ignorance, public esteem for our courts. (Judges, P-205)

The overwhelming majority of our judges do a difficult job fairly well, commanding confidence of the people. Nevertheless, as judge Cardozo elegantly observed, in his book The Nature of the Judicial Process, social philosophy does not pass the judges by. Unwitting infiltration of class bias may creep into their overt impartiality. Professor J.A.G. Griffith, in his book The Politics of the Judiciary, gave reasons to hold that judges, being but human, may not be immune to class bias, never intentional but subconscious in their surrender to partiality. He quotes Winston Churchill whom I reproduce instructively:

The courts hold justly a high, and I think, unequalled pre-eminence in the respect of the world in criminal cases, and in civil cases between man and man, no doubt, they deserve and command the respect and admiration of all classes of the community, but where class issues are involved, it is impossible to pretend that the courts command the same degree of general confidence. On the contrary, they do not, and a very large number of our population have been led to the opinion that they are, unconsciously, no doubt, biased. (Hon. Members: 'No, no', 'Withdraw' and interruption)

The Secretary of State for the Home Department (Mr. W.S. Churchill) on the second reading of the Trade Unions (No.2) Bill, 1911 (26) H.C. Deb. Col. 1022) (The Politics of the Judiciary, P-173)

Lord Justice Scrutton made a similar point:

The habits you are trained in, the people with whom you mix, lead to your having a certain class of ideas of such a nature that, when you have to deal with other ideas, you do not give as sound and accurate judgments as you would wish. This is one of the great difficulties at present with Labour. Labour says 'Where are your impartial Judges? They all move in the same circle as the employers, and they are all educated and nursed in the same ideas as the employers. How can a labour man or a trade unionist get impartial justice?' It is very difficult sometimes to be sure that you have put yourself into a thoroughly impartial position between two disputants, one of your own class and one not of your class.

Lord Justice Scrutton in an address delivered to the University of Cambridge Law Society on 18 November 1920 (1 Cambridge Law Journal, p. 8). (The Politics of the Judiciary, P-173)

Does it ring a bell in the bosoms of Indian brethren on the high bench? Our Constitution and Court have a vision which the Crown and Law Britannia do not possess.

Did not Lord Atkin in *Liversidge* v. *Anderson* hold the House of Lords: 'In this case, I have listened to arguments which might have been addressed acceptably to the court of King's Bench in the times of Charles-I'. Therefore, arguments at the Bar sometimes condition the conclusions of the Bench and public reaction and jurists' evaluation may be reflected in a reconsideration of the law laid down in a decided case. Law never stand still. It is in this liberal spirit and with a constructive purpose that I 'wash in acid' the ratio in *Rangarajan* and the anti-strike dicta of the Bench.

With due deference, I dissent from the macro-negative proposition based on broad assumptions and expressed in paragraph twelve of the judgment. 'Now coming to the question of right to strike, whether Fundamental Statutory Equitable. Moral Right—in our view, no such right exists with the Government employees.' The court's dicta, as pointed out in a passage earlier in this paper, have gone beyond Government servants and condemned strikes as unjustified 'on any equitable ground'. In a mood of benignant philosophy, the court counsels Labour on its patriotic duty.

> *In the prevailing situation, apart from being conscious of rights, we have to be fully aware of our duties, responsibilities and effective methods for discharging the same. For redressing their grievances, instead of going on strike,* if employees do some more work honestly, diligently and efficiently, *such gesture would not only be appreciated by the authority but also by people at large. The reason being, in a democracy even though they are Government employees, they are part and parcel of governing body and owe duty to the Society. (Para 21)*

This moral message, with a pulpit touch, reads like a judicial addition to Jesus' Ten Commandments. This hortative mantra is a spiritual mandate that workers of the world unite; when you have demands to gain from Government or other employer, *work harder, produce more* and *win the Management's heart!* No doubt, our country will be transformed if ministers travel less and work more, if Secretaries visit Delhi less and dispose of files more without paper-logging, if public offices slumber less and devote to duty more, if judges hear with more business-like thoroughness, bring down the appalling backlog of dockets and pronounce judgments to the point without prolonged procrastination. Indian judges have a tough job flooded by escalating litigation and medieval methodology.

In this very case, having tactfully and gracefully terminated the dismissal order using the good offices of K.K. Venugopal, a creative, compassionate counsel, the dubious incursion into ambiguous Labour law was perhaps obiter and superogatory. What did counsel, a battery of them, all eminent, do in countering the harsh criticism of strikes? The judgment is silent about their submissions on 'strike jurisprudence'. With curial cynicism, working class leaders and labour lawyers may pardonably be pejorative against this jurisprudence which may be more at home in President Reagan's country and bring solace to Super-Conservative Mrs. Thatcher and may be to multi-national corporations (MNCs) who are allergic to the presence of labour as a menace creating unrest.

Our judges on the high bench are aware not only that India is a socialist Republic but that several provisions of Part IV of the Constitution like Articles 41 to 43A, which are 'fundamental in the governance of the country' have welfare of workers at heart. Indeed, the learned judges persuaded the Government to take the dismissed workers back as a measure of urgent relief. That shows the concern of the courts for employees. What is hurtful to labour jurisprudence is the castigation of all strikes as vicious. Were we colonial, perhaps the conspiracy theory of strikes might have passed unquestioned. Not so now in Gandhi country. Why, in England of today, trade union law has nullified the view that strikes are conspiracies. There are situations where the Management is unreasonably recalcitrant and turns down just claims of workers. An observation by Lord Denning, in a dissenting judgment, is relevant. I excerpt a part:

> *Here we have to consider the right to demonstrate and the right to protest on matters of public concern. These are rights which it is in the public interest individuals should possess; and, indeed, that they should exercise without impediment so long as no wrongful act is done. It is often the only means by which* grievances can be brought to the knowledge of those in authority—*at any rate with such impact as to gain a remedy. Our history is full of warnings against suppression of these rights. (The Politics of the Judiciary, P-146)*

Freedom of speech and freedom of association are not mere abstractions nor purposeless inanities. Collective action is implicit in these basic freedoms. In express terms, there is no freedom to strike writ into the Constitution. But collective bargaining for legitimate causes is best served by a creative combination of speech and association, of course, without breach of law and order or transgression of other people's human rights. Once this perspective, sanctioned by constitutional initiative, is correctly and curatively interpreted, industrial jurisprudence becomes a process where both managements and workers have rights. When claims are justly made based on the contribution of labour to the progressive profit making capacity of the Industry an arbitrary refusal even to discuss may lead to tension which may mount to the point of peaceful, though militant expression by collective withdrawal from work, otherwise called strike. This is more to strengthen the demand than to destroy the industry or to disturb the peace of the community. Strikes are not a noxious novelty of Indian Trade Unions, but have been in every country where industrialization has been a part of organized production. Those who are familiar with the International Labour Organization are not jittery about strikes.

A profusion of citations may be avoided by a reference to *B.R. Singh's case* (1989 SCC 710) where Justice Ahamedi, speaking for the Bench, observed:

> *The right to form associations or unions is a fundamental right under Article 19(1)(c) of the Constitution. Section 8 of the Trade Unions Act provides for registration of a trade union if all the requirements of the said enactment are fulfilled. The right to form associations and unions and provide for their registration was recognized obviously for conferring certain rights on trade unions. The necessity to form unions is obviously for voicing the demands and grievances of labour. Trade unionists act as mouthpieces of labour. The strength of a trade union depends on its membership. Therefore, trade unions with sufficient membership strength are able to bargain more effectively reduced if it is not permitted to demonstrate. Strike in a given situation is only a form of demonstration. There are different modes of demonstrations, e.g., go-slow, sit-in, work-to rule, absenteeism, etc., and strike is one such mode of demonstration by workers for their rights. The right to demonstrate and, therefore, the right to strike is an important weapon in the armoury of the workers.* This right has been recognized by almost all democratic countries. Though not raised to the high pedestal of a fundamental right, it is recognized as a mode of redress for resolving the grievances of workers. But the right to strike is not absolute under our industrial jurisprudence and restrictions have been placed on it. *(1989) 4 Supreme Court Cases 710 para 15)*

The right to strike and the conditions under which it should be exercised are found in the Industrial Disputes Act. Indeed, the Bench, in *B.R. Singh case,* was dealing with a strike in a Public Sector organisation and the court, on an overall view of the facts and circumstances of the case, held:

> *Keeping the interest of the institution in mind and bearing in mind the economic hardships that the labour would suffer if the impugned orders are not set aside, we think that it would be desirable to restore the peace by directing the reinstatement of the workers. (1989) 4 Supreme Court Cases 710 para 22)*

A Bench of seven judges, in the Bangalore Water Supply and Sewerage Board Case, considered in great detail the meaning of the word *Industry.* A passage from the leading judgment therein is relevant: 'The International Labour Organization has had occasion to consider freedom of association for labour as a primary right and collective bargaining *followed by strikes, if necessary,* as a derivative right.' In para 62 of the ruling, the Court refers to the *Corporation of Nagpur case* where the

Education Department of Government was brought within the conception of Industry. A plethora of case-law relied on in the leading judgment (in the *Bangalore Water Supply etc.* case) takes the view that even a hospital run by Government is an industry. Industry implies employers and employees, demands and denials of claims, strikes and lock-outs and industrial adjudication. Therefore, to exclude the idea of strike from the scope of legality is naïve.

It is not without significance that in *Gujarat Steel Tube case* (1980 2 SCC 593) the majority on the bench held that it was a fundamental flaw to equate illegal with unjust strikes. A strike may be illegal by a technical violation, but need not be necessarily unjustified. All that I mean is that a token illegality does not make the strike a gross act of injustice. It is surprising that the dubious legality of the Ordinance, extraordinary in its character and timing, had not awakened the court's jurisdiction into considering the constitutionality of the executive legislation affecting a colossal number of public servants. Some day, some bench of the Apex Court may be conscientised into scanning the constitutional jurisprudence of Ordinance Raj.

In the USA where 'hire and fire' is the rule, strikes are considered economic terrorism by the mega-corporate controllerate of the U.S. economy. Industrial jurisprudence is labour-friendly in India. Our Constitution, with social justice and industrial equity writ large, shapes labour law. Our robed brethren offer a dignified place to Labour as almost a partner in the productive process.

Criticisms apart, the judges in the *Rangarajan* case need a meed of praise for restoring instantly most of the employees who were sacked by an ireful Government, although it baffles me that Government employees for helping themselves back into office have had to apologize and undertake not to strike ever thereafter. This condition is an ad hoc humiliation which I presume the court never meant.

An Afterword

In the provocative context of the contra-strike pronouncement, the learned Attorney General, with alacrity and authority, repudiated the theory that the right to strike is anathematic. This historic right cannot run riot nor turn berserk but, within socially sensitive bounds and liberal legal limits, has a permissible home in Indian jurisprudence. We are not a totalitarian State nor subject to Corporate Employer authoritarianism.

I never mean a pejorative reflection on the high bench. The learned judges, with a sense of relief after having secured reinstatement for the bulk of employees, relaxed into a censorious frown and presented a certain point of view not integral to the relief sought or the arguments at the bar. The Court is supreme but not infallible. In a Preface of lovely brevity, Justice Kirpal has rightly stated (in a semi-centennial publication by the Supreme Court):

> *Many a time, the Court has changed its mind and adapted the law and Constitution to suit India's need. If its work has been appreciated, it has not always escaped criticism. ....*
>
> *We would like to believe that the Supreme Court has gone about its task less conscious of its supremacy and more warily with the intuition that the Court, though final, is fallible. (Supreme But Not Infallible)*

Rangarajan is a case where the Court, though pro tem final, is perhaps fallible.

GUJARAT AND MARAD—IS INDIAN SECULARISM A CHARADE OR A SOUL UNDER SIEGE

India is a land of religions. It is a pluralist democracy with Hinduism, Islam and Christianity flourishing in fellowship. We have a constitutional order guaranteeing to the minorities their religious autonomy and identity. Yes; with all the facts of history and constitutional law a crisis has been brewing and escalating putting in peril and panic our secular system; Gujarat and Marad (near Calicut) being the latest terrorist syndrome, the first being molar and the next being molecular. The omens are bad and ideology calls for affirmation for the very survival of the nation. In this view, I discuss herein the various facets of the contemporary crisis and constitutional fundamentals.

Long years ago when India awoke to freedom, Jawaharlal Nehru, rose to tell the world that every member, be he Hindu or Muslim or of other faith, had an equal title to the country and its resources. Let me quote him.

> *India does not belong to any one party or a group of people*
>
> *At a time when we are on the threshold of freedom, we should remember that India does not belong to any one party or group of people or caste. It does not belong to the followers of any particular religion. It is the country of all, every religion and creed. We have repeatedly defined the type of freedom we desire. In the first resolution, which I moved earlier, it has been said that our freedom is to be shared equally by every Indian. All Indians shall have equal rights, and each one of them is to partake equally in that freedom. We shall proceed like that and whosoever tries to be aggressive will be checked by us. If anyone is oppressed we shall stand by his side. If we follow this path then we shall be able to solve big problems, but if we become narrow minded we shall not be able to solve them.*
>
> *(Pandit Jawaharlal on the midnight of 14th August, 1947)*

These great words gain sombre meaning now when we are gripped by a grim crisis because secularism, the cornerstone of our nation, is confused with and propagated by bigoted extremists as the tombstone of the body politic—a terrible outrage. If secularism ceases to be the bedrock of our Republic Swaraj becomes mirage. If we, as a people, do not belong to a single nation, politically cemented by a strong sense of human solidarity, we will splinter and founder. The British, in keeping India divided, played with the idea that we were not a people, a nation. It is the glory and irony of history that M.A. Jinnah, the betrayer of Indian nationhood and founder of the two-nations theory hen political opportunism and power allurement seduced his soul, did, long before the Round Table Conference, observed in a notable speech critical of the British divisive thesis:

> *India is not a nation, we are told. We were a people when the great war was going on and an appeal was made to India for blood and money. We were a people when we were asked to be a signatory to the Peace Treaty in France. We are a nation when we become a member of the League of Nations to which we made a substantial contribution. We are a nation or a people for the purpose of sending our representative to the Imperial Conference. We are your partners, but we are not a nation. We are not a people, nor a nation when we ask you for a substantial advance towards the establishment of responsible government and parliamentary institutions in our own country.*

While I condemn the insinuation that Indian Muslims are a separate nation I am convinced that every right thinking Indian, even during decades before Freedom was won, did think passionately of Indian Humanity as a single, substantive, inseparable people. This politically axiomatic reality has been reiterated as an inviolable rule of constitutionality. Surely the Founding Fathers were, fully aware during the debates when the clauses were discussed threadbare, that India was deeply rooted in religious pluralism and its fraternity embraced not merely the dignity of the individual but the sacred vision of ancient religions living in peaceful co-existence and cultural comity.

When we consider the excellence of a democracy which has religious minorities of ancient vintage we must gracefully respect the full freedom of faith which belongs to every denomination to practise without inhibition the imperative prescriptions constituting the credal essentials integral to their holy beliefs. Subject, of course, to public order, morality and health. This guarantee is inscribed in Articles 25 to 30 of the Constitution, progressively interpreted. Immunity and autonomy *vis a vis* religious matters do not extend to totalitarian untouchability with fanatical ramifications and obdurate obscurantisms asserted by bigots. What is protected are the basic structure and fundamental features, consistent with the civilised ethos of society—these values form the soul of a religion and enjoy inviolability, not as a tolerance of a necessary evil but as a magnanimous fellowship of faiths warmly welcomed into the spiritual-temporal treasury of culture about which we collectively feel happy without rivalry. When the religion of the majority community is different in religion from that of the minorities, the apprehension of sharp division and hostile imposition of restriction is natural, what with the memories of Partition based on a barbaric two-nation theory, massive migrations and savage barbarities. All right-minded Muslims resisted the theocratic politics of the two-nation theory but history has happened and geography has divided then sub-continent. What of us, one billion humans who are Indians? Every sixth person on our planet is an Indian, heir to a composite cultural heritage of ancient vintage and modern constitutional mintage. Defiantly resisting temptations of divisive communalism, devoutly adhering to the life-blood and life-breath of one nation—one people secularism, we must march, advancing towards a national unity and cultural integrity, and rejecting as repugnant to our radiant Indianness all vicious allurements of majoritarian authoritarianism and godist chauvinism inflicting humiliating inferiority and indignity on minorities siezing the power of the State or using the terrorism of larger numbers. We belong to each other and *sarva dharma samabhava* is *our* proud tradition. Secularism is the bed-rock of our nationalism. The arrogance of a majority community may drive to despair a minority and breed obnoxious minority communalism, even terrorism. Our national campaign is not pampering majority malignancy or minority prejudices. Vote banks strategies and foreign-funded game-plans are at work but we must avoid these pitfalls. We must be secular in every cell if we mean business. There are no ifs and buts and other exceptions in the sphere of public affairs and social life. Muslim history in India is as old as Islam. Arabic influence and Urdu literature are art and part of our composite cultural heritage. So too Christianity which is almost as old as Jesus. Let great thoughts blow in from all sides, to glorify the welfare of our land, runs the sublime call of the Rig Veda. This authentic Upanishadic perspective is hospitable and humanist, welcomes the divergent visions, voices and versions of Truth from whichever direction they blow into India. This is the spiritual dimension of secularism.

We need not look to the West with its materialist yen to gather the semantic essence of secularism. Post-modernist, Hedonist consumerism, sexism and vulgar materialism are the cultural syndrome which has spread into India *i.e.* Bharat through the current invasion of globalization, privatisation and marketisation. The soul of Indian Secularism is unalloyed humanism battling against the monoculture of the mind and never subjugated by neo-colonialism. All religions flourish in spiritual concord and temporal accord Fellowship without fend or fetish is our profound ethos.

In a long-ago lecture delivered at the Calicut University much before the Gujarat carnage I stated:

> *Whenever there is a potential for Hindu-Muslim clashes, the communal mafia (of both religions) take over. In Bombay and other cities, inflammatory beginnings are from the mosques and moulvis on the one side and the sants, acharyas, Shiva Sena and Hindu politickers on the other. But soon the underworld of both religions take over. Criminal gangs, not the fez and ochre, are guilty of murder, loot, arson and rape! The writ of the mafiariat, not the commissariat runs the lawless disorder of our country! There is money in blood and bigotry. Even the police force has a vested interest in tension a la Punjab. The death toll and loot are of innocent victims. Humanism and compassion are easy casualties and hate and hatchet soon take over when communal incineration starts somewhere. Of course, there are bigotries to be ended, appeasements to be eradicated and religious chauvinism and distorted history to be corrected. Pakistani pollution is India's curse. We cannot copy Islamabad but withstand it.*
>
> *Indian secularism, without borrowing from Western rationalism of Marxian materialism, must go to its roots of comity of religions, camaraderie of faiths, beautiful blend of divine light and cross-fertilisation of divergent teachings which made for a vibrant fellowship of church, mosque, temple and other shrines. Two thousand years ago, Christianity came to India (St. Thomas). As fresh as Prophet Mohammad preached his divine Revelations came the universal message to Kerala shores. The Buddha and Mahavira were of India and Saint Tukaram, Shirdi Baba, Guru Nanak, Shri Narayana Guru, Sufi Saints and the very quintessence of advaita promoted a rare and lively unity in diversity.*
>
> *A few instances of comradely co-existence of religions may be cited:*
>
> *The most famous shrine, with the largest pilgrim trek, is the Sabari Temple located in dense Kerala forests which attracts hindus from all over India and some non-Hindu pilgrims as well. The legend runs that the forest god Ayyappa was led to his present seat through dark woods by a Muslim guide called Vavar (Babar). People worship Ayyappa in their millions and they are Hindus, but before climbing the steps to the shrine, they make offerings to Vavar, the Muslim guide, whose hallowed spot is still there. The poojari or representative, himself a Muslim, offers vibhooti or holy ashes to the Hindu votaries and received dakshina in return. This confluence of Hindu-Muslim sacredness continues even now and the Muslim representative of Vavar recently issued a statement about this beautiful blend of worship. Similar mutuality occurs in many parts and myriad ways.*
>
> *In Central Kerala (Changanacherry town) there is a Chandanakudam festival on December 25th and 26th every year. (This year too). This vintage Muslim festival starts from an ancient mosque, winds its way to a Bhagavati temple nearby (Hindu) and the elephant procession, with the*

Chandanakudam, is given a glorious reception at the Bhagavathi temple premises. The authorities of the Jamayat are garlanded by the temple priests to the accompaniment of nadaswaram music and the Muslim organisers sprinkle rose water on the Hindu devotees. Both the Hindus and the Muslims gathered apply sandal paste on their brows and receive flowers and lemon fruits in token of fraternity. The Muslim procession proceeds to the Nair Service Society office, SNDP Union, St. Thomas Orthodox Church and other centres in a mood of reverence and rejoicing. According to legend, the ancient Hindu Maharaja was responsible for the glorious co-existence of the Bhagavati temple, the old Mosque and St. Mary's Church built on royal land grants.

Several other shrines where Hindus, Muslims and Christians worship or make offerings are not uncommon in Kerala, even in Tippu's Karnataka. Ajmer is witness to this synthesis of the worshipping communities and flowers from the hallowed Pushkar lake are fetched by brahmin priests to the Ajmir mosque. God is in peace and wills peace among His Creation, but man degenerates, falls from the Universal love (Christ). Eminent scholars like former Chief Justice Ismail (Madras) are among the best exponents of Ramayana and disciples of Kanchi Sankaracharya. Our Constitution has this eclectic vision and we shall be betraying our founding fathers if we travesty this great heritage.

Vivekananda laid the modern foundation for a new dimension of secularism. Of course, Ramakrishna Paramahamsa experimented with Christian and Muslim faiths. But Vivekananda, in a letter to a Muslim friend Sarfaraz Hussain, wrote in 1898:

"Amorah

10th June, 1898

My Dear Friend,

I appreciate your letter very much and am extremely happy to learn that the Lord is silently preparing wonderful things for our mother land.

Whether we call it Vedantism or any ism, the truth is that Advaitism is the last word of religion and thought and the only position from which one can look upon all religions and sects with love. I believe it is the religion of the future enlightened humanity. The Hindu may get the credit of arriving at it earlier than other races, they being an older race than either the Hebrew or the Arab; yet practical Advaitism, which looks upon and behaves to all mankind as one's own soul, was never developed among the Hindus universally.

On the other hand, my experience is that if ever any religion approach to this equality in an appreciable manner, it is Islam and Islam alone.

Therefore I am firmly persuaded that without the help of practical Islam, theories of Vedantism, however fine and wonderful they may be, are entirely valueless to the vast mass of mankind. We want to lead mankind to the place where there is neither the Vedas, nor the Bible, nor the Koran; yet this has to be done by harmonising the Vedas, the Bible and the Koran. Mankind ought to be taught that religions are but the varied expressions of THE RELIGION, which is Oneness, so that each may choose that path that suits him best.

For our own motherland a junction of the two great systems, Hinduism and Islam—Vedanta brain and Islam body—is the only hope.

I see in my mind's eye the future perfect India rising out of this chaos and strife, glorious and invincible, with Vedanta brain and Islam body.

Ever praying that the Lord may make of you a great instrument for the help of mankind, and especially of our poor, poor motherland.

Yours with love,

VIVEKANANDA".

[Vol. VI-Page 416-417]

Gandhiji, with political—cultural stress on fundamentals, told us:

"Hindustan belongs to all those who are born and bred here and who have no other country to look to. Therefore, it belongs to Parsis, Beni Israels, to Indian Christians, Muslims and other non-Hindus as much as to Hindus. Free India will be no Hindu raj. It will be Indian raj based not on the majority of any religious sect community but on the representatives of the whole people without distinction of religion".

Let us struggle to make this goal our religion, our politics, our economics, our social order. To behold a human being as human is the best tribute to secularism. All else is double-speak. An honest man is the noblest work of God. An honest God is the noblest work of Man.

Among the cultural pillars of Indian society is the ancient universalism which absorbed the best in every faith and made every religion which anciently arrived from outside India share native qualities and customs and language. Indeed, there is a certain catholicity in every religion and several schools and sects exist which promotes progressive interpretation and liberal traditions thereby establishing a happy proximity in praxis when plural religions have geographical co-existence. To behold a temple, church and mosque in a small locality is no serendipity. This generous empathy informs Indian secularism and makes for the *modus vivendi* of great religions without stubborn rigidity and hide-bound fads and fetishes. Dr. Singhvi has felicitously explained this passage:

> *"In religions there are wide options; in traditions there is ample flexibility. Each generation can choose for emphasis the elements that appeal to it most. Religion thus becomes a reservoir and a source of strength for social suasion and social change. It furnishes a rationale for new ethics, for a new age and facilitates, smooth transition in conditions of stability. That is a role religions have been fulfilling in India for the last many centuries and specially during the 19th and 20th centuries. That is a role which it would continue to fulfil for quite sometime in our society. It may be added that no statesman or social scientist can afford to underestimate or to undermine the role of religion. Nor can a social reformer reject religion and its role in the Indian society because of some assumed canons of the new "theology" of secularism. To try to cast Indian secularism into a fixed western mould or to prevent the State from intervening in some of the secular affairs or aspects of religion or religious practices would be unreal escapism or impulsive rashness. True religion need not be irreconcilable with the social and humanitarian ethos of our times. Nor would it be irreconcilable with reason. As Swami Vivekananda said, "real inspiration never contradicts reason but fulfils it".*
>
> *Secularism is not, however, merely the broad pattern of management of equations between politics and religion. Nor is it a mere matter of an institutional framework, important though that is. Secularism represents in a true sense the synthesis of reason and compassion, 'prajnya' and 'karuna'. A spirit of tolerance, universalism and freedom seems essential to secularism".*

Constitutional historians with puritan pedantry may argue that the word 'secularism' was introduced into our Constitution only through the 42nd amendment in the seventies. It has ever thereafter remained in the book although several times Parliament has brought in fresh amendments, varying other provisions but leaving untouched the glowing idea of secularism. A holistic study of the Constitution in its original form will convince any critique jurist that the Founding Fathers had always yearned for and fashioned a substantive secular fabric governing, with a social sense of justice and equality, all the people within the hallowed land of India. The Supreme Court of India has emphatically declared not only that India is secular but that secularism is inviolably integral to the basic structure of the Constitution, beyond parliamentary amendability. Therefore, we, Hindus, Muslims and Christians and others of different faiths or of no religion, are all Indians, never divided by religion and ever united by common nationalism. The Muslim minority, with its separate identity, has title to enjoy/equal rights and cultural guarantee—a profound dream of Hakeem Abdul Hameed, the founder of Jamia Hamdard.

The jurisprudence of secularism in its magnificent panorma, is spelt out in several parts of the Constitution. For example, the Preamble, freedom of expression, of liberty and thought, belief, faith and worship. Sublime are the ideas these words convey. The sweep and scope of this vast concept is subject only to public order, morality and health. Article 25 confers on every person the freedom of conscience and the right freely to profess, practice and propagate religion. The Preamble emphasises concord and goodwill among the people rooted in social justice. The freedom of everyone, whatever his religion, to reside and settle in any part of India gives territorial tangibility and anti-apartheid absoluteness to the rights of religious minorities.

The *right to life* (Art.21) of every Indian, regardless of religion, is implies an inviolable value of secularism, subject, of course, to conditions which are just, fair and reasonable but never pares down the dignity of the individual, the divinity of his being and his right to development in the plenitude of his personality. Articles 25 and 26 are an empowerment of religious autonomy while Article 27 forbids the State from compelling any person to pay taxes for the promotion of any particular religion or religious denomination. In this sense, there is a wall of separation between the fiscal power of the State and the convictions of a person belonging to a particular religion. Article 28, 29 and 30 grant protection to the affirmative dimensions of religious practice. In sum, secularism, in all its aspects of civilised life, has supreme standing *vis-à-vis* any minority and, no doubt, the majority too.

The law may be glorious, the court may be sentinel and the rights may be large, but society, in its actuality, must impart viability to secularity by breathing life and light into the law and investing confidence in each person whose freedom of conscience is his precious paramount and private right. How far has the social history of India, in the recent decade, lived up to the great promises of the Preamble and the other provisions of the Constitution?

An important fact of life relevant to the secular unity of India is that Muslims from Kashmir to Kanyakumari and, in a sense, all over India live interspersed so much so total segregation of the Muslim community is no feasible proposition. Nay more. Muslims and Christians are in most occupations and businesses together with Hindus, and their presence in Government, including in the officialdom, makes separatism an unworkable and immoral unreality. We have had Presidents of India, Governors in the provinces who have been Muslims with an outstanding record. The present President is a humble Muslim from the South, but is beloved of the masses everywhere. We have had judges and Chief Justices of the highest court from among Muslims. Why, in every walk of life, non-Hindus occupy high positions? Our colleges have heavy Christian management and we have Muslims running colleges and universities. It follows that the Hindu-Muslim mosaic is a political, social and economic ground reality highlighting a beautiful cultural blend.

Notwithstanding this geo-communal mix, the Muslim minority has legitimate grievances and aspirations to blink at which is unjust. Certain sections of the Hindus have developed prejudice and chauvinist attitudes in the shape of Hindutva. Muslims are around 12% of the population but in public posts and economic life, in educational level and professional participation they have yet to gain that proportionate presence which gives them democratic confidence. This deficiency has to be remedied by a national policy promotive of abolition of minority disparity. While political parties generally show no manifest discrimination against minorities, how many Muslims and Christians have dominant positions and radical influence in the principal political parties in the country? This needs special attention, not as a pathological communal problem but as a national homogenisation desideratum.

More disturbing is the gradual escalation of religions discord and estrangement with divisive consequences. More pronounced is this unfortunate development when we look at the reality of religious pluralism and communal amity as a national necessity. Hindu-Muslim riots occur more frequently, religious fundamentalism and desperate extremism are assuming terrifying proportions. Mistrust is striking die-hard roots. The demolition of Babari Masjid and all that happened before and after are a dire disaster and running sore which the nation can ill-afford. What a shock and shame that during the last decade Hindu-Muslim camaraderie is becoming a bleeding casualty. The decease is spreading, the solution is receding and the mentality of the people is being malignantly vitiated by a cultural distemper. Neither the court nor the parliament has been successful in banishing the distress and distrust of the minority. The most horrendous savagery since the days of the Partition has been the Gujarat tragedy where almost genocidal operation, perhaps with the connivance of the political administration, took place inflicting bleeding injury on the national psyche. The Babri Masjid vandalism remains an indelible stain and incurable wound aggravated by a gravely militant demand for construction of a temple in the same sport as Ram Janmabhoomi. The Sree Krishna Commission Report on the Bombay blast is grievous evidence of majoritarian communal violence with no effective action to implement the judicial report. The Gujarat Carnage was investigated by a People's Commission and an exhaustive report was produced with elaborate collection of testimony; and the thoughtful conclusions arrived at have led to short term and long term recommendations set out in Volume II of the Commission's Report. In a foreword to the report I wrote, as Chairman, the following poignant words:

> *There are tragic, traumatic conclusions and creative, corrective recommendations. There are measures, punitive and rehabilitative, for victimological constitutional action. My task is to place the report before the people. Know ye the Truth and the Truth shall make you Free—provided We, the People of India, act promptly and fearlessly.*
>
> *The melody of communal unity, the beauty of religious amity and the secularity of Indian humanity—these glorious values are the mission and message to the nation. Let us struggle to sustain this supreme value, lest we, as a people, perish by divisive ideology. The Gujarat episode is an evil event and disastrous portent. Let us battle for the success of our pluralist culture, secular heritage and social-justice-illumined democracy. India must win! The integrity of our fraternity shall never surrender to berserk, blood-thirsty political bestiality.*

Even so culturally liberal a State as Kerala is stricken with the noxious virus of communalism violently erupting in various parts of the State, disrupting the great composite cultural heritage and producing situations like the Marad Carnage.

Marad is a few miles from Calicut and is situated on the lovely beaches of the Arabian Sea. The population, all fisher families, is composed of Hindus and Muslims living separately but proximately. There is a temple where the Hindus worship and a mosque where Muslims offer prayers. This area of amity became a scene of bloodbath over a year ago where, as a result of a terrorist strike some Hindus and some Muslims perished. Bitterness between the two communities was simmering in their bosom. A year later (a few months ago) on one salubrious evening a gory group of Muslims blitzed, with knives and explosives, into a gossiping Hindu relaxers and butchered eight of them. They escaped immediately after, making it clear that the whole blood-thirsty process was perfectly preplanned. The Sangh Parivar exploited this savage sanguinary episode for inflaming the feelings of the Hindus. Even today the Muslim families in the neighbourhood, who had fled after the event, have not been allowed to return home safe. Muslims are a minority in Kerala but well entrenched. The Marad massacre was an act of communal terrorism which gave a big burst to Hindutva groups to destroy cherished secular amity in the State. Right thinking people, Hindus, Muslims and Christians alike, condemned this Marad terrorism. Those who are committed to humanism and secularism want the Marad community to bury the hatchet and live together. Peaceful co-existence is the only strategy to salvage swaraj lest national unity should become a mirage. Taking a larger view and a national perspective, we have to condemn terrorism and aggressive communalism certainly of the majority, which is more dangerous, but equally of the minority which is both vicious and incendiary because it offers a burning alibi for the Hindu communal constituency across the country. Obscurantist bigotry, Hindu or Muslim, engineered by homicidal hate, is a deadly menace to Indian integrity.

Citizens for justice and Peace stand resolutely for secular fraternity. There cannot be democracy if any section of society is discriminated against on the score of religion. "We the People of India", is a diamond-hard collective and does not mean we, the Hindus plus the people of other religions. Secularism, even in our pluralist society, vibrantly visualizes the principle of one people, one nation, not Hindu, Muslim and those of other faiths huddled locationally into the large territory of India. Secularism is the radical locomotive of social democracy.

MATA AMRITANANDAMAYI—
A VOTARIST SALUTATION

Amma is a sweet symbol of spiritual charisma, a sublime revolutionary of matchless simplicity, a cosmic conqueror of human hearts with immaculate missiles of mother's love and innocent manifestation of divinity that dwells in everybody. Her compassionate vision of a world where the humblest has a title to basic shelter, health care, educational access and ascent of the soul is global in its warm embrace, is hallowed by a universal grace and is free from colour bar, language barrier and desire to be popular. This gentle gender wonder, born half a century ago under backward circumstances in a backward region of India, has been destined to rise as the most mobile missionary of peace on earth and harmony amongst humanity. Her birthday is a golden jubilee marked not by dazzle but by dedication, not by pompous vanity but by affectionate austerity. This celebration gathers millions to dear Amma because millions adore her as mother dear. This is the law of Nature Love begets love. Mother is the symbol of love and love is sacred. Amma's power is a process and a presence, a guileless smile and holy hug, an arsenal with stock-piles of 'prem' cells, a synthesis of the spiritual and the temporal with a holistic appeal that transforms the social order to change a savage into a Samaritan. Amma has no magic or mantra, no transcendental course of meditation, no gold to give or take. Her inexhaustible asset is a devotee in flood. The science of being is the awakening of the Spirit in every person. The art of living, Amma's teaching, is the switching on of the heart, the receiving set which responds to her communication, the eyes and ears of the listener being the transmitting medium. This is universal motherhood in catalytic action. Be you man or woman, infinite is your potential. Realization of this great truth is religion at its noblest which is Operation Liberation. This lovely revelation of the divine that we are is the journey of our material existence to the divinity that is our high destiny.

Selfless service, identification of each with every other, the dharma that commands us to share and care, to wipe every tear from every eye, in short, to universalize our individuality—this is the only salvation of humanity free from materialist negativity and disease of 'affluenza'. Surrender to materialism as the summum bonum of existence is the bondage out of which we must break. We have nothing to lose but our chains but have a world of fellowship to gain. This is our cultural heritage. The Gandhian concept of development rejects the ideology of aiming primarily at the creation and consumption of material wealth and the satisfaction of insatiable and endlessly multiplied pleasures. "In so far as we have made the modern materialist craze our goal" Gandhiji said, "so far are we going downhill in the path of progress". The hedonist gluttony as a *tamasic* philosophy is the reason why "man was born free but is everywhere in chains."

Mataji's holistic message is no total negation of material needs or scientific discoveries and modern technology. We live here on earth and peace, harmony and happiness are the birthright of everyone—the needs of the many, not the greed of the few. Finer materialism and higher spirituality are twins and complementary. The integral yoga of the two unfolds the brave new world where the mind is without fear, knowledge is free and humanity is not fragmented by narrow, nationalist walls or exploitative globalization making even hunger of the masses a market for multi-national corporations.

To adopt whole villages for good, to gift free homesteads, to run hospitals and colleges are on the humanitarian agenda of Mataji. To banish poverty of mind and body is the burgeoning point of true humanism and compassion inspired by Amma.

Amma is motherhood in its ecstatic dimensions. Woman is no more suppressed in this scheme of things. Women, once in full stature with all their faculties free to develop uninhibited by the *status quo ante,* are the wealth of the world. The United Nations represents the people of all nations only when gender justice makes sisters and brothers united in equality and dignity. Children too, that generation of pure innocence—also is a paramount concern if the earth we inhabit is to be the home of a happy family, peaceful fraternity and nations in comity and cooperation. I know this is a dream. But more things are wrought by dream and the world will be lost in darkness without the glow and glory of dreams. Mata Amritanandamayi embraces our world with a dynamic dream of love, justice and truth. The great tribute that millions of us can pay to her gracious presence at age fifty is to enliven our mortal existence by an ounce of sincerity in actualisation, by our thoughts, words and deeds, of a world order worthy of the divinity of humanity.

A votarist salutation to thee, Mataji.

TWO CONTRASTING VISIONARIES

Deliverance from temporal bondage is the noblest ambition of human liberation. Two sublime spirits, visionary wonders both, strove to set free the whole of humanity and create a brave new world of uninhibited happiness. Karl Marx, a radical materialist in his global perspective, Vivekananda, a sublime revolutionary with spiritual-temporal synthesis, are contrasting personalities fired by the mission of mankind's manumission. Universal humanists they were, daring iconoclasts they were, flaming philosophers, with liberative rage they were. Marx operated on the logic of dialectical materialism geared to economic emancipation, while Vivekananda was a divine militant with a restless soul battling for the total redemption of the human race. Both struggled to break the chains of thralldom and found that man, though born free, was everywhere in chains. In a higher sense, both Marx and the Swamiji were religious. What is religion? The liberation of the mind and spirit from everything that creates a mundane cage from which there is no escape. The illusion of acquisition of wealth and power is in reality an invisible version of self-spun prison tenure. Rabindranath Tagore, in Gitanjali, beautifully versifies this temporal-spiritual incarceration.

> *'PRISONER, tell me, who was it that bound you?'*
>
> *'It was my master,' said the prisoner. 'I thought I could outdo everybody in the world in wealth and power, and I amassed in my own treasure-house the money due to my king. When sleep overcame me I lay upon the bed that was for my lord, and on waking up I found I was a prisoner in my own treasure-house.'*
>
> *'Prisoner, tell me, who was it that wrought this unbreakable chain?'*
>
> *'It was I,' said the prisoners, 'who forged this chain very carefully. I thought my invincible power would hold the world captive leaving me in a freedom undisturbed. Thus night and day I worked at the chain with huge fires and cruel hard strokes. When at last the work was done and the links were complete and unbreakable, I found that it held me in its grip.'*

The two great revolutionaries, Marx and Vivekananda, were truly religious in its finest definition. Romain Rolland, quoted by Jawaharlal Nehru in his Autobiography, (at page 380) writes in his work on Ramakrishna:

> *"….many souls who are or who believe they are free from all religious belief, but who in reality live immersed in a state of super-rational consciousness, which they term Socialism, Communism, Humanitarianism, Nationalism and even Rationalism. It is the quality of thought and not its object which determines its source and allows us to decide whether or not it emanates from religion. If it turns fearlessly towards the search for truth at all costs with single-minded sincerity prepared for any sacrifice, I should call it religious; for it presupposes faith in an end to human effort higher than the life of existing society, and even higher than the life of humanity as a whole. Scepticism itself, when it proceeds from vigorous natures to the core, when it is an expression of strength and not of weakness, joins in the march of the Grand Army of the religious Soul.'*

If this be the measure of religion, both Karl Marx and Vivekananda fill the bill. Both believed in the greatness of the human being and the radicalism of the rational approach to life. For instance, Vivekananda expressed his conviction.

> *"Experience is the only source of knowledge." The same method of investigation which we apply to the sciences and to exterior knowledge should be applied to religion. 'If a religion is destroyed by such investigation it was nothing but a useless and unworthy superstition; the sooner it disappeared the better.' 'Why religions should claim that they are bound to abide by the standpoint of reason no one knows… For it is better that mankind should become atheist by following reason than blindly believe in two hundred million gods on the authority of anybody… Perhaps there are prophets who have passed the limits of sense and obtained a glimpse of the beyond. We shall believe it only when we can do the same ourselves; not before.' It is said that reason is not strong enough, that often it makes mistakes. If reason is weak, why should a body of priests be considered any better guides? 'I will abide by my reason', continues Vivekananda, 'because with all its weakness there is some chance of my getting at truth through it… We should therefore follow reason, and also sympathise with those who do not come to any sort of belief following reason." Behave nothing until you find it out for yourself. (Discovery of India, Nehru, P.187/188)*

The basic conviction in human equality was shared by both the greats. Marx stressed the power of the proletariat while Vivekananda described it as *shudraraj.* Socialism, in its material dimension, appealed to Marx who was appalled by capitalist servitude. Socialism, spiritually charged, was the demand of Vivekananda who asserted: "I am a socialist because half a loaf is better than none." Organised religion, obscurantist and authoritarian, which blocked the ascent of the human spirit to its highest destination was allergy and anathema to both. Early in the day, the young Swamiji orated, with oracular power, at the historic Chicago Parliament of Religions (1993) over a hundred years ago:

> *Is man a tiny boat in a tempest, raised one moment on the foamy crest of a billow and dashed down into a yawning chasm the next, rolling to and fro at the mercy of good and bad actions—a powerless, helpless wreck in an ever-aging, ever-rushing, uncompromising current of cause and effect; a little moth placed under the wheel of causation which rolls on crushing everything in its way and waits not for the widow's tears or the orphan's cry? The heart sinks at the idea. Yet this is the law of Nature. Is there no hope. Was the cry that went up from the bottom of the heart a cry of despair? It reached the throne of mercy and words of hope and consolation came down and inspired a Vedic sage, and he stood up before the world and in trumpets voice proclaimed the glad tidings: Hear, ye children of immortal bliss. Ye are the children of God, the sharers of immortal bliss. Holy and perfect beings. Ye, divinities on earth. Sinners; it is a sin to call a man so: It is a standing libel on human nature. Come up O lions, and shake off the delusion that you are sheep. You are souls, immortal, spirits free, blessed, and eternal, ye are not matter: ye are not bodies; matter is your servant not you the servant of matter.*
>
> *(p XIV Marx and Vivekananda P.Parameswaran)*

Perhaps Marx and Vivekananda may well agree on Victor Hugo's statement. "I am for religion against religions (Les Miserables, preface). Albert Einstein put it best, if I may say so in all humility.

> *My religion consists of a humble admiration of the illimitable superior spirit who reveals himself in the slight details we are able to perceive with our frail and feeble minds. That deeply emotional conviction of the presence of a superior reasoning power, which is revealed in the incomprehensible universe, forms my idea of God.*

Indeed, the following quote from Swami Vivekananda reads like a marxian utterance.

> *The peasant, the shoe-maker, the sweeper, and such other lower classes of India have much greater capacity for work and self-reliance than you. They have been silently working through long ages, and producing the entire wealth of the land, without a word of complaint. Very soon they will get above you in position. You have so long oppressed these forbearing masses; now is the time for their retribution...*
>
> *But times have changed. The lower classes are gradually awakening to this fact and making a united front against this determined to exact their legitimate dues. The masses of Europe and America have been the first to awaken and have already begun the fight. Signs of this awakening have*

shown themselves in India too, as is evident from the number of strikes among the lower classes now-a-days. The upper classes will no longer be able to repress the lower, try they ever so much,

I consider that the great national sin is the neglect of the masses, and that is one of the causes of our downfall. No amount of politics would be of any avail until the masses in India are once more well educated, well fed and well cared for. They pay for our education, they build our temples, but in return they get kicks. They are practically our slaves. If we want to regenerate India, we must work for them.

On whose side are you? On the side of the millions of downtrodden, exploited, uneducated, supersitious, ignorant or on the side of the exploiting few?

Inspirational and historical was Vivekananda when he addressed the working class:

Our proletariat are doing their duty....is there no heroism in it? Many turn out to be heroes, when they have some great task to perform..."and it is you who are actually doing this, ye ever trampled labouring classes of India; I bow to you.

The materialism implicit in "Annam Brahma" was a credal component of his synthesis:

Feel, my children, feel for the poor, the ignorant, the downtrodden; feel till the heart stops and the brain reels and you think you will go mad.

We talk foolishly against material civilisation. The grapes are sour... Material civilisation, nay even luxury, is necessary to create work for the poor. Bread; I do not believe in a God, who cannot give me bread here, giving me eternal bliss in heaven. Pooh; India is to be raised, the poor are to be fed, education is to be spread, and the evil of priestcraft is to be removed...more bread, more opportunity for everybody....

He reiterates his faith in the power of the masses: "Disciple: Sir, what you say is true, but there yet seems to be a wide gulf between the higher and lower classes. To bring the higher classes to sympathise with the lower seems to be a difficult affair in India.

Swamiji: But without that there is no well-being of the upper classes. You will be destroyed by internecine quarrels and fights—which you have been having so long. When the masses will wake up, they will come to understand your oppression of them, and by a puff of their mouth, you will be entirely blown away. It is they who have introduced civilisation amongst you, and it is they who will then pull it down. Think how at the hands of the Gauls the mighty ancient Roman civilisation crumbled into dust. Therefore, I say, try to rouse these lower classes from slumber by imparting learning and culture to them.

When they will awaken—and awaken one day they must—they also will not forget your good services to them and remain grateful to you.

K. Damodaran says in his "Indian Thought:

It must be specially mentioned that two decades before the socialist revolution in Russia, this great man, (Vivekananda) raised the slogan of socialism in India. There is no wonder that he became a great source of inspiration for the new generation.

This spiritual radical was a tour de force on the Indian people. He came as a tonic to the depressed and demoralised Hindu and gave him self-reliance and some roots in the past, says Nehru. Truly, as Netaji Subhash Chandra Bose said: This cyclonic sadhu was the spiritual father of the modern nationalist movement.

V.K.R.V. Rao sums up the impact of Swami Vivekananda on India thus: "Though not in politics, Swami Vivekananda has played a great role in the shaping of modern India, second if not equal to the role played by the God-conscious patriot Mahatma Gandhi who followed him. Secularism, socialism, mass uplift and mass power, women's liberation, abolition of untouchability, inclusion of social service as a part of religious worship, Hindu-Muslim unity, universal literacy and informal education—all these constitute the contribution of Swami Vivekananda to the building of modern India.

Aurobindo made the best assessment:

Vivekananda was a soul of puissance if ever there was one, a very lion among men, but the definite work he has left behind is quite incommensurate with our impressions of his creative might and energy. We perceive his influence still working gigantically, we know not well how, we know not well where, in something genuine, grand, intuitive upheaving that has entered the soul of India and we say 'Behold, Vivekananda still lives in the soul of his mother and the souls of her children.'

This puissant sanyasin, with the energy of a tidal wave, raged against superstitions, roared for universal values and rhetorised to advocate the absolute monism of *vedanta*. A few excerpts from Nehru's Discovery of India thrill the soul:

Passionately, Vivekananda condemned the meaningless metaphysical discussions and arguments about ceremonials and especially the touch-me-notism of the upper caste. 'Our religion is in the kitchen. Our God is the cooking-pot, and our religion is; "don't touch me, I am holy."

There cannot be any progress without the whole world following in the wake, and it is becoming every day clearer that the solution of any problem can never be attained on racial, or national, or narrow grounds. Every idea has to become broad till it covers the whole of this world, every aspiration

> *must go on increasing till it has engulfed the whole of humanity, nay the whole of life, within its scope.*
>
> *He once wrote: 'I am a socialist not because I think it is a perfect system, but half a loaf is better than no bread. The other systems have been tried and found wanting.*
>
> *He condemned 'occultism and mysticism…these creepy things; there may be great truths in them, but they have nearly destroyed us….And here is the test of truth—anything that makes you weak physically, intellectually, and spiritually, reject as poison, there is no life in it, it cannot be true. Truth is strengthening. Truth is purity, truth is all-knowledge…. These mysticisms, in spite of some grains of truth in them, are generally weakening… Go back to your Upanishads, the shining, the strengthening, the bright philosophy; and part from all these mysterious things, all these weakening things. Take the world, simple as your own existence.' And beware of superstition. 'I would rather see everyone of you rank atheists than superstitious fools, for the atheist is alive, and you can make something of him. But if superstition enters, the brain is gone, the brain is softening, degradation has seized upon the life… Mystery-mongering and superstition are always signs of weakness.'*
>
> *(Discovery of India, P-337-339)*

Bread, bread for the hungry, Vivekananda urged with spiritual flame and material militancy.

The international dimension of the appreciation of Vivekananda has claimed a page from the Hindu scholar P. Parameswaran:

> *This new appraisal of the Swami is not confined to India alone. The Socialist countries have also started appreciating the personality and message of Swami Vivekananda. Both Russia and China observed his 120th birth anniversary on an official level, coinciding as it did with the death centenary of Karl Marx. His works are being closely studied and books brought out on them.*
>
> *E.P. Chelishev, a well-known Russian writer and an ardent admirer of Vivekananda, believes that 'the humanistic ideal of Vivekananda is to a certain degree identical with Gorky's Man with a capital letter…. The Socialist people who already know some of the works of Vivekananda published in the U.S.S.R. highly revere the memory of the great patriot, humanist and democrat, impassioned fighter for a better future for his people and all mankind.' Similarly, the Chinese Professor of History, Huang Xin Chuan paying handsome tributes to Swami Vivekananda recollects his historical association with China: 'Vivekananda stands out as the most renowned philosopher and social figure of India in modern China. His philosophical and social thought and epic patriotism not only inspired the growth of Indian nationalism but made great impact abroad… He paid high*

tributes to our glorious ancient culture and loved the Chinese people—We pay homage to him.' Huang has written a book on the Swami in Chinese entitled "Modern Indian Philosopher—Swami Vivekananda". (Page-3 Marx and Vivekananda)

Young Narendra, dynamic, tornadic and monastic was touched and transformed by Ramakrishna Paramahamsa into Vivekananda, a socially sensitive, spiritually volcanic sadhu, a founding father of India's cultural heritage—a confluence of scientific temper, soul force, vedantic vision, synthesis of the temporal and spiritual and eclectic wisdom indivisibly universal.

The misery of the Indian masses moved him; the imperialist exploitation of the country by the British angered him. The grand idea of Advaita, with the indwelling presence of the divine in every human, inspired him and the creative courage of transforming society as a hallowed habitat for living with dignity, equality and developmental opportunity made him a dauntless missionary travelling the world over and belighted the vision of the infinite and the absolute as the truth to be realised by everyone as the manifestation of the universal self. Narendra, turned Vivekananda, was a spiritual—material explosion for whom economic liberation was a creed, but what was more integral was the spiritual unfolding, the true discovery of the divinity within. Inevitably, divisive casteism and corrosive communalism were anathamatic to his universal humanism.

I cannot resist quoting what I wrote in a Foreword to Parameswarji's book Marx and Vivekananda:

"He preached the monism of the Advaita philosophy of the Vedanta and was convinced that only this could be the future religion of thinking humanity. For the Vedanta was not only spiritual but rational and in harmony with scientific investigations of external nature. This universe has not been created by any extra-cosmic God, nor is it the work of any outside genius. It is self-creating, self-dissolving, self-manifesting. One Infinite Existence, the Brahman. The Vedanta ideal was of the solidarity of man and his inborn divine nature: to see God in man is the real God vision; man is the greatest of all beings. But 'the abstract Vedanta must become living-poetic in everyday life; out of hopelessly intricate mythology must come concrete moral forms: and out of bewildering yogism must come the most scientific and practical psychology'. India has fallen because she had narrowed herself, gone into her shell and lost touch with other nations, and thus sunk into a state of 'mummified' and 'crystallised' civilisation."

Read Nehru again:

He condemned occultism and mysticism.... These creepy things; there may be great truths in them, but they have nearly destroyed us... And here is the test of truth—anything that makes you weak physically, intellectually, and spiritually, reject as poison, there is no life in it, it cannot be true. Truth is strengthening. Truth is purity, truth is all knowledge... These mysticism, in spite of some grains of truth in them, are generally weakening... Go back to your Upanishads, the shining, the strengthening, the bright philosophy, and part from all these mysterious things, all these weakening things. Take up this philosophy, the greatest truths are the simplest things in the world, simple as your own existence. And beware of superstition, I would rather see every one of you rank atheists than superstitious fools, for the atheist is alive, and you can make something of him. But if superstition enters, the brain is gone, the brain is softening, degradation has seized upon the life... Mystery mongering and superstition are always signs of weakness."

The indignant oratory of this ochre-robed rationalist is matchless and I quote from The Discovery of India to substantiate this thesis:

"Vivekananda, one of the greatest of the modern exponents of Yoga and the Vedanta, has laid repeated stress on the experimental character of Yoga and on basing it on reason. 'No one of these Yogas gives up reason, no one asks you to be hoodwinked or to deliver your reason into the hands of priests of any type whatsoever. Each one of them tells you to cling to your reason, to hold fast to it.' Though the spirit of Yoga and the Vedanta may be akin to the spirit of science, it is true that they deal with different media, and hence vital differences creep in. According to the Yoga, the spirit is not limited to the intelligence, and also thought is action, and only action can make thought of any value."

(Marx and Vivekananda XI-XII)

Again, let me excerpt:

But this oceanic personality shines forth in his radical splendour not so much in his rationalism, philosophical eclecticism, East-West humanism, power-packed, cultural patriotism and extraordinary evangelism as in his supreme spiritual egalitarianism and his sensitively militant harmonisation of materialism with Hindu thought, the fundamental focus being on the human masses and their spiritual-social transformation. Reading Vivekananda one sometimes wonders whether he is not a spiritually charged Marx minus obsessively materialist value base. The proletariat fascinated both, the super-emergence, in their own soulful right, of the suppressed and silent, yet potentially creative and numerically enormous underdogs. The freedom to unfold one's personality is everyone's spiritual birthright. Through purposive education and emancipative religion, man realises his cultural fullness. 'Education is the manifestation of the perfection already in man.' 'Religion is the manifestation of the divinity already in man.' In short human freedom and its cosmic dimension springs from the Upanishadic wisdom about the world process. Vivekananda, says Nehru, emphasised the root truth. The question is: "What is this Universe? From what does it arise? Into what does it go?" And the answer is: "In freedom it rises, in freedom it rests, and unto freedom it melts away." Freedom and fearlessness go together and so the revolution of the human spirit implies the imperatives of both freedom and abhay.

Equality and social justice are not mundane values nor ethical rules but the postulates of the divinity that dwells in each person:

'Thou art that:' (Marx and Vivekananda, P-XIII-XIV)

The cornerstone of the cultural basic structure of Nav Bharat, was laid with verve and vision by Prometheans like Vivekananda. Never in the finer field of higher human affairs have so many owed so much to so few as one billion Bharat brethren to so vibrant a visionary like Vivekananda.

Karl Marx, born in a city in Germany, belonged to a middle-class lawyer family with liberal views and progressive ideals. Karl was a brilliant student who became interested in history and philosophy and was fascinated by Hegel. He grew up into a radical who was critical of the German State. With great daring he wrote the Communist Manifesto in 1848. He lived in extreme poverty but was oblivious of everything except the great task he had set for himself. He evolved the science of dialectical materialism and envisioned the strategy of revolution:

"For nearly four strenuous decades, there flowed from Marx's pen, books pamphlets, articles and addresses, a 'corpus' of writings that has changed the world.... In August 1852, Marx's first article appeared in the radical American paper, 'New York Daily Tribune' where during ten years, Marx and Engels wrote more than five hundred pieces." All these years Marx worked under heavy financial strain. (Page 20 – Marx and Vivekananda)

He was too great intellectually and ideologically for those who claim to be his disciples. It is ironic but true, as P. Parameswaran writes:

By the 1870's Marx and Engels began to have apprehensions about some of their followers, who proclaimed themselves 'Marxists', that they would falsify the basic concept of scientific socialism and turn it into a dogma. By that time Marx had dissociated himself from such ''Marxists' with his famous reply, "All I know is that I am not a Marxist." This was not, as is sometimes assumed a casual remark, but a statement frequently repeated by Marx, expressing his growing misgivings about the 'Marxists' appearing at that time. Engels also shared these sentiments. He called many of these 'Marxists' as "people whose incompetence is matched only by their ignorance".

(Marx and Vivekananda, P-21)

His great work was Das Capital written with eloquent diction and burning conviction. Marx, according to Engels:

> *Before all else, Marx was a revolutionist. To collaborate in one way or another in the overthrow of capitalist society and of the State institutions created by that society; to collaborate in the freeing of the modern proletariat, which he was the first to inspire with a consciousness of its needs, with a knowledge of the conditions requisite for its emancipation—this was his true mission in life. Fighting was his natural element. Few men have fought with so much passion, tenacity and success.*
>
> *Because he was an active revolutionist, Marx was the best hated and most calumniated man of his time. He was shown the door by various governments, republicans as well as absolute. Bourgeois, ultra-democrats as well as conservatives vied with one another in spreading libels about him. Yet he has gone down to his death honored, loved and mourned by millions of revolutionary workers all over the world, in Europe and Asia as far eastward as the Siberian mines, and in America as far westward as California. I can boldly assert that, while he may still have many adversaries, he has now hardly one personal enemy.*

What has struck me as great in the personality of Marx is the set of answers he gave to a questionnaire prepared by his daughters in 1865:

> *What is your favorite virtue? Simplicity.*
> *Your outstanding characteristic? Singleness of purpose.*
> *Your idea of happiness? To struggle.*
> *The vice you detest most? Servility.*
> *Your favourite maxim? I am a man and nothing pertaining to*
> *Man is alien to me.*
> *Your favourite motto? One must doubt everything.*

Marx was not a religionist nor an antagonist. In his words "Religion is the sigh of the oppressed creature, the feeling of a heartless world, just as it is the spirit of unspiritual conditions. It is the opium of the people". Marx's position is widely misunderstood. When the essay in question was written, opium was used in Europe almost exclusively for relieving pain... Marx was using the word opium in this sense and not in the sense that religion is a stupifor deliberately administered to the people by agents of the ruling class—Weekly People, (official organ, Socialist Labour Party) January 31, 1959.

The most explosive call of Karl Marx is the oft-quoted words 'the workers have nothing to lose in this (revolution) but their chains. They have a world to gain. Workers of the world, unite!' The command of compassion we see in his teaching is again an oft-quoted slogan of communism 'from each according to his ability, to each according to his needs'. The philosophers have only interpreted the world in various ways; the point is to change it. (Karl Marx).

Friedrich Engels, whose writings are integral to Marxian thought, writes:

> *By it (Historical Materialism) History for the first time was placed on its real foundation; the obvious fact, hitherto totally neglected, that first of all men must eat, drink and have shelter and clothing and therefore work, before they can struggle for supremacy or devote themselves to politics, religion, philosophy, etc., this fact at last found historical recognition.*
>
> *The materialist conception of history starts from the principle that production of the means to support human life, ultimate causes of all social and with production the exchange of products, is the basis of every social order; that in every society which has appeared in history the distribution of the products, and with it the division of society into classes and orders, is determined by what is produced and how it is produced, and how the product is exchanged. According to this conception, the changes and political revolutions are to be sought not in the philosophy but in the economics of the epoch concerned.*
>
> *According to the materialist conception of history the determining element in history is ultimately the production and reproduction in real life. More than this neither Marx nor I have ever asserted. If therefore somebody twists this into the statement that the economic element is the only determining one, he transforms it into a meaningless, abstract and absurd phrase.*

What is emphatic is that while economics dominates the way of life Marx-Engels still left room for moral and spiritual forces to play. They stood for total human freedom but thought that economic bondage was the principal obstacle. Humanity Unbound was the mission of Marx. Liberation of peoples everywhere was his goal. The over-emphasis on materialism and lesser accent on the spiritual dimension was perhaps his western predilection. On the whole, his philosophy did not exclude the non-material values of life. That is why Swami Renganathananda described this great revolutionist as *Maharshi Marx* (I have heard him describe Marx using this lofty expression). Remember the selfless message and passion for change which motivated Marx when he said 'the philosophers have only interpreted the world in various ways; the point is to change it'. The challenge of change was beyond breaking economic chains but making the human person fully.

Karl Marx, with the power of his revolutionary doctrine, predicted that capitalism would be its own grave-digger and that a new classless society would emerge through the instrumentality of the dictatorship of the proletariat. The spectre of revolution did haunt the feudal-industrial world and the have-nots everywhere felt that the fire power of collective action could catalyse the collapse of the diehard order of thralldom. The Russian revolution demonstrated this dramatic change, People's China proved the power of this great idea, socialism became a philosophy seriously taken by the West. Marxism was, however, rooted in materialism but man is more than meat and body that *raiment*. Where the Promethean power of the spirit does not burn perennially to resist the captivating appetite of capitalism and its aggravated form of imperialism, it fails. In the final global march, when science and technology, through money power and profit hunger aggrandize capitalism, even the Soviet flag fails to fly triumphantly and China's Great Wall is cracking and its socialist conscience is in a mood to compromise. Materialist craving corrupts the soul, as Mahatma Gandhi drove home: In so far as we have made the modern materialistic craze our goal, he wrote, so far are we going downhill in the path of progress' Gandhiji's foresight about consumerist cannibalism is proven by events and portent. Karx Marx's mission, unless transformed by the talisman of Vivekananda's vision, cannot sustain the revolutionary global order as he predicted. Expropriators shall be expropriated, Marx predicted, but, in our age of globalization and privatization, the reverse process of expropriation ad *libitem* will continue to impoverish the world, as the North now does the South. But all is not lost if the will is not dead. John Pilger's last paragraph in Hidden Agendas gives hope:

> *Beware 'the rumbling out there', says the President of the Federal Reserve Bank. 'People are dangerously suffering from globophobia,' says a senior floor trader in New York. The magnitude of change in the world economy since the end of the Cold War,' wrote the eminent American economist, David Hale, 'has been so dramatic it has given rise to a new political phenomenon....voters now view trade issues in terms of domestic class struggle.' In his book, Has Globalization Gone Too Far? another Harvard high priest, Dano Rodrik, wrote 'The international integration of markets for goods, services and capital is pressuring societies to alter their traditional practices (so much that) in return, broad segments of these societies are putting up a fight.*
>
> *The fight has only just begun. (P-610)*

Vivekananda was a cosmic figure who did not deny the material base of the social order. But towering above the materialist interpretation of communist theory, he wrote in revolt against exploitation and demanded in militant tone that an egalitarian order, spiritually charged and temporally just, must come to pass, that the manifestation of the divinity and dignity of humanity is the salvationary route to a brave new world.

Rarely do personalities emerge who shake and shape the world. Vivekananda belongs to this rarest of the rare category. In my humble view, a spiritual revolution must shatter the materialist macro-mania of MNC gormandization. All Creation is one; universal compassion is the spiritual catalyst that can slay World capitalism Incorporated. The voice of Vivekananda gave the call to all mankind to fight the terrorism of Materialsm Unlimited. 'Arise, awake and stop not till the goal is reached'.

In a profound dimension, Vivekananda was a power for spiritual—temporal transformation and perennial locomotive of global regeneration and elevation of the human race. Karl Marx, operating on the materialist-humanist plane, was a puissant force for liberation of mankind and influenced the World Order with his doctrine of dialectical materialism. In the words of Engels "because he was an active revolutionist, Marx was the best hated and most calumniated man of his time.... Yet he has gone down to his death, honoured, loved and mourned by millions of revolutionary workers all over the world."

RANDOM REFLECTIONS ON OUR ANCIENT CULTURAL TREASURY

Let me confess, at the outset, to my gross inadequacy to deal, even summarily, with the Upanishads which scale the supreme height of cosmic comprehension humanity has ever attained. The esoteric meaning, the variorum of **bhashyams** and the perennial essence flowing therefrom are so blended and boundless that even a superficial presentation to initiate interest demands a measure of scholarship, a duration of contemplation and a degree of inner experience too overwhelming for smell me. Even so, as a lay **jijnasu** let me tell you a few things my peripheral pursuits enable me to mention.

The Upanishads are a Hindu heritage but go far beyond the Hindus. These scriptures are Indian but transcend its territory. The sublime science of the spirit these esoteric teachings enshrine is universal and soar to other spheres we may call trans-universal. They embrace the Manifest Phenomena but probe and unfold the Unmanifest Infinite of Brahman. The call of the Upanishads—harken to it, meditate on their message, live a line of these sacred texts which have inspired East and West and explained the cycle of Creation, before and after, so perfectly that saint and sinner may receive deliverance by an incisive understanding and penetrating experiencing of the teachings. But the process is not easy. That unrelenting commitment to self-enlightenment is rare to find, hard to acquire and difficult to practise. However, apart from that discipline and determination, there is the philosophical vision and unitive understanding which is the message and meaning of **Vedanta**. If we understand Dialectic as Emerson has defined it, we can apply dialectics to both materialist and spiritual forces:

> *"As there is a science of stars, called astronomy; a science of quantities, called mathematics; a science of qualities, called chemistry; so there is a science of sciences—I call it Dialectic—which is the Intellect discriminating the false and the true."*

When material phenomena are analysed and scanned by the dialectical method, by studying the opposites objectively, we get the truth of the universe through the physical sciences. But materialism does not exhaust the other dimensions. Spiritual truth must be apprehended through the dialectical approach or discriminating assessment of Reality in its non-physical attributes. In sum, dialectics, materialist and spiritualist, together in their holistic perception and integral yoga, give us the Truth in its fullness, not in partial projections. A science, which explains the material universe as **bhautic** and the spiritual as **adhyatmic**, arrives at a synthesis where the opposites lose their contradictions and project a Divine Presence everywhere. It is this unitive vision, this advaitic essence that is the Upanishadic fundamental.

We find great Western poets and seers like Eliot and Tennyson, Whitman, Emerson and Blake and a host of other earthly celestials in other literatures whose doors of perception did swing wide open and their souls directly did witness what the senses could not descry. Listen to William Blake:

"This life's five windows of the soul
Distorts the Heavens from pole to pole,
And leads you to believe a lie
When you see with, not through, the eye."

You tread on Vedanta, when you look at the universe through Walt Whitman's verses, beyond what the scientist could, with experiments in laboratories, tell us of nuclear power, heart transplant and the substance of the stars. When the bard burst out and said:

'I believe a leaf of grass is no less than the journey work of the stars'—

or read another little, profound piece:

"Come lovely and soothing death,
Undulate round the world, serenely arriving, arriving,
In the day, in the night, to all, to each.
Sooner or later, delicate death.
Prais'd be the fathomless universe,
For life and joy, and for objects and knowledge curious,
And for love, sweet love—but praise! praise! praise!
For the sure-enwinding arms of cool-enfolding death."

Yet another:

"The universe is in myself, it shall pass through me as a procession."

He wrote in anglo-saxon tongue but gave expression to Upanishadic vision. Emerson's poem on Brahma runs like this:

"If the red slayer think he slays,
Or if the slain think he is slain,
They know not well the subtle ways
I keep, and pass, and turn again,"

A thousand affirmations of vedic truth are found between, strewn in prose and poetry, in written and oral utterances. Aurobindo's Savitri also bears testimony. Inspired souls pour forth in great moments a vocabulary of ecstasy too glorious for human poetry. There is a touch of the Upanishads which makes the whole world of thinkers and poets kin.

Vachaspati, in this esoteric work, interprets to us the actual text of Shankara Bhasya on the world's most ancient and lofty attestation of the science of Self, which combines the eternal rules that govern the phenomenal universe and the intangible cosmos, too rational to be rejected by infidels, too experiential to be ignored by scientists, to rebelliously truthful to be bound by priestly rituals.

The hallowed land of Bharat produced the Upanishads for the benefit of generations of humankind on earth and other planets wherever life may flourish. Humbler mortals like me may only gain a moment's glimpse and be astonished but a Rabindranath may sing, a Radhakrishnan may expound, an Aurobindo may experience, a Ramana or Sai Baba, a Nityananda or Krishnamurti may realise. Likewise, other saints and prophets in other climes and countries may have had Upanishadic impulses, regardless of religion and sect. Truth is the same though it may have various versions and view-points. The greatest exponent of these songs Celestial or Upanishadic verses is Shankara whose brief mortal spell blessed mankind with boundless wisdom in its finest blossom, now in terse prose, now in superb poetry, now in bursts of devotional song, now in harsh admonition to blind materialists and bigoted ritualists. Jewels here, jewels there, jewels everywhere—such is the treasury of thought Sankara has left as legacy. We are heirs, but the heirs must become worthy of the heritage and the acharya.

For me the ideas expressed in the upanishads are not mere sanskritic stanzas for holy chant, sitting in meditative poses and mystic squint but the Reality behind Reality, the science of sciences, the Truth not to learn which is life missed. A person is never free until he masters knowledge, that alone makes him free. Says the Bible:

"And seek ye the Truth
And Truth shall make you free"

And what truth exists beyond **Tattvam** asi—thou art that! How scientific is the search? The stages who saw the universe around them began asking challenging questions. Inspired interrogations, authentic answers, verified experiences and systematised knowledge immortalised in songs codifying the science of the Spirit and all else in the Manifest and the Unmanifest—this unbounded, encyclopedic collection cannot be insulted by mere mechanical recitation coated with piety. To do justice to the grand text you must read, reflect, again reflect and stop not till a shaft of light awakens the slumbering soul. Alas, in our electronic age we have information revolution, maximisation of living in pleasure but not a wee bit of Life itself, that profound gift of Creation! T.S. Eliot sadly sings:

"Where is the Life we have lost in living?
Where is the wisdom we have lost in knowledge?
Where is the knowledge we have lost in information?

An introduction to the book cosmic vistarama of Shankara is best given by borrowing the beginning from the initiated author Panoli on Shankara's commentaries on the Upanishads. He opens thus:

"No expression can be chaster, none purer, and none more elevating than the Upanishadic utterances that came down to us from the saints and sages of yore who lived in the forests meditating on the Supreme."

"No thought can be more lofty, some more sublime, and none more inspiring than the thoughts conveyed through the naïve utterances of these Vedic sages, ancient seers of truth, who breathed into their words all that is auspicious for the whole of humanity."

"Upanishads voice forth in pristine purity all about the human experience of the Divine and every word issues from the depth of truth, from the inmost shrine of wisdom. Holy is their source; holy is their course. Holy indeed is the man chastised by them and the holiest he will ever remain who breathes the life-giving, ever-purifying air of the Upanishads."

"These immortal utterances are the quintessence of thought brought to bear upon the existence of the immanent God. Introspection could not proceed further when the Vedic sages rose up and declared in ecstatic joy, 'We and our creator are one'".

The Upanishads are often considered the further spiritual flowering; the finer development into the Vedanta or the final phase of the Vedas. The Vedic civilization of the Aryans in India has been one of the greatest mankind has seen. The author tells us that the *poorva bhaga* shows the way to ***pravritti dharma*** (the path of action) and the ***uttara bhaga*** lays the guidelines to the ***nivritti dharma*** (the path of liberation through knowledge). It is to this latter part Upanishads belong. It is interesting that there are 108 Upanishads, although what are considered most significant are the ten Upanishads:

"Isvasya, Kena, katha, prasna, Mundaka, Manudkya, Taittriya, Aitareya, Chhandogya and Brihadaranyaka."

Adi Shankara wrote his **bhashya** on these ten Upanishads and two more. The shortest is Mandukya and the longest, as the name indicates, is the Brihadarnayaka. The supreme spiritual contemplation of the Vedic Seers is condensed into the ten Upanishads, and to master them Adi Shankara's **bhashya** is the leading light. The quintessence, the highest message, the liberating truth is contained in the perennial philosophy of which the Upanishads are the nidus. The eternal interrogation which leads on to the supreme revelation is "Who am I; how is this cosmos evolved; who is its creator?"

The everlasting, ever fresh, ever baffling answer rings back from the ancient texts "I am Brahman—Thou art that—**Aham Brahmasmi—Tattvamasi."** The Bhagavad Gita, which has been for centuries upon centuries the lighthouse for humanity, is itself but the epitome of Upanishadic literature.

What is the etymological meaning of Upanishads? Only the very erudite Panoli must enlighten us:

"The formation of the word Upanishad is as follows:

Upa +ni+sad

"The words *upa* and *ni* are prefixed (***Upasarga*).** The syllable (*sa*) of sad will changes into shad the word *Upa-ni-shad* comes into being. The root *sad* has several meanings such as 'to destroy' (*visarana*), to attain' (*gati* or *prapti*), 'to disable' (*avasadana*) etc.

(That which destroys *samsara*, the cause of all evils, which dispels *avidya*, the cause of *samsara* and which conduces to the attainment of Brahman, is termed Upanishad).

"The word *upa* means near. Since the root sad is generally used in the sense of *gati* (i.e. to lead, to attain) the word Upanishad is interpreted as that which leads nearer to Brahman, the realest of reality.

Again, the word Upanishad embraces *Brahmavidya* to signify which there is no other better term. Also it is used in the sense of *rahasyam* or *guhyam* (secret), for the teachings of the Upanishads are ever regarded as (secret of all secrets), because there is nothing more of a secret nature than the *Atmatativa* (Doctrine of the self) which the Upanishads bear in their inmost recesses. Because the Gita is the epitome of the essence of the teachings of the Vedas, it is also spoken of as the secret of all secrets."

India, pregnant with the Vedas and the Upanishads, burst on the West, kindled the thinkers and catalysed the thinking of the West, with that cyclonic sadhu and eloquent torrent, Swami Vivekanands, storming the materialist citadels of America and Europe. He synthesized materialism and spirituality in the new chemistry of Vedanta, at once rationalist and humanist and amazingly fresh and holistic. The occidental philosophers who despised India as barbarian and philistine discovered the priceless treasures of the vedic age and burst into raptures.

Max Muller regarded Rig Veda 'the first word spoken by the Aryan man'. These Aryans envisioned Truth without inhibitions and asked deeper questions. Evolving from this vigorous investigation came the Upanishadic monism. Says Nehru:

> *The Upanishads are instinct with a spirit of inquiry, of mental adventure, of a passion for finding out the truth about things. The search for this truth is, of course, not by the objective methods of modern science, yet there is an element of the scientific method in the approach. No dogma is allowed to come in the way.*
>
> *(Discovery of India—by Jawaharlal Nehru—Page 89)*

So marvelous has been this philosophical continuity reaching civilization's acme, that Max Muller, more than a century back, paid a rare tribute to it:

> *If we were to look over the whole world to find out the country most richly endowed with all the wealth, power, and beauty that nature can bestow—in some parts a very paradise on earth—I should point to India. If I were asked under what sky the human mind has most fully developed some of its choicest gifts, has most deeply pondered over the greatest problems of life, and has found solutions of some of them which well deserve the attention even of those who have studied Plato and Kant—I should point to India. And if I were to ask myself from what literature we here in Europe, we who have been nurtured almost exclusively on the thoughts of Greeks and Romans, and of one Semitic race, the Jewish, may draw the corrective which is most wanted in order to make our inner life more perfect, more comprehensive, more universal, in fact more truly human life, not for this life only, but a transfigured and eternal life—again I should point to India. (Ibid., p.88-89)*

Rajaji, in an eloquent passage, writes of the Upanishads:

> *The spacious imagination, the majestic sweep of thought, and the almost reckless spirit of exploration with which, urged by the compelling thirst for truth, the Upanishad teachers and pupils dig into the "open secret" of the universe, make this most ancient of the world's holy books still the most modern and most satisfying.*

How emphatic is Nehru on the spirit of enquiry in the Upanishads:

> *The dominating characteristic of the Upanishads is the dependence on truth. Truth wins ever, not falsehood. With truth is paved the road to the Divine. And the famous invocation is for light and understanding:*

Lead me from the unreal to the real! Lead me from darkness to light! Lead me from death to immortality.'

Oft quoted is the tribute by Schopenhauer, the pessimist:

In the whole world there is no study... so beneficial and so elevating as that of the Upanishads....(They) are products of the highest wisdom... It is destined sooner or later to become the faith of the people. And again: 'The study of the Upanishads has been the solace of my life, it will be the solace of my death. (Ibid., p. 92-93)

This remarkable spiritual summation was based on scientific investigation, fearless interrogation, experiential validation, not priestly rituals and non-stop chants. However, clerical orthodoxy invaded the free thought and adventurous search of the Upanishads. And this decline and fall is mentioned with distress by Aurobindo:

If an ancient Indian of the time of the Upanishad, of the Buddha, or the later classical age were to be set down in modern India......he would see his race clinging forms and shells and rags of the past and missing nine-tenths of its nobler meaning.....he would be amazed by the extent of the mental poverty, the immobility, the static repetition, the cessation of science, the long sterility of art, the comparative feebleness of the creative intuition. (Ibid., p.96)

Vedanta, with its intellectual pursuits, had even ridiculed the rituals in the Vedas. Where the mind is free from purohit domination and the head holds direct conversation with the heavens, superstitious rites are pushed aside.

Adi Shankara gave life and power to the spiritual empire of India and restored the Upanishads to their sublime scientific status. Time and again when decadence infected Indian culture some vigorous spirit rose to win back its puissance and experimental élan. In a later era, Vivekananda imparted a revolutionary thrust to the emaciated spiritual poverty of India. "Go back to your Upanishads, the shining, the strengthening, the bright philosophy; and part from all these mysterious things, all these weakening things" thundered the swamiji." "I would rather see everyone of you rank atheists than superstitious fools, for the atheists of alive, you can make something of him. But if superstition entered the brain is gone....." With the tremendous power of the Upanishadic teachings coursing through his veins, Swamiji exhorted Indians in words which reflected the prestine strength of Vedanta:

In the words of the Christians—you cannot serve God and Mammon at the same time. Throw away everything, even your own salvation, and go and help others.... The nation is sinking; the curse of unnumbered millions is on our heads—those to whom we have been giving ditch-water to drink, when they have been dying of thirst, and while the perennial river of water was

> *flowing past; the un-numbered millions whom we have allowed to starve in sight of plenty; the un-numbered millions to whom we have talked of Advaita and whom we have hated with all our strength.... Wipe off this blot! "Arise and awake".*

The militant spirituality and the radical majesty of the Upanishads is urgently relevant and burningly important to India to-day and, in a larger sense, to the world itself. We cannot recite inertly the Isopanishads, for instance, without sharing the global, universal, cosmic sweep of the verses. There are no narrow walls, no barren deserts in the poetry of the Upanishads, and that is precisely the creed that we need in a warring world threatening to break up any moment because bloodshot materialism grips it in its deadly clasp and the moral and spiritual values, which are indispensable for man's ultimate destiny, are waning and withering. Even from an individual point of view, man is surrendering to bhoga and a few, going to the other extreme of asceticism, are giving up to tyaga or abandonment of material things altogether in a mood of foolish illusionism. Humanity must find a new material, spiritual synthesis, a divinised humanism, a vigorous compassion for creation and feeling of ecological integrity.

We live in a period of crisis, the crisis of character, of morality, of integrity. We are on the verge of collapse because a vulgar fall pulls down those higher values which are our lofty Upanishadic legacy. The Constitution of India speaks of fundamental duties obligated on every citizen. One of the principal mandates so laid is 'to value and preserve the rich heritage of our composite culture'. Dialectically speaking, this cultural factor, rooted in the Upanishads, is perhaps the most potent weapon in our battle for unity of the nation and even peaceful international co-existence. It is a pity, though, that humanity, Indian and other, is lost in high technology, and chases crazy satisfaction and power intoxication, subverting that noble synthesis where life and worldliness are real in a relative sense but the deeper spiritual springs, more enduring, fertilize and stabilize society and reduce entropy. We have, therefore, to focus much more on the positive message of the Upanishads, altho' the fact remains that where there is religion we sink in its ritualism and where there is crass atheism we sterilize our capacity to rise to the skies and crawl on the morass. Said Goethe:

> *The greater part of all the mischief in the world arises from the fact that men do not sufficiently understand their own aims. They have undertaken to build a tower and spend no more labour on the foundation than would be necessary to erect a hut.*

Adi Shankara, whose mortal life was brief but genius superlative, revolutionized our cultural fibre, fought cant and cult and specious erudition, and battled thro' the length and breadth of Bharat to establish, by conquests of reactionary critics, the authentic monism of advaita with a noble fire unparalleled in the spiritual odysseys of the world. He has been an Everest of light for the ages. As a teenage man he began his divine mission when Hindu India was dissipating its soul and Buddhist India, falling into degenerate days and vicious ways, was betraying the Buddha himself. No crusade or jehad could compare with Operation Renaissance, Shankara executed singlehanded, spanning on foot the vast land from end to end, walking and debating, composing and discoursing, and, with the powerless power of a sovereign sannyasin and energized by the boundless gifts of Sarada Devi, spreading the Upanishadic essence of the Self. He taught, like a master spirit the presence of the One in everything and everything in the Self, of the Reality which transcends relative realities, of the Truth which eludes grasp because of contradictory versions and perceptions of portions and the all-embracing realization 'Thou art That'! Be your religion what it may, the Shankara encyclopedia supports, not subverts, its indefinable, ineffable creedal core—provided you are ready to drop the dross, sacrifice the superficials and dare to seek its undying light. In that sense, he is a universal torch, humanity's missionary.

Each of the ten Upanishads is marvelous poetry and profoundest investigation, presentation of sublime truths in manner, neither before nor after, has been attempted or achieved. For me, it is only given to feel appalled, sense the awesome Infinite and hope that although I am far from home, one step is enough for me.

Let me conclude with Radhakrishnans' great words:

> *The Upanishads affirm the reality of a Supreme Brahman, one without a second, without attributes or determinations, who is identical with the deepest self of man, Spiritual experience centers round a sovereign unity which overcomes the duality between the known and the knowing. The inability to conceptualize and experience leads to such descriptions as identity, pure and simple. Brahman, the subsistent simplicity, is its own object in an intuition which is its very being. It is the pure subject whose existence cannot be ejected into the external or objective world.*

The man who finds a truth lights a torch, said Ingersoll. Learn what is true in order to do what is right, said Thomas Huxley. Thus the integral yoga of truth and righteousness is the course the world must take to redeem itself from downfall. Here come propitious forces to accomplish the renewal the degenerate human planet so progressively needs. Adi Shankara came in one such age of cosmic crisis. But humanity must be ready to absorb and act on his salvationary philosophy. When the degree of decadence is darkest, the soul of society is sick and it seeks a candle light that will drive away the moral tamas, The battle between adharma and the urge for dharma is then waged and a new synthesis of higher ethics in human relations arrives.

Yet Truth is afar. Who responds to the call of Truth in this fevered world?

The human race if it is to survive must in its millennial march carry the torch handed down to us by the great teacher Adi Shankara; a synthesis of the temporal and the spiritual with a mandate to realize in oneself the Universal Self.

A DEMOCRATIC DEFEAT WITHOUT PERSONAL DISAPPOINTMENT

A Superannuated Man

My age of retirement as judge of the Supreme Court was 65. This happened in November 1980 when, sans robes of judicial office, I continued my commitment to society without the authority and insignia of official power. Not that I was tired—indeed few who retire are tired—but the command of date of birth and Article 124 of the Constitution made me lay down office. Throughout my career on the Bench and the Bar, social activism in the larger sense has consumed my interest. Of course, at the Bar apart from court work, I was connected with quite a number of public organisations and spent a considerable part of my time in addressing public meetings of a miscellaneous sort. Fine Arts Associations and Sports Organisations too claimed my time. Assuming office as judge I did not jettison my association with people's organisations. Nor, indeed, did I give up public speaking under the auspices of legal and cultural bodies, taking care to see that I did not involve myself in issues which were likely to become problems in court. That would be an embarrassment to my office. Total insulation from public activities is not an obligation of the judicial office. In the words of Chief Justice Earl Warren 'Our judges are not monks or scientists, but participants in the living stream of our national life'.

Oftentimes experience in public life before elevation to the Bench may be an advantage, as the American judges from John Marshall to Earl Warren have demonstrated. The secluded life of judicial aloofness robs the functionary of the great advantage of activist involvement in national preoccupations. The rule of law and the rule of life run close together. I have found, speaking for myself, that my life as a minister, my membership of public organisations such as the Indian Association of Lawyers, All India Peace and Solidarity Council, Indo-Soviet Cultural

Society and the Free Legal Services bodies to mention but a few, only enriched my capacity, deepened my people-oriented convictions and widened my vision of life in its larger dimension while sitting on the Bench. When superannuation overtook me, I did not find life empty. Because, even while I was judge, I continued to be associated with public bodies of a non-controversial nature with a socially useful agenda. True, the great satisfaction of exercising judicial power is not replaced by being President or Patron of any number of other organisations. To do justice in court is soulful joy, to be activist on the Bench is a remarkable self-fulfilment. The robe is more than a symbol and a judge, to be worthy of earning the appellation of justice, has to have wide experience, large learning and a vistarama of values enshrined in the Constitution. The great judge Learned Hand did observe once:

> *I venture to believe that it is as important to a judge called upon to pass on a question of constitutional law, to have at least a bowing acquaintance with Acton and Maitland, with Thucydides, Gibbon and Carlyle, with Homer, Dante, Shakespeare and Milton, with Machiavelli, Montaigne and Rabelais, with Plato, Bacom, Hume and Kant, as with the books which have been specifically written on the subject. For in such matters everything turns upon the spirit in which he approaches the questions before him. The words he must construe are empty vessels into which he can pour nearly anything he will. Men do not gather figs of thistles, nor supply institutions from judges whose outlook is limited by parish or class. They must be aware that there are before them more than verbal problems; more than final solutions cast in generalizations of universal applicability. They must be aware of the changing social tensions in every society which make it a organism; which demand new schemata of adaptation; which will disrupt it, if rigidly confined.*

(Quote It-II, P-203)

I have always felt that my fighting faith in life have been formed by participation in people's causes. At the bar I was freer, but even on the Bench I never remained a cloistered virtue. I visited countries including the Soviet Union, read literature including Karl Marx and never shied away from patriotic issues and national concerns which may be allergic to the orthodox, on the measly alibi that I was a judge and, therefore, should confine myself to dockets, reported cases and judicial clubs. Felix Frankfurter was right although I never reached anywhere near his grand description:

A judge should be compounded of the faculties that are demanded of the historian and the philosopher and the prophet. The last demand upon him—to make some forecast of the consequences of his action—is perhaps the heaviest. To pierce the curtain of the future, to give shape and visage to mysteries still in the womb of time, is the gift of the imagination. It requires poetic sensibilities with which judges are rarely endowed and which their education does not normally develop. These judges must have something of the creative artist in them; they must have antennae registering feeling and judgment beyond logical, let alone quantitative, proof.

(General Quotations-II, P-534/535)

Back to my retirement and the days thereafter

My public speeches were on the increase. My public engagements were diverse, my cultural pursuits were multiplied, my time was consumed by writing articles and delivering lectures. In that sense, shorn of power though, I lived a fuller life. Of course, a great tragedy, my wife's demise, darkened my survival by the distress of separation of the dearest. Today, I can say as a poignant reality that there is no bar of limitation for the tears of separation. I search and research into life after death. Meanwhile, I remain immersed in the human issues engaging the nation and the world. I have often felt that an epitome of my autobiography was a pale but honest reflection of the answers to a questionnaire prepared by Marx's daughters. I reproduce it here because it brings out what I have lived for:

What is your favourite virtue? Simplicity.
Your outstanding characteristic? Singleness of purpose.
Your idea of happiness? To struggle.
The vice you detest most? Servility.
Your favourite maxim?
I am a man and nothing pertaining to man is lien to me.
Your favourite motto?
One must doubt everything.

(General Quotations, P-646)

I did frequent philosophers and saintly souls in search of profound light about life and after. Ranganadananda, J. Krishnamoorthy, Muktananda, Matha Amritanandamayi, Maharshi Mahesh Yogi and above all, Sree Satyasai Baba *et al.* Am I wiser about life after death; even after sittings and seances and other experiments on communication with the dead? Some light I have derived. Sometimes I feel with Scott Fitzgerald 'in the real dark night on the soul it is always 3 O'clock'. Maybe, Edward Fitzgerald may also fit in, though not wholly.

Myself when young did eagerly frequent
Doctor and Saint, and heard great argument
About it and about; but evermore
Came out by the same Door as in I went.

(Oxford Quotations, P-212-20)

I skip these sombre leaves of life since simultaneously I have been in the thick of public life, national issues and matters of common concern to humanity. I have written books, which are collections of writings, I have travelled and addressed lectures. With Edward Gibbon, I must reluctantly observe that two causes, 'the abbreviation of time, and the failure of hope, will always tinge with a browner shade the evening of life'.

Now I come to an episode which springs from my involvement in the political issues of our time. Long years ago, I did have political friends belonging to all parties; and public figures regardless of party affiliation have extended their friendship to me. This is due to a non-dogmatic and affable attitude, although I am generally and rightly known to have a slant to the Left. My integrity was generally accepted because I had no ambition for acquisition of wealth or position. Indeed, one of the early decisions I had taken on superannuation from the Supreme Court was to be totally free from the temptation for office or fabulous fee from consultation and arbitration income from which not many judges were exempt (and some have totally succumbed). How free I feel when lucrative lust fails to gain any purchase over my soul!

I had known Nehru with deep admiration and was reciprocated with a measure of affection. I had known Indira Gandhi while she was President of the Congress Party and I in the Opposition and later, when she was Prime Minister during two terms. Although as a judge I maintained the necessary propriety of aloofness I could still truthfully say that our relationship was good. Her assassination suddenly made Rajiv Gandhi the Prime Minister of the country. I had seen him but not known him although in later years I had a few occasions of friendly meetings with him. Of course, by then I had retired from the bench. I had known with some degree of intimacy, Comrade Surjit of the C.P.I (Marxist). My cousin S.K. Ananth used to bring him to my room in the Kerala House whenever I was in Delhi. One of the items of casual conversation was the suggestion that I should contest the election when the Rashtrapati's office fell vacant. This was a few months ahead of the vacancy. As a realist I dismissed the idea as preposterous for two reasons. Firstly, I had not the remotest idea of running for an office whatever the prospect be. (I had once dismissed a Rajya Sabha suggestion during V.P. Singh's tenure as P.M.). That was no longer my cup of tea especially after my defeat in 1965 in the Kerala Assembly elections. Secondly, there was not the ghost of a chance for any candidate set up by Leftists who made national noises disproportionate to their electoral muscles. Surjit and Ananth gave up the proposal knowing my mind and firm resolution. Then came the expiry of the term of Rashtrapati R. Venkataraman. Rajiv Gandhi, though young, was resolute. His candidate, whoever he be, would win hands down. So in any contest for Presidentship, the rival to Rajiv's choice would fail utterly. Nevertheless, the idea was mooted that in the largest democracy in the world, it should not be that the election to the highest office should go without contest in spite of the fact that there was a significant Opposition to the ruling party inside the House and outside. For these reasons, the diverse opposition groups toyed with the idea of setting up a rival candidate.

From now on, I speak from amnesic memory. One day while I was undergoing ayurvedic treatment at Kottakkal, my old friend, a C.P.I. leader, the late N.E. Balaram, landed up made his way to my room where I was resting. When I warmly welcomed him as an old friend he puzzled me with a ludicrous proposal that I should run for Rashtrapati's office. Balaram could advocate his cause cleverly. He tried his best to persuade me into an odd affirmation but I rejected as fantastic the proposal for candidature. When he found me diamond-hard, he left in disappointment. To wipe out the gossip of my being presidential candidate, I issued a clear press statement negating any such possibility. After my ayurvedic treatment, I returned to Kochi. One day while I was convalescing, the great E.M.S., who had given earlier intimation, sprang a surprise on me. He came all the way from Delhi and announced that the Opposition parties, many, though tiny, had collectively resolved that I should be their candidate. I had no hesitation to tell my respected friend Namboodiripad that I could not consider the opposition proposal. He insisted that he had come all the way from Delhi because that was a mandate entrusted to him and he had to carry it out. I had sanity enough to know the result of the election. I had resolution enough to remain firm on my decision. Namboodiripad, to our mutual embarrassment, returned to Delhi, although his errand proved to be a damp squib.

Let me correct my memory by reproducing the politically sensitive E.M.S. letter:

"My dear Krishna Iyer,

> The three-man Committee (NTR, Chandra Sekhar and myself) met yesterday when I told them about my talks with you. My two colleagues are agreeable to your name provided (a) you give your consent, and (b) they want to consult parties like the BJP whom I am not prepared to consult.
>
> In the meanwhile, it is clear that there is no prospect of a consensus candidate. Rajiv is determined to push his party candidate, making it appear that he (or she) is a 'consensus candidate'. There is, therefore, no possibility of our (opposition) candidate winning the election; it is a fight on policies.
>
> From this point of view, you are the best person to take up the challenge. Your widely-publicised article provides the political basis on which to fight. On the other hand, there is a real danger that, in case of your decision to stand down, the non-left opposition parties may float names which cannot be accepted.

I, therefore, plead with you that you should give your consent.

Yours sincerely,

E.M.S. Namboodiripad"

And now my reply personal:

"My dear Namboodiripad,

Your letter was delivered to me by Comrade Ramakrishnan at Calicut yesterday and I had a brief discussion on the subject with him but promised to send you a reply today. N.E. also met me and had a longer exchange of views. The issue of presidential candidature is one of decisive moment at this sensitive juncture of our country's democratic saga. I agree with you that the politics of that high office is not idle polemics but a facet of the dialectics of the current Indian crisis. Clarity is critical when confusion fertilises interested forces in their efforts to throw out polity into disarray.

I am heartened that my jural-political approach to the President-Prime Minister problem receives your approbation as well as of many progressive jurists and political thinkers.

Any serious social realist studying the political scenario of India in the context of the presidential election will agree with the conclusion you have indicated that the Congress nominee will numerically (not ethically) win hands down. The dynamics of political forces may, (?) in its evolutionary process, wreak slow or sudden changes upsetting conservative conclusions. Even after making an allowance for such developments, one must realise that in the short term the command performance of the Congress electorate, may be as directed by the 3-line whip. It is fair to accept the position that a rival has no real chance in the present mood of the Prime Minister and his fiat. What is regrettable is that the illusion about a national consensus was cultivated by him cleverly but without authentic will.

Proceeding on the footing that the contestant to the Congress candidate has no prospect of success, the crucial question arises whether I should agree to be a candidate at all. My general disposition has been against being a candidate even if the prospects were rosy. My physical health leaves much to be desired. (I have just returned from the Manipal Hospital and am going into the Kottakkal Arya Vaidyasala for treatment a little later). However, I had not banged the door of my mind on account of certain persuasions from friends whom I respect, including you. But I had not any time consented to be a candidate of the Opposition, even in the absence of a consensus, a position which is clear from your letter. Nevertheless, a few newspapers erroneously published some days ago that I was an opposition candidate and my consent had been secured. There was no need for me, who had been keeping out of the fray, to go to the Press and contradict. I had never agreed for President.

While I agree with you about the analysis of the situation in the event of my declining to be a candidate and while I deplore the emergence of more than one candidate for the Opposition parties, I find myself unable to run for President. Your few sentences in the last part of the letter have moved me beyond words and touched me to tears. But emotional reactions do not solve problems. My negative subjectivism based upon several factors, unnecessary to be detailed here, persuade me to tell you reluctantly that I do not find my way to be a candidate for the presidential election. My indifferent health corroborates my mood. Of course, in a rapidly changing situation, it is political prudence to keep one's eye open.

Dear Namboodiripad, I am deeply grateful to you and all the other parties which have chosen to put faith in me in the present presidential electoral race. Yet, I am unable to agree, and plead with you to forgive me for saying so. I deeply respect your sentiments and request you to reciprocate it.

With kindest regards,

Yours sincerely,

V.R. Krishna Iyer"

(Justice V.R. Krishna Iyer—A Living Legend, P-251/252)

I was the President of Indo-Afghan Friendship Society at that time when that finest-President Najibullah, a friend, governed the country admirably. The Vice President of Afghanistan was visiting Delhi and the Indo-Afghan Friendship Society decided to give him a warm reception. Necessarily, I had to be in Delhi for this purpose and I had a few other engagements. So I visited Delhi and stayed in the Kerala House. Sri. N.T. Rama Rao, a unique leader of Andhra Pradesh with large political support, was my affectionate friend and great admirer. He came to the Kerala House and pressured me to be the Opposition candidate. He assured me that all the Opposition parties would unite to support my candidature. I reluctantly surrendered and I was taken to the Andhra Bhavan where all the Opposition parties except the BJP had gathered to welcome me as their choice. N.T.R. told me that the BJP had told him they would support me as an anti-Congress candidate. Anyway, there was tumultuous announcement at the meeting of my choice as the opposition candidate. Democracy should not fail in India by not being able to find a candidate to contest the high office. This was the sentiment thrust on me. I do not think anyone had the illusion that I would win. What is more important than the victory is the principle of freedom to differ. Dean Inge is right:

Democracy is only an experiment in government, and it has the obvious disadvantage of merely counting votes instead of weighing them. (Oxford Quotations P-270:7)

Next morning I filed my nomination with due attestation. Thus did I enter the fray to fight on democratic credentials mindless of the eventual result. I began my campaign, but with total fidelity to the fair norms of elections. I was a little unhappy because Mr. Venkataraman, the Congress candidate, was my good friend and never expected that I would run against him. Alas! The political compulsions based on principles of democracy when pitted against personal friendship and lesser considerations, the former prevailed. I sighed like a friend but obeyed like a statesman. I too put up a manifesto where nothing but the truth was projected. I agreed in writing, followed by speeches in many centers, that a President in a parliamentary system of the Westminster pattern ordinarily reigns, but the Cabinet in daily governance rules. In exceptional circumstances, the President has supreme power and they are among the rare cases. While I was on the Bench of the Supreme Court, I had myself expounded every dimension of the status and powers of the President of India, so my mind was clear. My campaign was principled, my integrity unchallenged and my friend Venkataraman maintained perfect silence, his election campaign being left entirely to the mighty field marshal Rajiv Gandhi.

Nikhil Chakravarti inaugurated my battle for the ballot at Thiruvananthapuram, the Kerala State Capital. I gained national support in goodwill, not in more votes. N.T. Rama Rao introduced me to the MLAs at a large meeting in Hyderabad and sought their support. I too addressed the gathering. Karunanidhi did the same thing in Chennai, Somnath Chatterjee brought the Left MLAs in Calcutta together and urged them in battle mood to back my candidature. In Bhubaneswar, the tall leader Biju Patnaik powerfully pleaded for me and Nandini Satpathy promised her votes. The Chief Minister of Bihar, Devilal of Haryana and Barnala of Punjab movingly projected me as the best democratic symbol and I was deeply touched by their great gesture. Humility overwhelmed me and the prospect of defeat never disturbed me. I stood for a cause and every cause claims a martyr. Round the country I gyrated in a whirlwind campaign and my morale was high as I crossed the nation and felt the warmth of welcome. I knew my fate but how inspiring to behold India and be one with Bharat's elected surrogates!

An anecdotal divagation is of general interest. In one of my speeches, during the campaign, I explained that the Rashtrapati was not a glorified cipher but had strategic powers. One such sword in his armoury was to ask the Prime Minister to disclose or demand even the most embarrassing or confidential information, however secret it be. If the Prime Minister is implicated in a grave scam such as the Bofors swindle the President can compel full disclosure to him of reports on the alleged fraud although final action belongs to the province of the Cabinet. This point had a topical flavour at that time. To make it spicy I said in a vein of alliterative humour, 'If a big Kumbakonam shakes the nation the President cannot remain a sleepy Kumbhakarna.' What I meant was that when a large national financial scandal is reportedly alleged against the Government the President cannot sleep over it smugly but must alertly ask for full information and advise his Prime Minister. Kumbakonam is a well-known town in Tamil Nadu. But Kumbakonam had come to mean big fraud, a libelous insinuation about the people of that town. When my statement appeared in the press I received protest letters from Kumbakonam denizens against the defamatory innuendo. I wrote back saying that the Oxford English dictionary carried that meaning. The more knowledgeable Kumbhakonam citizens corrected me at once that on a protest from the City of Kumbakonam the Oxford Dictionary had, in its later editions, deleted this calumnious meaning. I withdrew and apologised my Kumbakonam illustration was proved wrong; my law about the President's powers stands good (*vide* Shamsher Singh's case).

Back to the ballot contest

On 25th June, 1987 Krishna Iyer wrote a letter to all the MLAs and MPs, it read:

Dear friend,

> A fateful hour of history has brought me suddenly close to you through this letter which I take the liberty to write. Kindly have the charity to consider what I have stated here not as a personal plea but as a national appeal to your responsible role as a navigator of this dear motherland of ours.
>
> Long years ago we made a trust with destiny, Pandit Nehru intoned from the Parliament House as India awoke to Freedom, and chose to redeem its pledge to the vast masses of the people, now 800 million strong. What was that profound promise, that solemn resolve which our Founding Fathers and architects of Independence made as the surrogates of the countless victims of feudal and imperial injustices? Mahatma Gandhi, that frail marvel who symbolised in his humane person the collective will of Indians sought to wage a ceaseless, conscientious war for the Dalits and the Soshits, for the women under gender discrimination and other minority segments and majority have-nots? Why are we, one nation, one people under one flag lost in communal commotion, regional tension and cultural fratricide burying the great traditions of our many religious and glorious legacy of historic reformers?

Our progress on many fronts has been proud and promising. Our scientific and technological advances have the potential to be the locomotives of social transformation. Our Constitution, with its Preambular commitment and Parliamentary imperatives, is a manifesto of justice to every citizen and especially those in the lowliest brackets.

There is, nevertheless, a paralysis, an instability, a political dilemma and more dangerous than these, a constitutional crisis of menacing proportions which may throw out of gear our national direction and plunge the creative processes of State Power into constitutional chaos. Indeed, unless this will-lessness and wilderness, this constitutional imbroglio and consequent panic and deadlock are immediately arrested we, as a nation, may fail to overcome the crises that currently grip the political process.

Dr. Ambedkar, whose contribution to constitutional history and struggle for social liberation of large, suppressed sector of Indian humanity remains an angry interrogation to Bharat's engineers of State Power. Jawaharlal's humanism and socialist world view is a living force guiding us. We have had mighty spiritual giants operating for the truer principles of diversity and dignity of every human being and a harmonious, composite heritage of religious pluralism and commitment to the unity, integrity and strength of the country. Numberless martyrs, with their sacred blood and suffering, have sanctified the value-based sage of Brave New Bharat. But where are we today? How do we dare into the coming millenium with the grave challenges, internal and external which is in peril. The Constitution is on institutional trial. The pathological politics of President-Prime Minister estrangement at a critical phase of the nation's history can prove disastrous. If there is no time or temper in the highest functionaries like the President and the Prime Minister to consider many issues of communal holocaust, Punjab tragedy, military security, Sri Lanka policy, Pakistan's escalating arsenal, multi-national infiltration, feudal-medieval fundamentalist epilepsies and so on, the future of India that is Bharat may be fractured. The current situation of President versus Prime Minister paralyses decision-making processes and hijacks the attention of Government to questions of negativity leaving the major problems of urgency to drift and inevitable collapse. Therefore, the Presidential Office and the electoral contest for it have come too critical to be routine, too grave to be treated as a mere matter of party loyalty, too historic to turn upon the prestige or permanence of a particular leader, who lives if India dies? Such is the crucial issue that revolves round the resolution of the constitutional confrontation which is the central question in the current presidential election.

Indubitably, high offices should have a harmonious equation based upon constitutional parameters laid down by our founding fathers. The Westminster pattern has been adopted and adapted and the Supreme Court has affirmed the cabinet system and the conventions which accompany it as basic to our constitutional order. The President cannot arrogate to himself powers of Government but he is beyond question, the head of the nation, the symbol of its unity, the legal power in whose name the administration is run. He has the right to advise, to encourage and to warn his Ministers and, for this purpose, to claim the information that he needs from the Government. There is no iron curtain nor system or secrecy between the Prime Minister and the President. Likewise, the Cabinet headed by the Prime Minister has the plenary power to govern although the President may ask the Cabinet to reconsider, to take note of warnings, to shape its policies in the light of the wisdom he may impart. To transgress the limitations by either side is to create confusion and cloak the wheels of the political processess. I have explained this position while on the Bench as a Judge and later in articles in journals.

Today we need a President who will re-establish healthy relations with the Prime Minister by playing an independent role as advisor, as sentinel, as auditor and as engineer of certain powers exercisable in exceptional situations. He cannot sit with folded hands even without vital information, when the national scenario is showing serious shocks of corruption charges at the highest levels. Of course, he cannot rush into rash action but must use his good offices to see that confidence in the administration is sustained. May be, even parliamentary innovations in the committee system on a permanent basis may be considered. These are matters for future action, of course. He must, however, give respect to the plenary power of the Government under our parliamentary system, and never take over any part of the administration lest he should become a despot, that is. Nor is he helpless if the parliamentary system is subverted. We need a President who is neither a parrot nor a puppet nor even a mechanical ventriloquist but a person of higher authority and dignity commanding through his presence as Rashtrapati respect for the norms and imperatives of our Constitution and its destination as a Secular, Socialist, Democratic Republic. Pt. Jawaharlal Nehru asserted in the Constituent Assembly that the President must be a person of high stature, independent authority and dignity and not merely the reflection of the party which has the majority in Parliament. Indeed, that is the reason why a broad-based constituency involving the entire nation and including every state legislature has been devised.

You, as an elector have the weighty responsibility in the fulfilment of the Constitution and its processes, including the important duty of choosing its highest functionary, the Rashtrapati. Ultimately, our accountability is to the Nation and we are all its servants. On this categorical imperative, I offer myself as a servant of India, as the servant of the humblest millions and its lowliest denizens. If you feel convinced that I have any claim on your confidence and judgment, you may render your verdict accordingly. If you feel otherwise surely you must act according to your wisdom.

May be, I will try to meet you personally but collectively if time permits. Whether we meet or not, I commend the nation's destiny to your navigational duty and best judgment.

With kindest regards,

Sincerely,

V.R. Krishna Iyer"

(Justice V.R. Krishna Iyer—A Living Legend, P-255/257)

The poll day arrived. My opponent, the official candidate, taciturn to the last, won by a huge count while I lost horrendously although all my supporters duly cast their votes in my favour but the BJP maintained a mystic neutrality. L.K. Advani wrote to me what still is a riddle and an enigma:

You are a handmaiden of the Soviet Union and therefore we are not in a position to support you. But the leaders of the BJP, units of Kerala and Maharashtra who met Krishna Iyer assured him that they would write to the party high command to stand by the decision taken earlier and support Krishna Iyer. BJP advocates in the Supreme Court also wrote to the high command but the BJP did not change its stand.

Maneka Gandhi in her letter to Krishna Iyer wrote that there were a fewer number of MPs and MLAs in her party but all those in her party would vote for him. They also stood by this assurance and voted for the Opposition candidate.

(Justice V.R. Krishna Iyer—A Living Legend, P-258)

To lose at the hustings is not to lose heart in life. Was not Winston Churchill, after World War victory, defeated? He writes in The Gathering Storm that when the enemy had surrendered 'I was immediately dismissed by the British electorate from all further conduct of their affairs'.

I am no politician and never was life is an experiment and the Presidential election is an experience. Venkatraman has been my friend before and after. I spent very little money but did a lot of travel. I acquired rare friends and learnt the art of having no enemies.

The tranquillity of vanquishment has a spiritual value. I had no disappointment because, in this election, my rendezvous with destiny was defeat. What a heroic tryst with democratic might to dare and differ! The glamour of success brings material pleasure denied to one who at the polls has been the victim of macro-mathematical majority, but in the deeper measure of life Longfellow's lines strike the true note:

Not in the clamour of the crowded street,

Not in the shouts and plaudits of the throng,

But in ourselves, are triumph and defeat.

Postscript

The fury of canvassing, contesting, counting and collapsing was over but I had secured several votes by way of supports. I had to express gratitude to them and to the nation and so I wrote an open letter with which I conclude this Chapter:

The presidential polls are over, the process of swearing in of the new Rashtrapati brings the chapter of contest to a close. On this occasion, I owe love and thanks to all those who have voted for me, and even those who have abstained or marked against me. My profound gratitude goes to those legislators, though in a sore minority, who have reposed confidence in me, despite powerful adverse winds. I stood for a democratic proposition, I campaigned for the presidential right to information, I ran the country round to awaken the nation to the functional relevance, invigilatory importance and the authority and dignity of the head of the Republic in the very process of the Executive's ultimate accountability to the people of the country without in the least, disturbing the paramountcy of Parliament and the abundance of the Cabinet's governance. My numerical defeat notwithstanding, those who responded to my voice with their ballot, have placed me in a deep debt of gratitude. Even those who dismissed my candidacy have by their very taciturnity affirmed by thesis. Silence is implied assent where speech is occupational risk. Pressures and compulsions in tense situations may bend discretion to avert the displeasure of Power. To sacrifice secrecy, even though it be a constitutional guarantee, to avoid discovery and consequent sanctions is, perhaps, pardonable human frailty, I have no grievance whatever. On the contrary, the eloquence of silence on the part of those who opposed me is a significant victory for the validity of my presidential ideology. I have great personal regard for the leader of the abstentionists but feel sad when I read poet Dante who once said:

The hottest places in hell are reserved for those who, in a time of great moral crisis, maintain their neutrality.

While thanking those who voted for me and against me, I once again place before the people, our ultimate masters, the principle that the President matters and, within the parameters of the Cabinet system, has promises to keep. However camouflaged by demagoguery, never can the power process be left to one man, be he great or no, lest our system insidiously slip into freuhrerism. I conclude with a quote from John Stuart Mill:

A people may prefer a free government; but if from indolence, or carelessness, or cowardice, or want of public spirit, they are unequal to the exertions necessary for preserving it; if they can be deluded by the artifices used to cheat them out of it; if by momentary discouragement, or temporary panic or a fit of enthusiasm for an individual, they can be induced to lay their liberties at the feet of even a great man, or trust him with powers which enable him to subvert their institutions—in all these cases they are unfit for liberty.

Indians, I dare to hope, will prove worthy of the imperatives of Independence. My millions of thanks to my countless countrymen.

I wind up, as a little man from a long distance, with felicitations to Sri. Venkataraman as he fills his high office, but cannot help reminding him of what a great philosopher once said:

History has no other way of answering old questions than by putting new ones.

V.R. Krishna Iyer"

(Justice V.R. Krishna Iyer—A Living Legend, P-262/263)

A NATIONAL JUDICIAL COMMISSION— A COMMAND FOR REFORMS

I am all against scandalizing the judiciary, but am all for responsible, though vigorous, criticism of the judiciary. Judges are human and have human feelings, failings and firm convictions; and so, judicial sanctity should not silence or gag exposure of judicial weaknesses and misconduct which jeopardize public justice using, or rather misusing, the power of contempt. Experience and escalating instances show that in many higher courts of the country frequent resort to contempt proceedings is crowding the dockets with a jejune jurisprudence where the same person, sitting on the Bench, is prosecutor and judge. The independence of the judiciary is an inviolable value but as Lord Justice Salmon Committee (1969) wrote: 'the right to criticize judges .... may be one of the same cast which helps to ensure their high standard of performance'. David Pannick QC rightly states: 'criticism of the judges will not damage the rule of law. It may, by identifying defects in the legal system, promote the cause of justice. (Page 128-Judges). When the Executive misbehaves or the legislature acts beyond the warrant of the Constitution, the court, by Judicial Review, strikes down that excess or aberration, but when judges jettison good conduct or are guilty of corruption and delinquency people's right to justice becomes a casualty. Once appointed, a judge enjoys a measure of immunity so much so his misconduct, unworthy deviance and other vices and menaces on or off the Bench, remain irremediable except by impeachment which becomes a political process and often fails to produce the desired punitive objective.

The appointments of judges end in disappointment when the instrumentality for selection and the criteria for choice are unguided and operationally shrouded in secrecy. The path of justice is a public process and the public are deeply interested in the grounds on which and the organs by which judicial appointments are made. Since judgments of courts are binding on the country under the Constitution, the voice of the public in what affects them must not be excluded altogether. I do not plead for election of judges as is done in some states in the USA nor do I plead for plenary authority to be vested in the Prime Minister or President whose favouritism or political considerations may undo the confidence of the people in the institution of judicature. In the Indian Constitution the power of appointment of the higher judiciary textually resides in the top Executive after consultation with the Chief Justice of India and such other judges of the Supreme Court and High Courts as he deems fit. Articles 124 and 217 dealing with appointment of judges of the Supreme Court and High Courts vests the final word in the President, which means the Prime Minister on whose advice the President signs the order. In the U.S. the President has plenary power to nominate the candidate who is grilled by a Senate Judiciary Committee. In the U.K. the Lord Chancellor virtually chooses, although he is a member of the Cabinet. In India, until 1998, the Law Minister and the Prime Minister process appointments of judges. The Chief Justice of India, and in the case of High Courts, the Chief Justice of the State and the Governor, have a right to be consulted. Consultation does not mean concurrence and Dr. Ambedkar made it categorically plain in the constituent assembly that the power of appointment will not be surrendered to the Chief Justice of India whose opinion would carry weight, but would not be conclusive. However, a nine judges bench of the Supreme Court (In re-Presidential Reference) serendipitously laid down the apparatus of a collegium of judges. Virtually, the power of appointment was wrested from the Executive by the Judiciary, contrary to the plain words used in the Constitution.

The gravitational pull of power invents arguments to rationalize the appetite for taking over what belongs to the Executive. The *raison d'etre* for this benign usurpation is the independence of the Judiciary. Indubitably, the guarantee and glory of such independence is a basic feature of our Constitution. But what are the parameters of this great principle? An ambitious expansion of the philosophy of judicial independence to go beyond functional limits and extend to the very selection of candidates for judicial appointment is neither logical, lexical nor textual. Whoever is chosen as judge must enjoy just independence. But how can the Supreme Court's seniormost echelons corner the power, pre-natally as it were, exploiting the concern for judicial independence? Our Founding Fathers (of the Constitution) have specifically negated anything more than reverential consultation with the top judicial functionaries. Independence of judicial incumbents is universally accepted but there are varying practices from country to country as to the manner of picking up the right candidate for that purpose. The nine judges bench has made history by claiming to itself the power not contemplated in the Constitution. Indeed, judges have no mechanism nor know-how to select the best from the entire Bar of India or from the subordinate judiciary of the country. Nor indeed, is there any process under their control by which the character and antecedents, the social connections, political associations, wider scholarship and unalloyed integrity of the candidate can be ascertained. They know only the High Court or Supreme Court Bar; and even there, favouritism, communalism and other irrelevant factors may play a part. Clever candidates have myriad ways of using clout with judges as well as with politicians. The claims of many excellent lawyers may not be known to the Chief Justices of the States or of India. Similarly, for selection and elevation to the Supreme Court from among six hundred odd High Court judges the Chief Justice of India and his senior colleagues have no methodology to ascertain or be aware of their capabilities. Thus many a more suitable candidate may fail to be considered. Moreover, the prejudices and regional affiliations, ideological alienation and other grounds not pertinent to the high office may prevail. There is no democratic country in the world where the monopoly for appointment of judges belongs exclusively to seniormost judges. Moreover, the whole process is kept confidential and the inner disputes among the members of the collegium are unknown to the Bar or the public. I have known cases where the seniormost judges furiously disagree out of personal pique, communal consideration and other reasons which are not legitimate. Even so great a Lord Chancellor as Lord Halsbury was guilty of appointing men of little or no legal learning but were largely in the service of the conservative party or else were relations of his own. Prof. Griffith writes in his book The Politics of the Judiciary:

Of the thirty judges appointed by Halsbury to the High Court, eight were MPs at the date of their appointment and of these six were Conservatives. Five others had been unsuccessful Parliamentary candidates, three of them being Conservatives. Heuston concludes that of Halsbury's 30 appointments to the High Court, four or five were men of real distinction, eighteen or nineteen were men of competent professional attainments, leaving no more than seven 'whose appointments seem dubious'. Four of these seven were Conservative MPs at the date of their appointment, one had been a conservative MP, and another had twice been an unsuccessful Conservative candidate. (P-21)

The Indian 'Halsburys' sitting in the collegium also have their weaknesses which are hidden in unrevealed discussions. Secret deals regarding appointment of judges, if they did operate in England, there is no reason to think that the Indian counterparts are morally superior or immune from extraneous influences. It is unpleasant to investigate the performance of the collegium in India and the inordinate delay inflicted on the country in failing to fill in time vacancies in the High Courts and the Supreme Court. Rajindra Sachar recently wrote of course, the negative aspect of arrears and long delays and even 150 unfilled vacancies of High Court judges (due to non-recommendation by the judiciary collegium) have cast a shadow on the effectiveness of the present legal system' (Hindu dt. 9th Oct., 2003) while the patronage of the political bosses has largely vanished, the patronage of the 'robed' bosses has not improved the quality of the judges selected. In short, there is a case for a National Judicial Commission, beyond the judicial coterie. This does not mean that we must revert to the earlier system of leaving the power in the hands of the North Block.

Few in the country absolutely trust the competence and impartiality of the ruling classes with their notorious political deviances in the matter of judicial appointments. We must also go beyond the oligarchic elitism of judicial echelons and the dominant decisional finality of the political branch of government. U.S. Presidents have openly declared their political preferences and pet prejudices in their judicial nominations; and with glorious exceptions, the nominees have stood loyally to the Presidential expectations, the last being 5:4 majority ruling of the final court on the election of Bush. In India, the ominous message of supersession of the natural claimants to the office of Chief Justice, the refusal to confirm a few additional judges of High Courts and the motivated transfers of judges during the Emergency, demonstrate the danger of abuse by the Prime Minister. Even after the Emergency, Chief Justices have played with the power of transfer, causing chaos in the cosmos.

There is another dimension to the need for a Judicial Commission. For Francis Bacon 'the place of justice is an hallowed place; and therefore not only the bench but the foot-pace and precincts and surprise thereof right to be preserved without scandal and corruption'. But the Indian Bench—Bar scenario is murky, with stories of scams and scandals circulating with miasmic exaggeration and inventive imagination and venomous velocity of the whispering gallery of rumour with none to investigate or expose the truth of their lies. In public interest, the citizen's right to know must find expression through a high-power judicial commission which has exclusive constitutional authority to investigate *suo motu* or on receipt of complaints any corrupt act, delinquent behaviour or outrageous misconduct of a judge in public or private life which adversely affects or stains the status, stature or people's confidence in the performance of the brethren on the bench. There are, though rare, black sheep guilty of dark deeds, shameful violations, moral lapses, moronic blunders, physical failings and professional abuses who, unless punitively corrected or peremptorily cashiered, may scandalize the judicature and shake people's faith in a noble institution where good and great judges abound and suffer in their reputation, morale and integrity because of generalized aspersions based on the performance of a venal few. An ombudsman or Performance Commission will protect the vast number of fine judges but weed out the unworthy minority. There is a widely shared view that, unless arrested institutionally by ombudsman operation by an eminent body prestigiously composed and comporting with principled respect for the high office and independence of the peer fraternity, avoiding blackmail by irresponsible maligners and never allowing losing litigants to adventure into vengeful terrorisms, the court system may suffer decline and fall. Once the gravity of the Commission and the regulation of its procedure are solemn and scrupulously becoming of the high purpose, there is no need to fear that judicial independence will be jeopardized or intimidatory tactics will vitiate the instrumentality into an oppressive organ. David Pannick is instructive in this context:

In many parts of the world, individuals who are dissatisfied with judicial conduct have a right of access to a Judicial Ombudsman or a Judicial Performance Commission. The vast majority of American States have such mechanisms. The relevant bodies have the power to investigate whether the judge has acted in other than a judicial manner. In some jurisdictions they have the power to impose sanctions, including dismissal, on an errant judge. Many of these States give the accused judge the right of appeal to the State Supreme Court, which has the power to reconsider any finding made and any sanction imposed. In 1980, for example, the Supreme Court of Wisconsin upheld the decision of the State judicial conduct panel that Christ T. Seraphim, a Circuit Judge in the County of Milwaukee, had engaged in judicial misconduct. He was found guilty of, among other matters, unprivileged and nonconsensual physical contacts with offensive sexual overtones, the totality of which is gross personal misconduct and of 'a temperament unsuited for judicial office', as illustrated by 'his berating and disparagement of defence counsel and defendants, his use of bail as an instrument of retaliation, his disrespect for other trial and appellate courts, his refusal to listen to defence arguments......' The Supreme Court of Wisconsin suspended him from judicial office for three years without pay.

The commissions or tribunals in different States vary in the scope of their jurisdiction, the procedure they adopt, the powers they possess, and the efficiency and competence they display. But they share four important objectives: to deter injudicious conduct; to provide a means by which judges can be disciplined in appropriate cases; to vindicate by an independent report a judge who has been unfairly criticized; and, most important of all, to enable aggrieved litigants or others to air their complaints.

(P-96-97—Judges)

The Bill for A Constitutional Commission for Judicial Affairs—A Critique

The Bill for a Constitutional Commission for Appointments and Performance (for Appointment and Performance of Judges) Commission with Constitutional Authority is a felt necessity of the time. Jurists, lawyers, parliamentarians and the public generally have been discussing this issue in India for some years. Now a bill to constitute a National Judicial Commission is before Parliament. The composition of the Commission is somewhat traditional and marginally an improvement on the present protocol; with the Chief Justice of India as the Chairperson, two seniormost judges of the Supreme Court, the Union Minister of Law and Justice and 'one eminent citizen to be nominated by the President in consultation with the Prime Minister being the other members. Functionally, the Commission makes recommendations for appointment of judges of the Supreme Court, Chief Justices and Judges of High Courts. The Commission recommends transfers of justices of the High Courts. The Chief Justice of the High Court and the Chief Minister of the State shall be associated with the Commission in cases of appointments or transfer. Importantly, the Commission may draw up a code of ethics for judges of the Supreme Court and the High Courts. The Commission has been vested with the power 'to inquire, *suo motu*' or on a complaint or reference, into cases of misconduct or such deviant behaviour of a judge other than those calling for his removal and advise the Chief Justice of India or the Chief Justice of a High Court appropriately after such inquiry.' The Commission's procedure is left to itself, but what is the scope of appropriate recommendation in the event of misconduct and deviant behaviour is not specified, except to the extent that the removal of the judge is not within the purview of the Commission's function. The bill is a good beginning, but falls short of sensitive specifications; purposeful guidelines and popular expectations from such a Commission.

The Select Committee of Parliament before which it now pends, I hope, will make meaningful and democratic changes, break out of the oligarchic bias of the bill and fill the vacuum that now weakens the draft bill. An extensive consultation with the Bar Councils, Bar Associations, the higher judiciary on a wider basis, leading non-partisan and well-informed citizens, legal aid bodies and public interest, pro bono, elements will harvest constructive suggestions about the merits of candidates which will effectuate the objectives of the Commission. So strategic and democratic an institution as the Judicial Commission cannot be the product of an elite group unless countrywide sittings and nationwide collection of views are undertaken. I take the view, departing from the Victorian practice which hardly illuminates the mission of the legislation, that the Preamble must find eloquent expression in the Preamble like in our Constitution. The Objects and Reasons must also state the teleologic thrust of the bill so that it may be of semantic significance and carry a message while interpreting the provisions. That is the modern trend. The National Judicial Commission has a message to the nation and those concerned with the judicial administration. The overwhelming majority of our judges do a good job and have nothing to fear from the existence of a Commission. The case for such a Commission is that it would help to ensure the candidate for judgeship are chosen openly and wisely, that all judges truly hold office without deviant behaviour and are seen and recognized to do so since the institution is under the ombudsmanic oversight of a high-powered body which represents the executive and judicial wings as well as the people's selective surrogates. What we need is not a blank, non-speaking, formal, conventional print but an invigilating instrument vibrant, articulative, collective, accessible. The composition of the commission also calls for a closer examination. As at present constituted, the Chief Justice and his two senior-most colleagues have a dominant presence which is fair, although experience shows, left to themselves they differ among themselves, delay the process and rarely consult a wider constituency or consider others beyond their personal ken. Nor have they the facility to investigate deeper. Sometimes it is a bargain and other judges have no voice. Patronage, favouritism and other prejudices have, at times, procrastinated the process. Moreover, it is a superstition that the senior-most are the wisest. So there is a case for provision of consultation with the other judges of the Supreme Court and the judges of the relevant High Courts. Federal fairness may justify this consultative expansion. On the side of the executive; the minister for law and justice is ordinarily an insular entity who is not professionally aware of the state of the Bar in the country nor of the qualities of members from a socio-economic angle and other factors relevant for elevation to the Bench. The Home Minister may, perhaps, be too political, or guided by police reports, but a consultation with him may serve some purpose. The entire bar is altogether ignored in the present scheme of the bill. That vacuum weakens the selective wisdom of the Commission. Moreover, the 'eminent citizen' (now provided in the bill) who is the nominee of the President, is likely to belong to the party in power. Therefore, I suggest that there be more than one nominee, a representative of the Opposition in Parliament and also a senior non-party statesman who has opportunity to have a look at the subject through informal popular contacts. The bar is not uncommunicably untouchable but must be discreetly heard. I am not dogmatic about these suggestions, but do commend an element of democratization in the composition and operation of the Commission. Perhaps, a look at the Nepal Constitution which also provides for a 'judicial council' may be edifying. In Switzerland, the approach is different and all political parties have a voice. The members of the federal court there are elected by the federal assembly which shall ensure that the three official languages are represented. Perhaps, in India the Commission must include a woman of outstanding stature in public or judicial affairs, a scheduled caste/tribe representative, care being taken to ensure that there is broad representation from the north, south, east and west of the country. I do not mean to argue for reservation at all (which will ruin the process) but do feel that the country as a whole must feel itself duly, though vicariously, present in the overall composition and perspective of the Commission. Not an oligarchic club with a class bias but a democratic, instrument with a high vision so that, we, the people of India must not be alienated or are out of bounds *vis-a-vis* the Judicial Commission's functional ambit.

Apart from the composition of the Commission and the provision for a code of ethics everything else is a blank in the present bill. In a pluralist society like India with regional variations, religious minorities linguistic diversities, underprivileged classes and other divisions which the Constitution itself takes note of, the Commission cannot be given a blanket power to choose whomsoever it likes for High Court judgeship or elevation to the Supreme Court. Clear guidelines, indicating constitutional values while selecting candidates, are desirable. Similarly, when prospective appointees are under consideration of the Commission, it is but fair to inform the public, especially the bar, the judiciary and enlightened groups, including jurists and leading academics, to offer their views, if any. The decision will be of the Commission, but the sources of information must be as broad as possible or relevant. Judicial remedies, what with public interest issues and litigation gaining more space and time in court, justify freedom of information gathered confidentially from several sources, which will strengthen the democratic content of the choice. I am against propaganda publicity or lobbying, but there are decencies and proprieties for processing public opinion on potential appointees. This may alarm the orthodox as an unconventional proposal, but a Socialist, Secular, Democratic Republic is itself a radical idea whose time has come. Judges are no longer mere dispute-adjudicating agents. They have a constitutional agenda for transforming the social order and be a sentinel on the *qui vive.*

Rules and regulations and other discretionary procedures in these matters may well be left to be filled in appropriately but positive, dynamic signals must be given. Unfortunately, the bill leaves a void in these matters. That cannot be. Even in the U.S. great judges have told us what a judge should be. If India is to have more creative courts the vision of the Commission must cognise the wisdom of Frankfurter and Earl Warren:

A judge should be compounded of the faculties that are demanded of the historian and the philosopher and the prophet. The last demand upon him—to make some forecast of the consequences of his action—is perhaps the heaviest. To pierce the curtain of the future, to give shape and visage to mysteries still in the womb of time, is the gift of the imagination. It requires poetic sensibilities with which judges are rarely endowed and which their education does not normally develop. These judges must have something of the creative artist in them; they must have antennae registering feeling and judgment beyond logical, let alone quantitative, proof. (Felix Frankfurter: Address: N.Y. Times Magazine, November 28, 1954)

Our judges are not monks or scientists, but participants in the living stream of our national life, steering the law between the dangers of rigidity on the one hand and of formlessness on the other. Our system faces no theoretical dilemma but a single continuous problem; how to apply to ever-changing conditions the never-changing principles of freedom. (Earl Warren: Fortune, November, 1955)

The Judicial Commission, in the contemplation of the bill, is also a Performance Commission. How should enquiries be held? Who should receive and process the grievances and complaints? Should any publicity be given to the enquiry at all? Are the proceedings to be in camera? In all these matters, the bill should not be totally silent but must speak, briefly though. There must be some delineation of the ideology of the code of ethics which is now a judicially consensual convention but good so far as it goes but has no statutory force and is toothless. This may be scanned by parliament, refined and modified and included in a schedule. What is the scope of punishment, in the event of breach of ethics? Surely, the Commission must have authority to recommend appropriate punishment. But what are the various punitive alternatives open to the Commission? They must be codified. Otherwise, it will be impotent and its recommendations mere brutum fulmen. The statute must speak on this subject as well as the mode of hearing. Even in the case of removal of a delinquent for gross misbehaviour, the Commission must have the power to recommend to the Parliament, a motion for impeachment.

It is perfectly possible that a complaint may be against the Chief Justice himself. In that event, who is to hold the enquiry. The bill is blank on this point. There are other omissions too; about the venue of enquiry, the exclusion of the media from undue publicity once the Commission is in seisin of the matter. Are judges whose children flourish in practice in the same court, liable to be transferred, lest a racket should spoil the repute of the 'sunstroke' judges. How about judges who never pronounce judgments or take unpardonably long gestation for pronouncing judgments in cases heard years earlier. A little more homework should have been done before launching on so great an issue as the National Judicial Commission. These and other shortcomings must be remedied before the bill blossoms into Constitutional law. We need judges who are free from fear or favour, whose impartiality and excellence lend lustre to the institution and confidence in it to the people.

"As people grow ever less willing to accept unreservedly the demands of authority, the judiciary like other public institutions, will be subjected to a growing amount of critical analysis. The way in which 'Judge & Co' is seen is a matter of public interest and will increasingly become a matter of public debate." (David Pannick)

A sagaciously constituted reasonably accessible, circumspectly operational judicial commission with constitutional power to grave aberrants with robes on and make impregnable the integrity and authority of the vast majority of judges who are incorruptibly impartial, undeviantly dedicated to the delivery of justice tuned to the noble values of the Socialist, Secular, Democratic, Constitutional Order.

A VIBRANT VISION AND MILITANT MISSION

Empowerment, egalite and dignity of women are the desiderata of contemporary womanhood, long subject to undeservedly humiliating inferiority of status, discrimination in civil and political rights and subordination in developmental opportunities. Women are human and, as of right, a radical transformation in women's position is just, fair and necessary to put an end to the current invidiously arbitrary situation. To actualise this dynamic dimension of women's upgradation we need planned action which, in turn, must result in a project for change sufficiently comprehensive to meet the challenges in the civil, political, cultural, social and economic dimensions. That is why a vibrant vision which inspires a militant mission, is necessary. Civilised humanity considers the norms of equality and liberty as the basis of just society. The notion of equality has many nuances even as the vice of discrimination operates in many fields. The Universal Declaration of human rights adopted by the United Nations way back in 1948, claims that all human beings are born free and equal in dignity and rights. This egalitarian versatility postulates not merely equality of opportunity in social and economic affairs but realistic unfoldment of personality in all faculties. Only then is it possible to feel that womanhood has gained an environment wherein her worth can blossom as a full human being. The holistic development of man and woman is impossible without social justice which protects the weak and inhibits the strong and in a gender dimension makes the woman no less than the man.

Global jurisprudence, through various Conventions, Declarations, Resolutions and other instruments, has affirmed that the female of the species shall not be invidiously treated from foetal state to final exit, from the cradle to the grave. The world's largest conference where women's rights found full acceptance and special consideration for womanhood was treated as integral part of the equalisation process was the Beijing Declaration, ratified by India. It binds and obligates initiation of national laws to incorporate the Beijing decisions. What is equally important is that international legal instruments, ratified by nations, enable the courts to read into municipal laws, the larger jurisprudence evolved at the global level. Thus a variety of universal instruments which deal with the girl child, with status of women and with gender discrimination have become invisibly part of India's justice system. The Supreme Court of India and the High Courts have used these International Instruments in interpretation of Indian Laws and in applying those principles where there is vacant space in the India *corpus juris*. In short, we have a universal gender jurisprudence applicable to India and beneficial to Indian women consisting of international instruments, Indian statutes and case-law which judicially bind.

Indian constitutional jurisprudence has emphatically accepted equality of station and opportunity and prohibits discrimination on the basis of sex. Article 14 of the Constitution, proclaiming equality before the law, goes beyond that bare equality through judicial interpretation. Women as a class are different from men as a class in so far as they are entitled to special treatment as a class. Article 15, not merely frowns on discrimination against women but permits especially favourable treatment to women based upon the social realism that they are weaker in economic and social status. The special disabilities of women can be counteracted by special provisions in their favour. The truth is that the fair sex has had an unfair deal in law and life and therefore legal activism at the judicial and legislative levels need to abolish the shameful inequality, indelible stain and incurable wound which is the lot of Indian womanhood. In *Muthamma's* case (1979 SC 1868) the Supreme Court condemned a rule of victimisation of women in the Foreign Service Rules. The court said, "discrimination against woman in traumatic transparency is found in this rule". The court struck down the Rule as naked bias and violation of equality. In short, not merely is equality guaranteed but discrimination in favour of women has found favour with the Constitution and the court. Protective discrimination supportive of women is a permissive classification under the Constitution. Special laws can be made and have been made in favour of women and children. Women's physical structure and performance of maternal functions places her at a disadvantage in the struggle for subsistence and her physical wellbeing becomes a matter of public concern in order to preserve the strength and vigour of the race.

Disabilities and Discriminatory treatment Women undergo

Globally speaking, civil and political rights, social and economic rights, cultural and gender rights have been unfair to womanhood. Indeed, human rights are not fully enjoyed even now by our daughters, sisters and mothers. It is heartening that the United Nations, in its great instruments, has upheld gender dignity and egalite. It is equally gratifying that the Indian Constitution has, in various provisions, shown special compassion for the weaker sex. We must be proud that our constitutional jurisprudence unreservedly grants equal status and guarantees equal opportunities to both sexes. We live at a time when Kalpana Chawla has blazed the trail to demonstrate that a woman can excel even in space travel (although the second experiment ended tragically). There is none in India who does not agree with the proposition that woman, if given unbiased environment, can perform in every field with signal success what men may claim they can. We, therefore, proceed from the fundamental fact that socially and politically woman must have equal rights. The reality is a different story and so women have to fight on every front as sisters and daughters, as wives and mothers, as partners in public affairs, as heirs under succession law and economic equals in every field of human activity, not for condescension nor concession but social justice and equal recognition. This is integral to the gender vision of the nation sans which slavery in disguise may still be the feminine fate. The rule of law is not fair unless the rule of life so transforms women's status as to be equal with that of men and opens up equal opportunity for women in every walk of life. Suffrage is necessary but the ballot alone not win power for the subject gender. So it is that we have to go beyond the vote to actualisation of equality as a social reality. The glory of the equal gender becomes a fact of history only when, from an angle of pragmatism and jurisprudence, it can be demonstrated that the aspirations of womanhood, regardless of religion, region, caste and creed, are not inhibited, but are promoted, by the sex factor. The mensuration of gender justice is not in international instruments, constitutional provisions and political platitudes but in the dynamics of life itself.

Our statute book, in some measure, supports equal rights but truth to tell, invidious discrimination weakens women's potential. It is heartening however, that the higher judiciary has been gender-friendly, has upheld constitutional equality and has exposed the practice of inequality against women. Nevertheless, there is much in the law which is lawless if equality is the test. There is much in politics that reveals prejudice because her very presence in Parliament or public office is negligible although by numerical strength equal power must be shared by both sexes.

Woman and the Law

In constitutional theory there is equality but diehard discrimination harms the claim of women in matrimonial life and divorce rights, in guardianship law, in succession and inheritance laws. Special provision protective against discrimination is distances away. Even in executive matters there is bias against woman. Just one instance, *Muthamma's* case, out of many:

The writ by Miss Muthamma, a senior member of Indian Foreign Service, speaks a story which makes one wonder whether Articles 14 and 16 belong to myth or reality. It was a unique example of sex discrimination *ultra vires* Articles 14 and 16 of the Constitution of India. Rule 8(2) of the Indian Foreign Services Rules, 1961 provided that *"a woman member* of the Service shall obtain the permission of the Government in writing before her marriage is solemnized. At any time after marriage, a woman member of the service may be required to resign from service, if the Government is satisfied that her family and domestic commitments are likely to come in way of the due and efficient discharging of duties...." "Discrimination against woman, in traumatic transparency, is found in this rule.... In these days of nuclear families inter-continental marriages and unconventional behaviour one fails to understand the naked bias against the gender of the species". Both the rules were declared violative of the principle of equality and held discriminatory. (*C.B. Muthamma* v. *Union of India*, AIR 1979 SC 868)

The political presence of Indian woman-hood either as legislators or as ministers is grossly inadequate. Considerable noise was made promising at least 1/3rd of the membership of the House to women. But this tantalising proposition suffers procrastination with no hope of implementation. In many political parties and trade unions the situation is no different. If woman is to matter, a change in her representation in public life is a *sine qua non.* In the professions, women's competence notwithstanding, they have no proportionate standing. Few woman lawyers, why? Few women judges, why? Very few women professors, why? Scarce is the presence of abundantly available women,—*a la* Kiran Bedi, in the police force or other strategic walks of life. Surely there is invisible discrimination and the process of social justice *vis-a-vis* women is iniquitous. In sum, there is a fundamental distortion which demands correction. Occupational injustice coupled with the burden of motherhood, house wife functionalism and other inevitable chores, aggravates her iniquitous fate. There is therefore need for a campaign for gender justice in plural dimensions if equality of the sexes is not to be abracadabra.

In law, there is the room for grievance. Family law, whichever the religion, is tilted against the woman. In Hindu law, where discrimination was writ large, statutory reform has gone a long way in doing justice. There is still room for making law equal in favour of the Hindu woman even now. Christian women patently suffer from discrimination. Luckily, the Travancore Christian Succession Act and the Cochin Christian Succession Act have been struck down by the court. Still, in the matter of inheritance, the law is not fair because implementation of the Supreme Court ruling in *Mary Roy's* case is resisted. In Islam the situation is worse. Orthodox Islamic opinion protects clamping down pardha on woman and banishing her to the kitchen and bedroom. This is being perpetuated despite constitutional equality. Even regarding maintenance to divorced woman, *Shah Bano* case notwithstanding, there is legislative discrimination although the court has interpretatively ameliorated the lot of the forsaken partner. Talaq is trauma for the victim even like the 'four wives privilege'.

The girl child is the Cinderella of law and life. She is neglected and survives under adverse conditions. She suffers dowry terrorism and even Sati homicide. Law, in its majestic equality has not helped her at school or place of employment. Sex has become a sombre liability. We have to rewrite the law to defend Helen, Fazulin Bi and Sita to secure what is their due. Her heroic exploits thrill the world but women are looked down upon as less than equal. A comprehensive gender code which assures equal opportunity and equal protection as indefeasible norms of justice. This masculine world must change its ethos and eidos. The gender sector has to wage a battle for a fair deal. In this context, the courts come out with flying colours because judicial pronouncements have challengingly upheld women's claims through girlhood and womanhood. A few leading cases may be an apt illustration of the great vision the judges have projected. Case-law, in profound value-set, can be cited to support how the judges have, by their powerful pen, salvaged women from their parlous lot.

Way back in December 1969 a judge of the Kerala High Court (Krishna Iyer, J) rejected the argument that a Muslim woman was not entitled to claim maintenance on the distressing ground that her husband has discarded her and married a second wife. The plea that Islam provided for four wives for every Muslim male was exposed as fallacious and section 499 of the Criminal Procedure Code granting maintenance to a neglected wife was applied. Here is a part of the head note in that case:

> *Section 488 provides a summary remedy and is applicable to all persons belonging to all religions and has no relationship with the personal law of the parties. It is distressing for a Court to discriminate against Muslim women who have for ages been subjected to several social disabilities clamped down on them in the name of personal laws. The Indian Constitution directs that the State should endeavour to have a uniform civil code applicable to the entire Indian humanity and, indeed, when motivated by high public policy. Section 488 of the Criminal Procedure Code has made such a law, it would be improper for an Indian Court to exclude any section of the community born and bred upon Indian earth from the benefits of that law, importing religious privilege of a somewhat obscurantis order. It behoves the Courts in India to enforce section 488(3) in favour of Indian women, Hindu, Muslim or other. It follows that Muslim women should not be denied the advantage of para 2 of the proviso to section 488(3). There is*

hardly any doubt that neither the reliance on Art. 25 of the Constitution of India nor the refuge under the sanctions of the Koran can save a Muslim husband from meeting his statutory obligation under section 488. (K.L.T 1970 p-4)

In another Muslim matrimonial case the court (same Judge) upheld a woman's claim to divorce in a case of total breakdown of wedlock. It may be useful to excerpt from the head note the following proposition strengthening the women's case:

Modern legal systems are veering round to the view that while no party can be permitted to benefit by his own wrong conduct and obtain divorce, pleading a break-down of marriage, public interest demands that formal ending of marriages which remain marriages in name only is but right. When an intolerable situation has been reached, the partners living separate and apart for a substantial time, an inference may be drawn that the marriage has broken down in fact and so should be ended by law. This trend in the field of matrimonial law is manifesting itself in the Commonwealth countries these days. This principle is of Quoranic vintage.

Muhammedan Law—Divorce—When to be granted—Dissolution of Muslim Marriage Act (1939), section 2(ix)—Applicability.

The sanctity of marriage is preserved not merely by the morality that permeates it, but by the reality that holds the family together; one without the other spells a breakdown; and so the ground for divorce may well be made out if there is a total irreconcilability between the spouse. The Muslim law, independently of Act 8 of 1939, accepts this ground for dissolution of marriage. (KLT 1971 p. 664)

A string of cases abbreviated but bringing out the essential concern of the Court may now be given:

1. *State of Maharashtra* v. *Chander Prakash Kewalchand Jain,* (1990) (1) SCC 550 this case dealt with the rape of a newly married girl—the Supreme Court observed that the prosecutrix cannot be put on par with the accomplice. She being a victim of the crime, not only is she a competent witness, her evidence should carry the same weight as said, "ordinarily the evidence of the prosecutrix who does not lack understanding must be accepted. To insist on corroboration except in the rarest of rare cases is to equate a woman who is a victim of the lust of another with an accomplice to a crime and thereby insult womanhood."
2. *State of Maharashtra* v. *Madhukar Naain Mardikar*, JT 1990 [4] SCC 169, the Supreme Court held that even a woman of easy virtue is entitled to protect her person. Her evidence cannot be thrown koberboard on that count. The Court expressed its unhappiness over the manner in which the investigation by the police was casual and defective.

3. *Government of A.P.* v. *P.B. Vijayakumar,* 1995 (3) SCALE 163 – Reservation of posts for women has been upheld under Art. 15[3] though Art. 16 does not specifically provide for such reservation for women.
4. *Vishaka* v. *State of Rajasthan,* 1997 (6) SCC 241 relying upon CEDAW and the country's official commitment to it, in addition to the Constitutional mandate, the Supreme Court has laid down guidelines to be followed by employees to prevent sexual harassment of women employees. The guidelines are mandatory till they are replaced by legislation.
5. *Mangatmul* v. *Punni Devi,* 1995 (5) SCALE 199, the Supreme Court said "Maintenance as we see it necessarily must encompass a provision for residence. Maintenance is given so that the lady can live in the manner more or less to which she was accustomed. The concept of maintenance must, therefore, include provision for food and clothing and the like and take into account the basic need of a roof over the head. Provision for residence may be made either by giving a lump sum in money or property in lieu thereof".
6. *Saleem Basha* v. *Mumtaz Begum,* CRL R.C. No. 1000+999 of 1995- decided on 22-4-1998. Judge S.M. Siddickk of the Madras High Court said, "Quran discourages divorce—it permits only after pre-divorce conference attempting for reconciliation" and mediation by both parties. Reference was made to the case of *Fazlenb* v. *K. Khader,* AIR 1980 SC 1730, Justice Krishna Iyer speaking before the Supreme Court quoted CJ Behard Islam—an elaborate judgment replete with quotes from the Holy Quran has exposed the error of early English authors and judges who dealt with Talaq in Muslim law as good even if pronounced at whim or tantrum by the husband........in the absence of serious reasons, no man can justify a divorce either in the eye of religion or the law. If he abandons his wife or puts her away in simple caprice, he draws upon himself the divine anger, for the curse of God, said the Prophet, rests on him who repudiates his wife capriciously.

Actions that outraged the modesty of female employees constitute sexual harassment and it is importantly laid down by the judges that physical contact may be absent but still sexual harassment may take place. The court imported international instruments in imparting a liberal approach to the issue.

1999 (1) SCALE 57, AIR 1999 SC 625, [2000] 1 LRC 563, (1999) 2 CHRLD 455

The respondent was removed from his post as an employee of the appellant council after the relevant disciplinary authorities found him guilty of sexually harassing X, a junior employee. He filed a writ petition before the High Court challenging his dismissal. A single judge allowed the petition, finding that the respondent's dismissal was unjustified on the grounds that he had only tried to molest X and had not actually established any physical contact with her. The appellant was ordered to reinstate him. The Division Bench of the High Court upheld this decision and the appellant appealed to the Supreme Court. The appellant, *inter alia*, relied upon the fundamental rights to equality (Art. 14) and life and liberty (Art. 21), as well as India's international obligations under the Convention on the Elimination of All Forms of Discrimination against Women, the International Covenant on Economic, Social and Cultural Rights (ICESCR) and the Beijing Declaration.

In allowing the appeal, it was held that:

1. In the absence of procedural irregularity, the High Court was wrong to interfere with the findings of fact recorded by disciplinary authorities and with the punishment which they imposed. It is a well-settled principle that, in exercising the power of judicial review, the court is not concerned with the correctness of findings of fact which are reasonably supported by evidence, but with the decision-making process itself (*Union of India* v. *Parma Nanda,* (1989) 2 SCC 177 (Ind SC); *B.C. Chaturvedi* v. *Union of India,* (1995) 6 SCC 749 (Ind SC); and *Government of Tamil Nadu* v. *A. Rajapandian,* (1995) 1 SCC 216 (Ind SC) followed).

2. Sexual harassment is a form of sex discrimination projected through direct or implied unwelcome sexual advances, requests for sexual favours and other verbal or physical conduct by the female employee may affect her employment, unreasonably interfere with her performance at work and create an intimidating or hostile working environment for her (dicta of Verma, J. in *Vishaka* v. *State of Rajasthan,* (1997) 6 SCC 241, [1999] 2 CHRLD 202 (Ind SC) followed).

3. Each incident of sexual harassment in the workplace is incompatible with the dignity and honour of women and violates the fundamental rights to equality, life and liberty.

4. The respondent's behaviour did not cease to be outrageous for want of physical contact and the observations made by the High Court to the effect that the respondent did not actually molest X because he did not establish such contact with her are unacceptable. The courts should examine all the evidence to determine the genuineness of the complaint and should rely on the evidence of a credible victim.

5. The respondent's conduct offended against morality, decency and X's modesty. It constituted an act unbecoming of the good

conduct and behaviour expected from a superior employee and undoubtedly amounted to sexual harassment. It follows that the punishment imposed on the respondent was commensurate with the gravity of his objectionable behaviour and there was no justification for the High Court to interfere with it. Any reduction in punishment is bound to have a demoralising effect on women employees and is a retrograde step.

The courts are obliged to give due regard to international conventions and norms when construing domestic laws particularly when they are consistent and where there is a void in domestic law. Moreover, the Convention on the Elimination of All Forms of Discrimination against Women, ICESCR and the Beijing Declaration impose obligations on India to gender-sensitive its laws.

Expression

Women

Depictions of social evils allowed where they advanced film's serious message

Supreme Court 1 May 1996

A.H. Ahmadi, CJI, S.P. Bharucha, J, B.N. Kirpal, J, (1996) 4 SCC 1: AIR 1996 SC 1846: (1997) 3 LRC 1

The film *'Bandit Queen'* deals with the real life story of PD, a poor, lower caste rural girl who is brutalised by her husband, the upper caste community and the police and is transformed into a revengeful bandit. The film contains scenes including female frontal nudity, a bare male posterior, rape, violence and generally strong language. The Appellate Censorship Tribunal unanimously upheld the film's 'A' certification (*i.e.* for adult viewing only) without requiring the cuts which had been sought by the Censorship Board. When the fim opened for public viewing, the first respondent, a member of the upper caste community depicted in the film, filed a writ petition before the Delhi High Court seeking a ban of the film on the ground that it depicted members of his community as rapists and the portrayal of PD was 'a slur on the womanhood of India'. The writ petition was allowed by a single judge, who quashed the certificate granted to the film and suspended its screening until the Censorship Board carried out modifications and excisions in terms of his order. This decision was upheld by the Division Bench of the High Court. The appellants appealed to the Supreme Court.

In allowing the appeals and restoring the film's 'A' certificate, it was held that:

6. The censorship guidelines under section 5B of the Cinematograph Act, 1952, which echo the constitutional restrictions on the guarantee of freedom of expression (Art. 19(2)), are broad standards that cannot be read as one would read a statute. The film certification authorities are required to be responsive to the values and contemporary standards of society while ensuring that artistic expression and creative freedom are not unduly curbed. The film must be judged in its entirety from the point of view of its overall impact (*K.A. Abbas* v. *Union of India,* (1970) 2 SCC 780 (Ind SC); *Raj Kapoor* v. *State,* (1980) 1 SCC 43 (Ind SC), *Samaresh Bise* v. *Amal Mitra,* (1985) 4 SCC 289 (Ind SC) and *State of Bihar* v. *Shailabala Devi,* (1952) SCR 654 (Ind SC) considered).
7. No film that extols or encourages a social evil is permissible but a film that illustrates the consequences of a social evil necessarily must show that social evil. The scenes of nudity and rape and use of expletives in the film, permitted by the Tribunal, were in aid of the theme of the film showing the psychological and physical effect of rape and violence on a village child. They were intended not to arouse prurient or lascivious thoughts but revulsion against the perpetrators and pity for the victim.
8. The court should recognise the message of a serious film and the test that should be applied to the individual scenes is whether they advance the message. If they do they should be left alone, with only the caution of an 'A' certificate. Adult Indian citizens as a whole may be relied upon to comprehend intelligently the message and react to it, not to the possible titillation of some particular scene.
9. Whether the depiction of a social evil is necessary is best left to the sensibilities of the expert Tribunal which gauges public reactions to films. Except in cases of a stark breach of the guidelines, the Tribunal should be permitted to go about its task.
10. Nakedness does not always arouse the baser instinct. The guidelines permit scenes of sexual scene where PD is humiliated, stripped naked, paraded and made to draw from a well within a circle of a hundred men was intended by those who stripped her to demean her. The scene was central to the powerful human story and its effect could hardly have been better conveyed than by showing the scene explicitly. It helps to explain PD's rage and vendetta against the society that had heaped indignities upon her.
11. The rape scene also helps to explain why PD became what she did. Rape is crude and its crudity is what the rapist's bouncing bare posterior is meant to illustrate. Rape and sex are not being glorified in the film. On the contrary, it shows the terrible and terrifying effect rape can have on the victim.

12. Too much need not be made of a few swear words the like of which can be heard every day in every city, town and village street. No adult would be tempted to use them because they are used in this film.

Bodhisattwa Gautam v. *Subhra Chakraborty*

Family remedies women

Interim award made to rape victim pending acused's trial

Supreme Court 15 Dec 1995

Kuldip Singh, J. v. *Saghir Ahmad, J.*, (1996) 1 SCC 490: AIR 1996 SC 922: (1995) 2 CHRLD 159

The Respondent alleged that the appellant induced her to have sexual intercourse with him by giving her false assurances of marriage. She claimed that when she subsequently became pregnant the respondent agreed to marry her secretly, despite knowing that the marriage was not valid, but later insisted that she have an abortion. She became pregnant again a few months later and underwent another abortion allegedly at the appellant's insistence. The respondent claimed that, having spent several years cohabiting together, the appellant finally abandoned her. The appellant was charged with committing various criminal offences under the Indian Penal Code and filed a petition to quash the proceedings. The High Court dismissed the petition and the appellant sought special leave to appeal to the Supreme Court. In refusing leave to appeal, the Supreme Court considered whether any further order could be passed compelling the appellant to pay maintenance to the respondent pending the resolution of the criminal proceedings against him. The appellant submitted that he should not be burdened with the liability of paying maintenance to the respondent as he was unemployed. Under Art. 32 of the Constitution, the Supreme Court has the jurisdiction to enforce fundamental rights, including the right to life (Art. 21). In ordering the appellant to pay interim compensation to the respondent pending the resolution of the criminal proceedings against him, it was held that:

13. Fundamental rights can be enforced even against private bodies and individuals.

14. It is not necessary, for the exercise of the Supreme Court's jurisdiction under Art. 32, that the person who is the victim of the violation of his or her fundamental right should personally approach the court. The court can itself take cognizance of the matter and proceed *suo motu* or on a petition of any public-spirited individual.

15. Rape is a crime against basic human rights and is also violative of the victim's most cherished fundamental right, namely, the right to life.
16. *Delhi Domestic Working Women's Forum* v. *Union of India*, (1995) 1 SCC 14 (Ind SC) recognises a rape victim's right to compensation by providing that it shall be awarded by the court on conviction of the offender, subject to the finalisation of a Criminal Injuries Compensation scheme by the Central Government. On the basis of the principles set out in that case, the court's jurisdiction to award interim compensation shall be treated as part of their overall jurisdiction to try rape offences and this power should be included in the above scheme.
17. The Supreme Court has, in any event, the inherent jurisdiction to pass any order it considers fit and proper in the interests of justice or in order to do complete justice between the parties.
18. The court is *prima facie* satisfied as to the truth of the serious allegations made by the respondent and accordingly orders the appellant to pay to the respondent Rs. 1000 (approximately US $ 27, as at 15 December, 1995) every month as interim compensation pending the resolution of the criminal proceedings against him. The appellant shall also pay arrears of compensation at the same rate from the date on which the complaint was filed by the respondent to the present date.

Observation

The right to life means more than mere animal existence; it means the right to live with human dignity and includes, therefore, all those aspects which go to make a life meaningful, complete and worth living.

Valiant has been the role of the judiciary in the vindication of gender justice. But case-law, creative, imaginative and gender friendly, has its logic and limitation. Judges cannot make law but only interpret it and decide specific cases and controversies within defined bounds although in that process they do make law interstitually. But legislation is essentially a wider function covering vaster spaces and free to weave fabrics of fundamental mutation. So it is substantive codification, radical in transformation of the social order, that we need, an *avant-garde* operation parliament must perform. Magnificently as the judiciary has acted, they have not and could not usurp legislative functions. It follows that while paying a tribute to the progress achieved by the Bench we still need a *great gender code* to render unto womanhood empowerment, which is her due. Subjection over centuries must be manumitted, not only by judicial daring but by legislative liberation. Operation Empowerment is legislation in action and goes beyond the passive declaration of equality of the sexes. Grant power to the subjugated sector, make her independence a source of strength, install her in seats where power resides and generate in her, a suppressed half of humanity, that confidence, courage and capacity which will sustain her worth and dignity so as to enhance the human resources of our generation to the common advantage of the world community. No society is free until the last girl child and the last damsel in distress is free. That is the dynamics and dialectics of our age, rewriting vintage subordination, restoring to our vast sister sector the victory of empowerment which belongs to her by human rights culture. Brave new Bharat belongs equally to sister and brother in power, property and pursuit of happiness. That is the militant vision social justice and cosmic jurisprudence project. Coda: We are active partners and march together. We have a world to conquer.

NUMEROLOGICAL NOSTRUM FOR PATHOLOGICAL PROCRASTINATION OF THE JUDICATURE

What has happened to the Indian Judicature? Great judges, classic pronouncements and memorable performance as the sentinel on the *qui vive* of people's rights have made the court system the final sanctuary of the humblest victims of injustice and ultimate authority to interpret the Constitution, the source of all State Power. And yet, this historic, humanist and high powered display of judicial statesmanship notwithstanding, justices, justicing and judgocracy have come in for sharp criticism as untouchable and unapproachable for the commonalty, anfractuous and expensively interminable procedurally and unpredictably expansionist jurisdictionally. Early litigative finality is an utter unreality since appeals, remands, visions and reviews offer tantalizing opportunities for dilatory holidaying at each judicial deck for the dawdling docket. Paper-logging with wasteful, though avoidable, prolixity is a chronic forensic pathology. Precipitous, procrastinatory and procrustean justicing processes often mar people's confidence in courts. Frequent reversals of decisions in the judicatural hierarchy promotes uncertainty and gambling proclivity. Judicial mediocrity, elitist affront and class bias shake the faith in judges even as indignant or indolent hearing, hustling or somnolent sitting spoil forensic fairness. A judge who does not know the law or the art of controlling counsel in pointless or offensive examination of witnesses or argumentation without a sense of time or relevance is a liability on the bench. Overbearing ignorance, loquacious pretensions, myriad mannerisms and open differences with brother judges on the bench blemish the decorum, dignity and credibility of the court. One thing more. If judges are to fill their office with functional success they must possess, beyond legal scholarship and reasonable measure of standing at the bar, the qualities elegantly expressed by Justice Frankfurter:

A judge should be compounded of the faculties that are demanded of the historian and the philosopher and the prophet. The last demand upon him—to make some forecast of the consequences of his action—is perhaps the heaviest. To pierce the curtain of the future, to give shape and visage to mysteries still in the womb of time, is the gift of the imagination. It requires poetic sensibilities with which judges are rarely endowed and which their education does not normally develop. These judges must have something of the creative artist in them; they must have antennae registering feeling and judgment beyond logical, let alone quantitative, proof. (Felix Frankfurter: Address: N.Y. Times Magazine, November 28, 1954)

The powerful point that I seek to stress, with marginal exaggeration, is that the protagonist of the judicial process is the presiding judge. Secondly, the functional success of access to justice is governed by the modern technology competently made operational daily in court, abandoning colonial medievalism still in vogue in the new millennium. The judge matters in many dimensions, particularly in the promptness and clarity of the judgments to be delivered. The delinquency in non-delivery of the judgments by many judges even by months and years, even in interlocutory matters, is like 'malignancy' afflicting the legal system deserving punitive correction. Not numerical ballooning, with judges dragging on without disposal of dockets, but transparently accountable justicing is what we need now. I agree with the prescription of aloofness of judges from political controversies, communal issues and other bitterly polemical problems which may embarrass the court if it presents itself as a litigation:

In 1954 Sir Winston Churchill told the House of Commons that judges are required to conform to standards of 'life and conduct for more severe and restricted than that of ordinary people', 'What', the Prime Minister asked rhetorically, 'would be thought of a Lord Chief Justice if he won the Derby?' (Page 11 – Judges)

Membership of secret organizations with ultimate loyalty to its members *e.g.* Freemasonry, may be an impediment to absolute impartiality in doing justice under the Constitution, without fear or favour, affection or ill-will. No one should be considered for judgeship if his past conduct, social milieu and party commitment run gravely counter to the values of the Constitution. Judges must remember that they must be loyal to the values of secularism, socialism, democracy and fundamental rights because they dispense justice under the Constitution, not over it. What we find these days is that some 'robed brethren,' with notable exceptions, violate the code of ethics, voluntarily adopted for judicial behaviour at a Chief Justice's conference. Everything that I have said above brings into focus the fundamental importance of choosing the right personnel. Not numbers, but quality of candidates is the mensuration which must weigh with those who select judges. Judges are what they wear and therefore, the robes symbolize high standards of public and private life, impartiality, integrity and intelligence. I hear from many sources that what was once rare has become unfortunately frequent *viz.* fall short of their dharma.

The pertinence of my observations must be appreciated in the context of the Central Law Minister's announcement that to save the country from the flood of litigative arrears, he proposes to increase in a big way the number of judges in the High Courts of the country. He is substantially right about the alarming quantum of arrears. But he forgets the intricacies and interlocutories and other insufferable delays of disposals and the unpardonable default in not delivering judgments long after arguments have been closed, a disease from which even the Supreme Court is not entirely free.

If we mean serious business in annihilating Himalayan arrears we have to consider the major factors contributing to the creation of arrears in court. So long as the civil procedure and criminal procedure codes are not streamlined, simplified and surgically reduced in the hierarchical tiers, no magic can produce a short-eat to disposal of such cases. Except for tinkering with the codes no real radicalization has been undertaken until now. A writ petition under Article 226 or 32 does not have the cumbersome and clogging processes which the codes weave into the hearing system as a consequence of which we are stuck with the confusing skein of miscellaneous trivia which block effective hearing. What is more, there is a provision in the Civil Procedure Code for examining the parties on their first appearance in court before they are tutored to take up specious pleas and hide the truth. But rarely is the provision used by the judges in the trial courts. If this were done most false pleas could be avoided at the first flush and the dispute can be narrowed down resulting in a just settlement. Indeed, the Gajendragadkar Law Commission, recommended that this provision be made mandatory, but although decades have passed, this measure has not been accepted. Secondly, modern technology is alien to the medieval methodology prevailing in court. Even a retail shop has more technological advance than a court. A simple computer or small Xerox machine in every court or tribunal can reduce delay considerably, if these gadgets are effectively used, not kept as idle adornments. Today making a decree in terms of the judgment is a delaying process while the suggestion of the Gajendragadkar Commission that the last paragraph in a judgment may be drawn up by the judge in decreetal terms so that a separate proceeding for drawing up of a decree can be eliminated. I remember, in Rajasthan, a Chief Justice introduced a system of commissioners attached to trial courts as a permanent arrangement. They would examine witnesses and where commissions have to be taken out for local inspection or otherwise, they will straight away carry out the court's orders. This would eliminate delays in the court and maximize judicial time for hearing cases. None of these simple changes have been thought through by official reformers and we are still in the archaic world. Moreover, half the time of the court is consumed by what is called 'roll-call' and verification of service of summons etc., which could as well be done by a legally trained officer of the court. The judge, in that event, can begin his day with hearing of the cases before him and function as a fast track court. How bizarre that obvious reforms are ignored and the pathology of huge arrears is put forward for creating new judicial jobs and necessarily of other staff. Litigation explosion has been a long ago companion of the court system. To relieve the court the Constitution was amended for creating Tribunals. In exercise of this Constitutional power, Central Administrative Tribunals were set up. But thanks to the habit of the judges, arrears in the High Courts continued and arrears in the tribunals were created. We have family courts, tribunals for consumer justice with a hierarchical structure, dispute settlement adalats which have been given legal sanction. However, the established courts are too remote, too legislistic, too expensive and too supine and slow. Tribunalisation has not been anything more than placebo gesture, not a panacean solution. In the words of Lord Justice Megary 'if our business methods were as antiquarian as our legal procedures, we would have been a bankrupt nation long back'. This applies to India as well, because the system is static and stratified, 'its ugly features are that it is highly technical, extremely formal, totally dilatory, atrociously expensive and highly professionalised' (Justice D.A. Desai). Law Day speeches by Chief Justices have revealed the poignant fact that the judicial system is under severe stress. The strength of the judges in the Supreme Court has been augmented, but with little marked improvement in the matter of reducing the backlog of cases, according to a former Chief Justice. In every High Court more judgeships have been created, in every state more tribunals have been set up, but alas, the chronic disease of terrible delays has defied the numerical nostrum. Interim stays and injunctions, and then forget about the case for years, is a 'stay' syndrome in vogue. Public interest litigation has pollutively been exploited and judicial jurisdiction quantum-jumped and publicity-prone brethren on the bench avidly hear long-winded submissions. Courts, without self-restraint, flood the cause-list with contempt petitions with intimidatory hauteur, making the court process an imperium in imperio. Tribunals were created for early finality but High Courts have claimed a supervisory power under Article 227 thus another incarnation for the litigation. In brief, more work is spun into the system, defeating the very object of tribunalism (presided over by the equivalent of High Court judges). The die-hard phenomenon of judicial dereliction demands Performance Commission. Anniversaries of cases pass without botheration, the sluggish system having suffered induration. Imagaine serious criminal matters pending for a decade or more, while the highest court rhetorises about speedy disposal as a fundamental of fair trial. It is fallacious to put all the salvationary eggs in the judgeship basket. More Lordships without substantial procedural reforms and more incompetent elevations leading to dilutive devaluation of the Bench and poor disposal are pathological prospects. (Parkinson's Law and Peter Principle). Parkinson's Law states that work expands to fill the time available for its completion and subordinates multiply regardless of the amount of work produced. Applied to the judiciary, a single judge hears long arguments, then refers a matter to a Division Bench, a Division Bench discovers the need for a Full Bench to decide the issue, thus expanding judicial work for six judges which could have been disposed of by one. More lawyers get employment and Their Lordships will hear cases leisurely, pronouncing judgments after unfair procrastination, keeping litigants in suspense and then the journey to the apex court begins. The Supreme Court practices the same game in different forms and yet all the judges are busy, overworked and create a good case for more numbers. Jawaharlal Nehru, inaugurating an all-India Law Ministers' Conference dismissed the demand for more judges citing Parkinson's Law way back in 1958 (I was Kerala Law Minister then). The story is complete only when we realize the application of Peter Principle. Parkinson's Law generates otiose work for more functionaries to keep themselves idly occupied. Peter Principle promotes arrears and injustice by incompetence of incumbents, a factor highlighted by Lawrence Peter. Peter widely publicized as Peter Principle:

Peter Principle is the theory that in a hierarchy people rise to the level at which they are incompetent.

Chambers 21st Century Dictionary Lawrence Johnsten Peter

Another version in the American Heritage Dictionary

The theory that employees within an organization will advance to their highest level of competence and then be promoted to and remain at a level at which they are incompetent.

(Lawrence Johnson Peter)

The judicature is a pyramidal structure with various decks from bottom to the top. A law person with experience in the trial court may be good as a trial judge, and when he is promoted as a district and sessions judge, he may manageably be competent. His jurisdiction will not familiarize him with the constitution and the myriad uses of Article 226 or other laws rarely figuring in the subordinate courts but frequently coming for consideration in the High Court. But if a District Judge, for reasons of seniority or successful disposal, is elevated to the High Court he may be incompetent in that office, not because he is a mediocre hand but because the jurisdiction and jurisprudence is somewhat new, the type of hearing is different and judgments have a different texture. There he is incompetent (not a personal reflection, but an occupational inadequacy). Unfortunately some Supreme Court decision which I consider decided wrongly, has directed that around 40% of the High Court judges should come by promotion. The result is that Peter Principle applies, more time is taken for grasping the constitutional issues, raised in the case, and incompetence is writ large in the end product. When an advocate is directly appointed as a judge in the High Court appreciating his competence at that level, he may be satisfactory on the bench. But an elevation to the Supreme Court summons a wider constitutional vision, familiarity with law in a new dimension and pronouncements which become final under Article 141 or Article 32 may expose the incompetence of the midget judge in the Supreme Court, although, he was a senior judge in the High Court. Sometimes we find some benches of the High Court and even the Supreme Court function as a kind of glorified District Court. There are other instances possible to prove Peter Principle, especially because the philosophy of the Constitution and the protean applications to fundamental dimensions of jurisprudence may be beyond the reach of the judge elevated from the High Court. Indeed, there are unique features in the remedial jurisprudence of the High Court which may be serendipitous for appointees from subordinate courts. The creative genius required at the highest level may not be his cup of tea. The appointee may be a good man, and trial judge but not necessarily of the Supreme Court grade. True, some district judges do perform with excellence at every level, but a good proportion may drag their feet to make the noble institution a wee-bee moronic. The Supreme Court is often called upon to face many of the dominant social, political, economic and even philosophical issues that confront the nation. Archibald Cox writing on the nature of Supreme Court litigation observed:

One who argues cases from time to time and sits in the Supreme Court day by day during both oral arguments and the delivery of opinions soon acquired both admiration and affection for the Court and all the justices. The problems with which they deal are so difficult, the number and variety of cases are so overwhelming, the implication are so far-reaching that one sits humbled by the demands upon them. That the judges are human—that some opinions seem inadequate and some decisions may be wrong—makes the experience more moving because the whole attests to the sincerity and capacities of man. (Quote It, Vol. I, P. 162)

The Court finds its finest hour not when, to fill the quota and rotary second-rates spiral up in numbers to reach the bloated Bench, but when distinguished subordinate judges, luminous leaders at the Bar or celebrated members of the High Courts lend dynamic luster to the rule of law governing the nation.

Not that I debunk the anodyne of judicial addictions when there is a glut of dockets in special situations but the superstitious addiction to the numerological nostrum as a pharmacopical curative is an illusion as the numbers experiment has proved in the past. A crowd of robed brethren is chaos in the cosmos while a brilliant batch with a sharp grip on backlog makes all the difference.

Another contributory to judicial delays and mounting arrears is the innocence of Chief Justices in court management which is an art and product of training. Not all judges are versatile geniuses in all branches of law. The chief must assess the worth and aptitude of brother judges when constituting the benches. An ill-tuned, neophyte in judicial administration may be a disaster as chief.

I mean no disrespect to any judge but do feel that each person has limitations which must be taken into consideration, so that the institution may not have large patches of incompetence. I have been at pains to prove my case that multiplication of judge-strength will not give the country the quality of justice which is the promise of the Constitution. A numerical nostrum without more is infantile therapeutic for tiding over the pathological crises that the Indian judicature currently faces. A last word: the unhappy rulings in A.K. Gopalan, Emergency and POTA notwithstanding, the nation pays a tribute to the Supreme Court collectively for functioning, by and large, as an impregnable, fortress of Indian humanity's right to justice.

PARLIAMENTARY PRIVILEGES, PEOPLE'S FREEDOMS AND JUDICIAL INVIGILATION

The political sovereign, expressed in constitutional diction, is 'We, the People of India'. The Constitution itself, legally speaking, is the creation of the political sovereign. The three great instrumentalities *viz.* the legislature, the executive and the judiciary, are created by and derive power under the Constitution. The ultimate value and operational purpose of the constitution and the instruments thereunder is to guarantee to all the citizens those fundamental freedoms set out in the Grand Preamble and spelt out in Part III thereof. The vision of the framers of the Constitution foresaw the need for harmonious hermeneutics in the event of friction, conflict of jurisdiction and occasion for a just resolution of clashes among the trinity and in situations of imbroglio. Indeed, confrontations between the legislature and the judiciary have risen and reconciliation, avoiding a brakedown, has been achieved in some measures in the light of the genius of the Founding Deed. Nevertheless, infrequently though, conflict and confusion have created tension paralyzing the paramount processes of power. Having crossed the semi-centennial of the Constitution it is time that the jurisprudence of parliamentary privileges and the parameters and perimeter of judicial invigilatory jurisdiction are settled by national consensus and if need be, by creative amendments. One fundamental fact should be remembered that the legislature, supreme with its limits, and the judiciary, supreme in the space carved out for it, have only under the Constitution and never over it.

Certain quintessential imperatives must enlighten our judgment on any question of constitutional law. The first consideration is that which we interpret our Constitution, not an anglophilic, bias but a posely Indian perspective must govern our construction which affects the life and liberty of every member of our Republic. Any ruling must therefore be rooted in Indian vintage semantics, not in British jural-regal sanguinary vicissitudes. Again, it is good to warn ourselves that the Commons fought for privileges against Royalties and the Lords to gain the status of the High Court of Parliament with power to punish. This judicial pretension cannot hold good in India where the constitution has exclusively vested, in entirety with a sense of finality, in the judicature under the supreme control of the Supreme Court of India. Article 141 categorically proclaims "the law declared by the Supreme Court shall be binding on all courts within the territory of India." Article 142 empowers the Supreme Court, in the exercise of its jurisdiction, the power to issue commands necessary for doing complete justice in any cause or matter pending before it, and any such direction can be enforceable throughout the territory of India. Article 144 obligates that without any exception 'all authorities', civil and judicial, in the territory of India shall act in aid of the Supreme Court. If language has any meaning, the legislature is a civil authority operating within the territory of India and must support the Supreme Court directives. The parliamentary institutions in the country are no oasis beyond the bounds of India and must therefore be subject to the constitutional limitations impressed by Articles 141, 142 and 144. This broad perspective, pregnant with value-laden authority, must inform our approach when the question for consideration is a conflict of jurisdiction between.

Yet another dimension of our constitutional order falls for notice. Article 32 invests "the right to move the Supreme Court for the enforcement of fundamental rights and this itself a fundamental right guaranteed in absolute terms. The Court cannot abdicate this jurisdictional obligation without being guilty of contra-constitutional jettison. The Court shall not make the constitution a casualty. It is a paramount principle, emphatically laid down by the Supreme Court, that the basic structure and features of the constitution cannot be amended at all and is non-negotiably enduring. The rule of law and the independence of the judiciary, secularism and democracy are basic features of the constitution. No parliament, even if unanimous, no party in power even if it commands national consensus, can alter these basic features or structure. So viewed, the rule of law prevails *vis-a-vis* the House and even the court. What is arbitrary is violative of the rule of law, as the Supreme Court has laid down. What is plainly not just, fair and reasonable is arbitrary and void. If a preposterous privilege is alleged to have been violated and an opportunity in terms of natural justice is not given to the alleged violator of being heard by an impartial body, the end product *viz.* the order of the legislature will be *ultra vires.* If the alleged privilege is unknown and unknowable, is archaic and arcane and involves intricate and alien research for discovery, the citizen cannot regard it as law, since law, as has been held by the Supreme Court, must have the quality of being available and of access to know. The secret decision in the chamber of a prince which ordinary people cannot reach has been held to be not law. Similarly, if the legislature claims some hoary immunity buried in British medieval history beyond Indian Ken, such ancient vintage assertion cannot be regarded as part of the *corpus juries* of Bharat. Our Founding Fathers could not be deemed to have contemplated as within the ambit of Articles 105 and 194 such enigmatic material as enjoying the status of constitutional law. Therefore, we have to exclude from the scope of privilege of the House such recondite restraints on the people of India. A vague and vagarious power to imprison a victim for contempt, without so much as notice with specific charges, is non-est as a rule of law. Everyone is deemed to know the law and law therefore cannot be "a riddle wrapped in a mystery inside an enigma". There cannot be an iron curtain between the people and privilege jurisprudence. The sequitur: A code clearly presenting the powers, privileges and immunities of our legislatures and legislators tuned to the cultural heritage and human rights vintage of our Democratic Republic, upholding the dignity of the individual and the majesty and authority of the House.

All right thinking people will liberate themselves from the obdurate obscurantism of obsolescent and misty majesty of the "omnipotent" comments. A code is overdue if people's rights to life in similitude and every speech are to have valued in the new millennium.

During our Constituent Assembly Debates, almost all members wanted to know what are the privileges of the House of Commons. Sir Edward Coke had said long ago that many look, but few find, the law of Parliament. When Mr. Naziruddin Ahmed remarked that he would have to be accompanied by an English attorney or counsel to know a member's privilege, little did he know-and nobody told him-that even English courts were supposed to be ignorant about anything bearing the name 'privilege of Parliament'. This ignorance was supposedly dictated by the *lex parliamenti* itself and was meant to be perpetual! Having said this much, the rest is governed by the great judgment in Special Reference No. I of 1964 under Article 143 which is a *locus classicus*. The lucubrious learning and explorative exhaustiveness of the judgment of Gajendragadkar CJ, the creative and clear declaration of law in an ambiguous and dilemmatic domain of law remain the radiant light to guide lawyers and legislatures alike. In England, the common law has unlimited power, uncommon in written constitutions. We must be wary of borrowing from such a *nidus* with a history incompatible with our story of swaraj. We must not forget the words of Coolidge J, in *Stockdale* v. *Hansard* that "it is in the very nature of irresponsible power, particularly in the hands of a large body, to run into excess. I illustratively read the statements of the House of Commons in 1593: "this court for its dignity and highness hath privilege, as all other courts have, and as it is above all courts, so it hath privilege above all courts, and as it also hath jurisdiction too, so hath also coercion compulsion, otherwise the jurisdiction is nothing in court, if it hath no coercion." An angry Commons may for gross contempt sentence a victim to go to the gallows, an outrage if we transplant such punitive atrocity to the Indian Parliament oblivious to and obnoxious of the fact that (a) we have a Bill of Rights in Part III, (b) that our Parliament is not and can never be a court, (e) that we have a judiciary as a separate and co-ordinate branch of the state, (d) that whatever the historical reasons in Great Britain for the House of Commons to have acted in the past as it did, the punishments meted out did impinge on the liberty of the subject and no court could save him.

Another imbroglio which mires the privilege issue is that under Articles 105 and 194, it must be shown that power claimed by the Commons had subsistence at the commencement of our Constitution, an impossible proposition. The fundamental condition which we must never forget is that the Indian provision articulating privileges opens with the words 'subject to the other provisions of the Constitution'. Inevitably, the tall and unbounded claim that the Indian legislature is the highest court above the Supreme Court must collapse. Outside the four walls of the Assembly, Articles 105 and 194 do not empower infliction of punishment for contempt beyond inscrutability by the judicial instrumentality under Articles 32 and 226. Gajendragadkar, CJ, rightly holds that it is not competent for the Legislative Assembly to direct the production of the said two judges and the advocate before it in custody or to call for their explanation for its contempt and that it was competent for the Full Bench of the High Court to entertain and deal with the petitions of the said two judges and the advocate and to pass interim orders restraining the Speaker of the Legislative Assembly and others from implementing the aforesaid directions of the said Legislative Assembly. Any action by any citizen outside the House is amenable to judicial jurisdiction and it would be egregious to reject this power on the bizarre ground of limitless power of the House. But within the House, the freedom of speech and other 'proceedings' are within the exclusive power of the House and the speaker and beyond the pale of the judicature.

Article 19(i)(a) must be read in harmony with Article 194 and so interpreted, 'proceedings' inside the House, including free speech, are beyond the bounds of the court. In this context Article 21 which specifically deals with the right to life and liberty claims our focus and locus. It is reasonable to hold that when life and liberty are put in jeopardy by the House on the ground of breach of privilege, the Court's verdict about the privilege is final. Whenever there is a dispute on any question of law, Article 141 clothes the Supreme Court with the final power of declaration. This provision binds the legislature when we read the relevant provisions harmoniously. The law has been repeatedly declared by the Apex Court that any procedure for deprivation of life or liberty of a person shall be just, fair and reasonable and if that condition is contravened the deprivation is unconstitutional. The Supreme Court and even the High Courts, have jurisdiction to examine this question. Here we cannot accept the British practice because the source and growth of the privileges claimed are radically alien. Luckily, it is now well-understood that neither House by itself can create a new privilege. There is something significant, in one case (King's Bench), which should not be overlooked. There were two offences (i) '**words** spoken' and (ii) the **assault** on the Speaker. The House of Lords, while holding that words uttered in Parliament were for Parliament **alone** to deal with, did not rule out the assault part as proper to be dealt with by the court. Presently, we find in India and elsewhere, members exceed, in excitement, offensive oral processes into unbecoming mayhem and obscene versions of injury to person. Operations with **fists** and **lips** differ. This branch of jurisprudence which defines where 'free speech' ends and violence begins is of importance when the Penal Code and the policeman seek their functional relevance and scope. If we are to preserve the dignity and utility of parliamentary debate for its appropriate purposes we must show concern for these values and their slow farewell. The opinion of a Canadian judge is instructive in this context:

I desire it to be understood, however, that I do not hold that a Member of Parliament is not amenable to the ordinary courts for anything he may say or do in Parliament. I merely say he is not so amenable for anything he may say or do within the scope of his duties in the course of parliamentary business, for in such matters he is privileged and protected by *lex et consuetude parliamenti'* (O'Connor J, in *R.* v. *Bunting*)

Can a Member commit homicide inside a House and get away with it on the score of 'privilege' under the umbrella of 'proceedings' in Parliament? Here a broad-spectrum defense for **words spoken** seems to be the rule. Says May:

> *"It may be regarded as established that a Member is not amenable to the ordinary courts for anything said in debate, however criminal in its nature. The language of Article 9 of the Bill of Rights is designed to make this clear. Except by some forced construction words spoken in debate cannot be taken out of the category of proceedings in Parliament. This principle is also established by the decision of the House of Lords in reversing the condemnation in the King's Bench of Sir John Eliot and his fellow Members on the ground, partly, that speeches of whatever character made in Parliament could not be inquired into out of Parliament."*

Criminal acts may not claim absolution even in the land of the Bill of Rights and supremacy of Parliament. The House of Lords, in Eliot's case, (supra), left the question open, suggesting that an assault by a Member may be cognizable by courts.

"In *Bradlaugh* v. *Gossett,* Mr. Justice Stephen said that he knew of no authority for the proposition that an ordinary crime committed in the House of Commons would be withdrawn from the ordinary course of criminal justice."

Another aspect of the matter falls for consideration here. The House, apart from the police, may feel that the crime was a contempt or breach of privilege and take action on its own. Can it do so and can there be two punitive trials then? One may read May's observation:

> *"With regard to a crime committed in Parliament, the House in which it was committed might claim the right to decide whether to exercise its own jurisdiction or to hand the offender over to the criminal courts. In taking this decision, it would no doubt be guided by the nature of the offence, and the adequacy or inadequacy of the penalties, somewhat lacking in flexibility, which it could inflict."*

The confused, complicated, historically obfuscated saga of parliamentary privileges is so riven with doubt that it is fair in a democracy like ours not to leave as an imbroglio an important branch of jurisprudence. Indeed, our Constitution expressly provides, as a lasting solution, that privileges and immunities of the House and its members be codified. The reference to the law in England is only a transitory provision. If Parliament makes a law regarding privileges the Court gains jurisdiction to interpret it. There is no reason why a transitory provision holding good until a permanent legislation is enacted should not also be amenable to judicial hermeneutics. I agree with the editorial in the Mainstream dated 15th November, 2003:

> *....every citizen has a right of offer fair criticism and/or comments on a matter, which is of public concern and that it is not correct to suggest that a Member of Parliament is not liable to be criticized in the performance of his duties as such member. Fair comments or criticisms by a citizen....particularly a statement couched in proper language in which he puts forward his own version of certain facts, which may be contrary to something said on the floor of the House by a Member or Minister, will not be objectionable.*

It is only when a point is reached and the writing ceases to be journalistic vapouring and becomes an improper obstruction to the functioning of Parliament and its members by patent falsehood or otherwise, that action to the extent of punishment is called for. Then the House will never hesitate to do its duty towards itself.

This is where the issue of codification of legislative privileges assumes importance and urgency. The Editors' Guild has already raised this demand. This becomes all the more essential as the Constitution has not comprehensively spelt out the privileges of Parliament and State

Assemblies. And it is also necessary that this exercise should result in what The Hindu described as a "carefully crafted statute that explicitly recognizes the application of the power of judicial review to cases of breach of privileges, especially cases where legislative privilege comes into conflict with fundamental rights.

Even in England the court has resisted the judicial authoritarianism of the Commons. In *Stockdale* v. *Hansard* Coleridge, J, made luminous observations:

> *"But it is said that this and all other courts of law are inferior in dignity to the House of Commons, and that therefore it is impossible for us to review its decision. This argument appears to be founded on a misunderstanding of several particulars; first, in what sense it is that this Court is inferior to the House of Commons; next, in what sense the House is a court at all; and, lastly, in what sense we are now assuming to meddle with any of its decisions. Vastly inferior as this Court is to the House of Commons, considered as a body in the state, ...yet, as a court of law, we know no superior but those courts which may review our judgments for error; and in this respect there is no common term of comparison between this court and the House. In truth, the House is not a court of law at all, in the sense in which that term can alone be properly applied here; neither originally, nor by appeal, can it decide a matter in litigation between two parties; it has no means of doing so; it claims no such power; powers of inquiry and of accusation it has, but it decides nothing judicial, except where it is itself a party, in the case of contempt. And to them no question of degree arises between courts; and, in the only sense therefore in which this argument would be of weight it does not apply. In any other sense the argument is of no force.*

British experience has created a dualism which makes law a jungle. Erskine May sums it best:

> *"The decisions of the courts are not accepted as binding by the House in matters of privilege, nor the decisions of the House by the courts. Thus the old dualism remains unresolved. In theory, 'there may be at any given moment two doctrines of privilege, the one held by the courts, the other by either Home, the one to be found in the Law Reports, the other in Hansard; and there is no way of resolving the real point at issue should the conflict arise'."....*
>
> *"The field of agreement is thus wide. With respect to rights exercisable within a House, the jurisdiction of the House is complete; and it is in practice so with respect to rights exercisable outside a House in the principal way in which the courts might come into contact with such rights, namely, in punishment for contempt or breach of privilege. The remaining opportunities for conflict with the courts are therefore narrow. Speaking of these possibilities in 1884 Lord Coleridge, CJ, could say: 'But, while I do not*

deny that as a matter of reasoning such things might happen, it is consoling to reflect that they have scarce ever happened in the long centuries of our history, and that in the present state of things it is but barely possible that they should ever happen again. If such a conflict should arise however, the House has its remedy in recourse to legislation, just as it solved the dispute with the courts over the protection of papers published by its orders by means of the Parliamentary Papers Act.

Since the House of Commons has not for hundred years refused to submit its privileges to the decision of the courts, it may be said to have given practical recognition to be jurisdiction of the courts over the existence and extent of its privileges. On the other hard, the courts have always, at any rate in the last resort, refused to interfere in the application by the House of any of its recognized privileges.

A pervasive impression may gain democratic legitimation of parliamentary pusillanimity and dereliction of duty to inform the people of their constitutional right to know what their 'free expression' parameters are *vis-a-vis* legislative privileges. Why should the Houses of our Sovereign Republic clings colonially to the laws of our royal masters of yester-years. We have a written Constitution and a Sovereign Republic with its own national ethos and eidos and it is time to elevate a borrowed, time-barred transitory provision into great code promulgating the law fine-tuned to the liberties and parliamentary privileges of a free people. We shall not suffer the humiliation of subjection to Hansard reports of half a century ago since it is a dependencia syndrome repugnant to our Republic's supremacy. One billion Indians have a basic right to be informed about and respond positively a jurisprudence and justice which validate the powers, privileges and immunities of our legislatures in a complete code, lest so great a branch of jurisprudence that governs their life be an oracular mystery and unpredictable infliction. People's rights cannot be banished, burlesqued or burked if democracy is to survive through elected surrogates.

"...the only breaches which are really amenable to the law of privilege and contempt are those which seriously interfere with the working of the House and its institutions, or its committees as institutions, or...to undermine the public respect and confidence in parliament and its institutions."

The rule of law commands that privileges jurisprudence be crystalised and codified.

THE JURISPRUDENCE OF CONSTITUTIONAL CAMARADERIE AMONG THE GREAT INSTITUTIONS

Judicature & Legislature

The pageantry of Indian constitutional instrumentalities is textually impressive and exhaustive, but in pragmatic experience, as between the Legislature and the Judicature, embarrassing situations, ambiguous interpretations and antimony of operations confront the nation. The three major pillars which support the constitutional cathedral are the legislature, the judiciary and the executive. Constitutional comity expects institutional harmony, so that the great vision of the Founding Fathers about a creative social order may fulfill itself without contradiction, contretemps and conflicts marring the national march in governing the life of the people. However high the expectation, confrontations have arisen leading to extraordinary occasions of head-on collisions. One such unhappy instance which exploded as a constitutional crisis is the case of Keshav Singh (under Article 143 Constitution of India).

The legislature and the judiciary are paramount institutions enjoying sovereign powers to the extent assigned to them and enshrined under the Constitution. Specific provisions have been made in our Founding Deed vesting authority in each and so long as they function within their bounds a happy *modus vivendi* prevails. But occasions may arise when operational friction and perception of jurisdiction may bring the Court and the House into a scenario of jurisprudential jujitsu, constitutional combat and interpretational imbroglio. The functional felicity of constitutionality alone makes the rule of law a process of good governance. Therefore, the boundaries of operation of the judiciary and to legislature must be clearly drawn so that the rights of the citizen may not be drowned in confusion and the pellucid stream of law may flow smooth and transparent, without hitting hard rocks of paralysing disputes leading to chaos in the cosmos.

The judiciary is charged with the solemn duty of upholding the fundamental rights and forbidding legal injury to citizens. In this sphere, the robed independence of the Court is a high guarantee under the Constitution. None whose rights are in jeopardy or violated is without remedy so long as Article 32, 142 and 226 reign supreme as inscribed in Part III and Chapter V Part VI. The power to declare the law is finally vested in the Supreme Court under Article 141. Of course, the High Courts, while granting relief under Article 226, do lay down the law subject to the overriding jurisdiction of the Supreme Court. In short, any aggrieved citizen can seek relief when his rights are infringed from the High Court or the Supreme Court. They are the haven of human rights under the Constitution. The independence of the judiciary is essential for the discharge of its plenary obligations to defend rights and to prevent wrongs. Indeed, judicial power is the central source of remedial armour to guard human rights such as are granted by the *corpus juris* of the country.

We have a Government of laws and the legislatures make the law. They are also a grand inquest of the nation and have vast powers of discussion and debate and law making decisions. Inevitably, the autonomy needed for the proper exercise of parliamentary power makes it appropriate for these majestic institutions to enjoy the authority required to exercise their constitutional obligations. Inevitably, the Constitution vests in the legislature powers, privileges freedoms and immunities which are necessary for functional attributes of the Houses and of the members and committees of such legislatures. The nidus of the privileges and what not can be located in Article 194 read with the restrictions in 211. To preserve the dignity of the judiciary and the majesty of its power there is a specific provision that no discussion shall take place in the legislature of a State with respect to the conduct of any judge of the higher court in the discharge of his duties. To protect the legislature from judicial interference, there is Article 212 which inhibits judicial investigation into proceedings of the legislature with a clear stipulation that no officer or member of the legislature in the conduct of his business in the House shall be subject to the jurisdiction of any court in respect of the exercise by him of those powers. Freedom of discussion inside the House is if the very essence of legislative *raison d'etre*. Therefore, under Article 194 (2) no member shall be liable to any proceedings in any court in respect of anything said or any vote given by him in the House. Curiously enough, the powers, privileges and immunities of the House and the members have not yet been codified and are as a fact what prevailed in the House of Commons when the Indian Constitution was framed. Verbal attempts to get out of this colonial vestige have been made, but the fact remains that we have to look to Westminster even today for the rights of the Indian legislature and legislator.

Such in broad outline is the constitutional conspectus of the relationship between the House and the Court.

Constitutional Camaraderie

There are occasions of institutional aberrations when one or other of the instrumentalities runs berserk. They are rare but still may occur. Therefore we must be clear about the fundamentals to eliminate absurdities. One such instance may be mentioned more by way of extreme illustration than by way of grave apprehensions. There was an Hon'ble Speaker in Tamil Nadu Assembly called Hector Pandiyan a few years ago. I speak from memory and newspaper reports and may not therefore be too accurate. A certain convict was sentenced to imprisonment by the High Court of Madras in the criminal jurisdiction. The next day Hector Pandiyan, in hectoring style, told the Tamil Nadu Assembly that he represented the House and the House represented the people and the people were supreme. Therefore, in exercise of this fabricated supremacy he released the accused who had been convicted and sentenced the previous day by the High Court and directed the D.G. of Police to release the arrestee. What power was vested in Pandiyan to travesty a sentence imposed by the High Court none that the Constitution knows of, except the arrogant usurpation by Hon'ble Pandiyan in exercise of some bedlam jurisprudence. This was a shock to the public and to the House. Luckily, sanity prevailed and, at the instance of the leader of the House M.G.R., the decision of the Speaker was reversed by a resolution of the House and the egregious error was not allowed to mar the law of the land.

A more horrendous and, indeed, historic episode which gave a rise to a cause celebre must be referred to. That was a case where the Hon'ble Speaker of the U.P. Assembly issued arrest warrants against judges of Allahabad. Let me quote the late great Palkhivala who sums up tersely the introduction to the story:

What had never happened in England since 1689, occurred in India in 1964. One Keshav Singh was committed and imprisoned by the U.P. Legislative Assembly (we shall call it "the House") for contempt. He moved a *Habeas Corpus* petition through an advocate before two Judges of the Allahabad High Court who admitted the Petition and granted him interim bail. The House could have filed a return showing how the detention of Keshav Singh was legal and within the powers of the House, and the petition would have been heard and disposed of on merits at a later date. However, immediately after the petition was presented, the House took the view that the citizen who moved the High Court, and the lawyer who presented his *Habeas Corpus* petition and the Judges who heard it were all guilty of contempt. The House resolved that the High Court Judges and the advocate should be brought in custody before the House. Thereupon the two Judges and the advocate presented petitions, which were admitted by the Full Bench of twenty-eight Judges of the Allahabad High Court, wherein they challenged the validity of the resolution of the House against them. Under a later clarificatory resolution the House withdrew the warrants for the arrest of the two Judges and the advocate, but the Judges and the advocate were still required to appear before the House and offer their explanations as to why the House should not proceed against them for contempt.

Fortunately, the President made a timely Reference to the Supreme Court under Article 143(1) of the Constitution (Special Reference No. 1 of 1964) asking the Supreme Court's opinion on five questions. The essence of the five questions may be summed up in just one issue which constituted the jugular vein of the whole Reference:

> *"If a citizen is committed for contempt by the Legislature, has the right to seek redress in a Court of Law, or do the Judges who hear his petition and the advocate who presents it commit contempt of the Legislature?" ((Privilege of Legislatures—Supreme Court's Opinion in President's reference, 1964, Page 2 & 3)*

It may be noted that between the Commons and the Judges there had been a battle of warrants against each other bearing on the contempt of Parliament. This 'deplorable irresponsibility' displayed by the Commons in 1689 was never repeated and no judge has ever been called upon to answer a change in England ever since, although the British judges have heard and decided petitions by citizens committed for contempt by the Commons. What we need is statesmanship on the part of judges and parliamentarians where a larger vision of comity of institutions will obviate stultifying collisions. The Supreme Court, with that great statesman judge Gajendragadkar presiding, cleared the law of possible confusion and ambivalence pettifogging obfuscation. We must remember that India has never suffered the stresses, tensions which were the result of historical causes and rival claims of the Crown, the Courts, the Commons and the Lords. That has no relevance under our Constitution. Let me cite Palkhivala:

> *Article 194 (3) must be construed to refer only to those privileges of the House of Commons which were definite, certain and judicially recognised as existing in 1950; and, further, the line must be drawn at the point where the privilege would erode the Supreme Court's jurisdiction under Article 32 and the High Court's jurisdiction under Article 226 to issue writs, directions or orders at the instance of the aggrieved citizen.*

The Court has jurisdiction to entertain and deal with the petition of a citizen committed for contempt by a Legislature, and to quash the committal where the Legislature has exceeded its privilege, even if the warrant is un-speaking or general. An unspeaking warrant cannot silence the Constitution.

In any view of the matter, even assuming the House of Commons could at all claim the right to commit a Judge for contempt in a case which was the subject-matter of the Reference, Article 211 is an absolute bar against the State Legislature's claim to exercise such a privilege against a Judge of the Supreme Court or of a High Court.

((Privilege of Legislatures—Supreme Court's Opinion in President's reference, 1964, Page-7)

The Supreme Court's view is thus summarised in the head note to the relevant AIR Report:

1. that it was competent for the Division Bench of the High Court to entertain and deal with the petition of K challenging the legality of the sentence of imprisonment imposed upon him by the Legislative Assembly for its contempt and for infringement of its privileges and to pass orders releasing K on bail pending the disposal of his said petition; (Paras 143, 197)
2. that K by causing the petition to be presented on his behalf to the High Court, the Advocate by presenting the said petition, and the two Judges of the Division Bench by entertaining and dealing with the said petition and ordering the release of K on bail pending disposal of the said petition, did not commit contempt of the Legislative Assembly; (Paras 143, 200)
3. that it was not competent for the Legislative Assembly to direct the production of the said two Judges and the Advocate before it in custody or to call for their explanation for its contempt; (Paras 143, 201)
4. that it was competent for the Full Bench of the High Court to entertain and deal with the petitions of the said two Judges and the Advocate, and to pass interim orders restraining the Speaker of the Legislative Assembly and others from implementing the aforesaid direction of the said Legislative Assembly; and (Paras 143, 203)
5. that in a case arising out of a contempt alleged to have been committed by a citizen who is not a member of the House of Legislature outside the four-walls of the legislative chamber, a Judge of a High Court who entertains or deals with a petition challenging any order or decision of a Legislature imposing any penalty on the petitioner or issuing any process against the petitioner for its contempt, or for infringement of its privileges and immunities, or who passes any order on the said Legislature; and the said Legislature is not competent to take proceedings against such a Judge in the exercise and enforcement of its powers, privileges and immunities. (AIR 1965 SC 745-746)

A certain lofty courtesy, innocent of measly rivalry, must inform and illumine the mutuality between the two high institutions. It must be remembered that Judge power is central to the constitutional order and so the legislature must deal with reverence towards the judiciary. Judicial independence and immunity are an unassailable value. This is fundamental. At the same time, the House in large measure has a representative character of a high order and the court can never act as a third chamber of the House, even though it has power to strike down unconstitutional legislation and pronounce upon excesses outside the legislative chamber. Having said this, our law lords must know their limitations. The high power to interpret law and adjudicate upon disputes is vested in the Court. This ultimate authority of hermeneutics and decision-making must be unreservedly accepted by the legislators and the Hon'ble Speaker. There is no competitive spirit but fair accommodation by each of that portion of sovereignty which is assigned under the Constitution to each institution. Once this is grasped in the right temper, the resentment by the Speaker towards the Court when request, by way summons, to comply with natural justice is issued is a misunderstanding. Of course when the court addresses the Hon'ble Speaker great respect must be shown, not a command to appear in the Court. The purpose of the judge issuing the summons (which must be dressed as a request) is not to exercise authority but to give opportunity. Once this aspect is understood, the Speaker's point of view, if any, may be brought to the notice of the Court through the Advocate-General who is himself a constitutional entity. The Secretary of the Assembly can give the necessary instruction and bring to the notice of the House that the proceedings in the House are altogether beyond the Court purview. It must be remembered by the court that there is an absolute bar to enquiry by the Court into proceedings inside the House. This is an oasis, as it were, and is out of bounds for the Court to enquire or adjudicate. Likewise, the freedom of speech of the members inside the House is a great guarantee of democracy. The debate in basic and what is said cannot be censured by any curial process. Judges are protected in their conduct even inside the House since they are beyond the pale of intra-mural criticism. Unfortunately, this ban or taboo is violated out of ignorance and arrogance by some members. When the conduct of a Judge comes under censure in the course of hot debate the Chair must pull up the member and expunge the violative portion of the member's expression. Unfortunately, when the Chair fails in this duty there is no specific provision in the Constitution to set right the deviant. Can the Court intervene when its conduct is debated in violation of the constitutional provision? This is a grey area. Again, it must be noted that what is absolutely protected inside the House is freedom of speech and to vote—nothing beyond. Supposing a member attempts to murder and there is bleeding violence in violation of proper conduct, what happens to the offences so committed? I should assume that when the House becomes a babel or bedlam or runs berserk and violent mischief breaks out, the Speaker is the supremo and may summon police help but beyond, that the Court does not lose its jurisdiction to try a murder merely because the venue is the House. It is not unusual these days for personal injury being caused inside the House. The penal law is not eclipsed inside the Chamber. Where lawlessness, departing from the rules of conduct, takes over the law of the land and the authority entrusted with the administration of justice do not blink at the scene. These are matters which Speakers' Conferences must discuss and take decisions, where judges and jurists must ponder and consider solutions. What our Founding Fathers did not dream of are becoming raw and vulgar realities. The law of contempt enjoyed by the House and by the Court may be pressed into service upto a point, but there is still need to examine these contra constitutional developments, so that orderly administration of the legislative business and judicial business may be ensured as part of our civilised democratic order.

A source of functional confusion relating to the Hon. Speaker *vis-a-vis* the higher judiciary needs specific mention. The Tenth Schedule to the Constitution vests in the Speaker the power to decide on questions of legislators' defection. When he rules under Schedule Ten he acts as a tribunal and his finding, if arbitrary, is vulnerable to judicial review. The provisions in Articles 6 and 7 notwithstanding, the Court can examine the validity of the Speaker's holding. A Division Bench of the Kerala High Court, speaking through Narayana Kurup J, has eruditely expounded the law:

By applying these well-known and accepted tests of what constitutes a Tribunal, the speaker or the Chairman, acting under paragraph 6(1) of the Tenth Schedule of the Constitution has been held to be a Tribunal. In *Kihota Hollohon* v. *Zachilhu*, AIR 1993 SC 412 the Supreme Court held that the Speaker while exercising powers and discharging functions under the Tenth Schedule acts as Tribunal adjudicating rights and obligations under the Tenth Schedule and his decisions in that capacity are amenable to judicial review. It was also held that the concept of statutory finality embodied in Paragraph 6(1) does not detract form or abrogate judicial review under Arts. 136, 226 and 227 of the Constitution in so far as infirmities based on violations of constitutional mandates, *mala-fides*, non-compliance with Rules of Natural Justice and perversity are concerned. Therefore, the question relating to the jurisdiction of the High Court to entertain writ petitions challenging the orders of the Speaker now stands concluded by the aforesaid judgment of the Supreme Court in *Kihota Hollohon* v. *Zachilhu*, AIR 1993 SC 412 (supra) wherein the provisions of Paragraph 7 of the Tenth Schedule which bars jurisdiction of courts in respect of any matter connected with the disqualification of a member of a House under the Schedule have been held to the unconstitutional and it has been held that the Speaker while passing an order in exercise of his powers under sub-paragraph (1) of paragraph 6 of the Tenth Schedule functions as a "Tribunal" and the order passed by him is subject to judicial review under Arts. 32, 136, 226 and 227 of the Constitution. (KLT 2000 (3) P-54)

Another Full Bench ruling on reinforcement of judicial review

The parliamentary jurisprudence bearing on House-Bench comity is of daily relevance to the ordinary citizen. The privileges of the House are sometimes an invisible violence and the media is vulnerable to Assembly authoritarianism. I have already referred to the great case arising from Uttar Pradesh and the Supreme Court's binding advice. I have also referred to the constitutional clarity brought into the juridical scenario where Justice Kurup exploded the myth of unquestionability of Speaker's rulings even when it affected adversely by arbitrary action against a citizen's fundamental rights. In the same strain runs the Ananda Vikatan case (1994-Writ L.A. 638) where a full bench of the Madras High Court set aside a resolution of the Tamil Nadu legislative assembly sentencing the editor of a Tamil weekly, Ananda Vikatan, to rigorous imprisonment for breach of privilege of the House. The basis of the breach of privilege was not anything that happened inside the House. The resolution for breach of privilege was adopted in respect of the publication of a cartoon which was alleged to be a pickpocket depiction of an MLA and a masked dacoit picture of a minister. The apology demanded was not forthcoming and so the House resolved to punish the editor. A Full Bench considered whether the collective will of the Assembly, albeit it deprived a citizen of his fundamental right under Article 21 would be amenable to judicial review. The Court held:

It is by now well-settled and there could be no serious controversy over the position reiterated by more than one decision of the Supreme Court that the Constitution reigns supreme and the rights, powers and privileges of the various limbs of the State are subject to the provisions contained in the Constitution, the basic and fundamental law which provides for the governance of the State. It is equally well-settled that the final authority to state the meaning of the Constitution and to settle constitutional controversies exclusively belongs to the Supreme Court and the High Courts which are constituted as the sentinels of both the Constitution and democracy as well as the fundamental rights of the citizen—inclusive of their life, liberty and freedom. That apart, the Legislatures in India have to function within the limits prescribed by the material and relevant provisions of the Constitution of India and adjudication of any dispute as to whether legislative authority has been exceeded or fundamental rights have been contravened is solely and exclusively left to the Judicature of his country and, therefore, inevitably the decision about the construction of Article 194(3) of the Constitution, the privileges, powers and immunities claimed or action taken in vindication thereof cannot be said to be in the exclusive domain or of the sole arbitral or absolute discretion of the House of Legislature. Of course, the Courts having regard to their own self-imposed limits would honour the sentiments, particularly keeping in view the plenary powers of the Legislature within the constitutionally permitted limits, so long as such action of the Legislature does not result in the negation of the fundamental rights secured under the Constitution or the life, liberty, freedom and dignity of the citizen. The all powerful postures or claims of sky-high powers or suzerain claims of sovereignty or over-Lordism are to be brushed aside as nothing but fossils of the tyrannical and anarchical past and not in keeping tune with the basic and fundamental principle of rule of law, the bed rock of the Constitution or the democratic ideals which are the avowed object of the Republic ushered in by the Constitution of India. The contentions to the contrary have no basis or recognition of law and do not have the merit of acceptance by courts in this country.

The Court gave monetary redress too by way of compensation under the Public Law for the wrong done to the citizen by way of detention. The expanding universe of human rights prevails over privileges of elite groups clad in pro tem power. It is right to conclude this dissension with the wisdom of the Madras Bench articulating the peril to freedoms if confusion creeps into make Public Law murky.

There is, if we may say so, considerable confusion still in the minds of some people as to the scope of the undefined "powers, privileges and immunities" of a House of a State Legislature so much so that it has sometimes been imagined that a House of a State Legislature has some judicial or quasi-judicial powers also, quite apart from its recognised powers of punishment for its contempts or the power of investigations it may carry out by the appointment of its own committees. Arguments of the kind which have been sometimes advanced in this country could not have been advanced if it was clearly understood that, even in England, where the Constitution is largely conventional, the exercise of judicial powers directly by Houses of the legislature, including powers such as those of impeachment, are practically obsolete. Whatever remained of the power enjoyed once by the High Court or Parliament, when the King could himself sit, as a part of Parliament with the Houses of Parliament, to administer justice is now concentrated in the House of Lords, exercised through a Committee of Law Lords.

Sum-Up

The constellation of propositions which crystallizes from this long exposition may be presented as pervasive principles which possess constitutional paramountcy. The first fundamental is that judicial independence never bends or bows before the Executive or the Legislature, as laid down authoritatively by the nine judges bench in the Judges Case. This indefeasible doctrine puts the judges in their forensic performance beyond the contempt power of the Legislature. Be you ever so high, the judges, in their curial capacity, are not answerable to the House or its officers.

Secondly, judicial supremacy derived from the Constitution and specified in Articles 32, 142, 136, 226 and 227 empower the court under public law to decide any case brought by any aggrieved citizen against any order, fiat or ukase emanating from any authority in the House. The legality of such a directive, if it operates from any conduct of a citizen outside the House, is amenable to judicial jurisdiction. However, if the action is taken by the Speaker inside the legislative chamber the court cannot sit in review the plenary authority being vested in the House. Even here, if what is alleged as the basis of action is a *privilege* of the House or member, it is open to the Court to examine whether such a privilege exists provided that the Assembly's action infringes *prima facie,* a fundamental right of the citizen.

Thirdly, whatever is spoken (or voted upon inside the House) is beyond the power of the Court to investigate or adjudicate. The member's conduct inside the chamber is immune to judicial scrutiny.

Fourthly, even if a member, contrary to the express provision of section 211, does indulge in improper speech the corrective mechanism is the Speaker, not the Court. This position requires constitutional reconsideration so that the comity of the House and the Court may be preserved in dignified camaraderie.

Fifthly, when the Court, in connection with any matter pending before it, requests the Hon. Speaker for information (or for the purpose of affording an opportunity for explanation makes a request) it behoves the Speaker, in courtesy to the Court, to respond in a spirit of co-operation and not reject in a spirit of confrontation.

Sixthly, the Court shall hold the Hon. Speaker and the proceedings of the House in all solemnity. Seventhly, when the Speaker decides a matter bearing on the defection law, judicial review is integral to constitutional law.

A Pertinent Divagation

In a petition under Article 226 of the Constitution an alleged gross impropriety of a Speaker setting himself up as a party candidate in a parliamentary election was challenged. Justice Sivaraman Nair wrote what is luminous wisdom *vis-a-vis* the *modus vivendi* between the Court and the House:

In the parliamentary system of Government, which we have adopted, the office of the Speaker is a high and exalted office. He represents the entire House of elected representatives of the people and holds a place next only to the Head of the State in protocol. To that office are attached privileges which are inalienable. Under Article 179 of the Constitution of India, he holds office till he ceases to be a member of the Assembly until immediately before the first meeting of the Assembly after dissolution. Though the Advocate-General submits that the British Parliamentary Practices shall not be applicable to India. I have to rely on the celebrated treatise of Erskine May on the mother of Parliaments due to lack of any other alternative source suggested by him. Dealing with the Speaker of the House of Commons, it is stated in "Parliamentary Practice", 20th Edition, at pages 234-235:

The chief characteristics attaching to the office of Speaker in the House of Commons are authority and impartiality. As a symbol of his authority he is accompanied by the Royal Mace which is borne before him when entering and leaving the chamber and upon state occasions by the Serjeant at Arms attending the House of Commons, and is placed upon the table when he is in the chair. In debate all speeches are addressed to him and he calls upon Members to speak—a choice which is not open to dispute. When he rises to preserve order to give a ruling on a doubtful point he must always be heard in silence and no Member may stand when the Speaker is on his feet. Reflections upon the character or actions of the Speaker may be punished as breaches of privilege. His action cannot be criticised incidentally in debate or upon any form of proceeding except a substantive motion. His authority in the chair is fortified by many special powers which are referred to below. Confidence in the impartiality of the Speaker is an indispensable condition of the successful working of procedure, and many conventions exist which have as their object not only to ensure the impartiality of the Speaker but also to ensure that his impartiality is generally recognised. He takes no part in debate either in the House or in committee. He votes only when the voices are equal, and then only in accordance with rules which preclude an expression of opinion upon the merits of a question. Until recently his seat was often uncontested at a general election. (1985 KLT P-40 at 41)

When the Indian parliamentary system comes of age, and excels Westminster emerged from its antics. Bharat will become the paradigm of the glory of our Constitution desiderates mutual reverence between the legislature and the judicature in such manner that comity and camaraderie become the majestic *modus vivendi.*

The Goal

A land of settled government,
A land of just and old renown,
Where Freedom slowly broadens down
From precedent to precedent.

A Post Script as a Caveat

The glow is gone and darkness alarmingly spreads. A conservative Chief Justice like Barucha has deplored that twenty per cent. of the judges are corrupt; nay more, other Chief Justices, before and after Barucha, have lamented likewise without quantifying the correct proportion. Shameful allegations have been made in the public about judges in their private conduct. One has been sought to be impeached in vain while some have resigned in shame. Yet, others have retired and escaped incrimination. 'In House' enquiry commands poor credence. "The time is out of joint; O cursed spite"—"there is something rotten in the State of Denmark"—if we may view our time through Hamletian lenses. This decay desiderates corrective therapy, not abuse in the legislature. Statesmen of the judiciary and great men in the political theatre must sit together to make Indian justice a glorious instrument.

Now to our elected representatives, our legislators at the Central and State levels are becoming notorious for dismal deviance, profligacy and even shocking corruption. A recent e-mail communication on my computer (from the Internet) reads like what I wish were never there. I quote :

Can one imagine working for the following Company?
It has a little over 500 employees with the following statistics?
29 have been accused of spouse abuse.
7 have been arrested for fraud.
19 have more than three criminal cases pending against them.
117 have been charged and are being investigated for Murder, Rape, Assault, Extortion and Robery.
71 cannot get credit or loans due to bad credit histories.
21 are current defendants on various lawsuits.
84 have been involved in offences and have paid fines.
Can you guess what mighty Organization this is?
It is the 545 members of the Lower House of Parliament of India

that works for you and me. The same group cranks out on hundreds upon hundred of laws designed to keep the rest of us in line..........

Can we do something about it?

At least, we'll spread the word around using this mighty medium called Internet and e-mail, create on awareness (as if people don't know already!!)

HELP SAVE THE COUNTRY!!!

People, we the people of India, must without delay awake to this alarming decline in moral values by making our elections cleaner and our candidates finer.

A CASE FOR NATIONAL PRISON POLICY

Our Constitution is on trial in our prison houses, our cultural credentials are tested behind stone walls and iron bars, our penal panaceas are in peril, what with the deterrent no-return and recidivist escalation despite long incarceration. The law cannot hang limp but must lash out to restore order, correct deviance and stabilise that personal integrity which is the best guarantee of behavioural normality and societal harmony. Barbarity in sentence and torture in prison are a trend, which aggravates the malady and so self-defeating that punitive cruelty is a curative futility and preventive disutility. From a practical range, criminologists have concluded that benumbing, long prison terms and inflictions within the walled campuses are ineffective drugs in the penological pharmacopoeia.

Therefore, a reformative philosophy, rehabilitative strategy, therapeutic prison treatment and enlivening of prisoner's personality through a technology of fostering the fullness of being such a creative art of social defense and correctional process activising fundamental guarantees of prisoner's rights, is hopeful not of national prison policy struck by the Constitution and the Court. This is my thesis but I must argue my case and establish the justice of this policy. Tersely put, the State must discover and engineer the highway to human rehabilitation and put it into practice in the prison system.

At this point we may begin with the basic question: Do we have a national prison justice policy? To be honest, the *Raj* had a prison programme at the services of its imperial policy, but the Republic, with all its boasts and all its hopes, has no penal policy, no prison, no humanism, no jail justice, even though almost every minister who was wielded power, regardless of party, has suffered incarceratory laptism. Regrettably, the judiciary has parrot-like, carried over precedents of Victorian vintage, being innocent of progressive penological thought and the nexus of constitutional values with prison praxis. Judicial illiterarcy about criminology, rehabilitative technology and of the court's responsibility in purposeful sentencing projects and restorative penitentiary procedures is appalling.

On the legislative front, the less said, the better. In a country where the majority of legislators have served a jail spell almost as a qualification for candidacy, is it not surprising that the Prisons Act, 1894, codifying the repressive policy of Whitehall, continues "red in tooth and claw", come freedom, come Constitution. The harassing and hamstringing traditions validated by Prison Manuals, are preserved thoughtlessly, decades after prisoner patriots assumed power (wearing a Gandhi cap is, under the Punjab Jail Manual, a Jail offence even now). Parliamentary apathy is matched by executive insouciance. Of course, at seminars and conferences, ghost speechwriters cover up minister's conscience with glittering inaugural exhortations and even policy formulations. And criminological workshops the academia's, never taken seriously by the politician, the bureaucrat, the judge and the warden who alone matter in executing prison justice. Thus, the battle for a national policy on prisons and imprisonment has been lost by apathy, insensitivity and 'eminent' ignorance.

The people—the political swashbucklers and professional jargon-mongers apart, are unaware, doped by hopes, and are inertly irresponsive to the sentencing mystiques. If only a human transformation inside the walled world of offenders were planned and executed, through a circumspect, yet intelligent project to invigorate benignly the inner man in custody, a crime-free society, why, a prisonless State may dawn in the distance, given creative courage and national vision in perspective of human values. This is not a moonly ideal but largely practical, as several social scientists and sublime pragmatists claim. I know, ever science has been an out caste. I may sound unorthodox but orthodoxy is the Bourbon of the world of thought. It learns not, neither can it forget.

Among the three alternatives, the retributive, the deterrent and the rehabilitative, modern penologists opt for the last with a sprinkling of the second. To be retributive is to claim an eye for an eye-and, logically, a murder for a murder, a rape for a rape, a reprisal barbarity for brutal burglary and so on. Soothing for the sadist, heartening to the little Hitler lingering in many bosoms, this form of blood-thirsty justice, which still is prevalent in a few countries, has become obsolete, what with the dignity and worth of the human person receiving better recognition in civilised societies responsive to the new international legal order. Not quite dead is *lex talionis*, as is evident from the lively controversy about death penalty.

Don C. Gibbons in his recent edition of "Society, Crime and Criminal Careers" writes: "What purpose does the infliction of suffering on lawbreakers serve? Tappan has offered an incisive summary of the purposes of punishment. He notes that punishment is designed to achieve the goal of retribution or social retaliation against the offender. Punishment also involves incapacitation, which prevents the violator from misbehaving during the time he is being punished. Additionally, punishment supposed to have a deterrent effect, both on the law-breaker and on potential misbehaviours. Individual or specific deterrence may be achieved by intimidation of the person, frightening him against further misbehaviour, or it may be effected through reformation in which the law-breaker changes his deviant sentiments. General deterrence results from the warning offered to potential criminals by the example of punishment directed at a specific wrongdoer".

The theory that savagery must be fought by savagery dies hard and if that philosophy holds good, judges must welcome prison torture and police third degree. Anyway, these primitive strands of thinking, decked in different apparel, are found among judicial, legislative and executive agencies. Is this our penal policy? Then, do jail the delinquent in, gouge his eyes, publicly flog him, dismember his limbs and hang him to the delectation of ghoulish crowds. Blinding Bhagalpur justice par excellence.

British justice once hanged even children for petty offences and some great judges were unhappy when some in the long list of capital sentence offences were sought to be jettisoned. "Sir Rober Peel regarded it 'as a most dangerous experiment' when stealing £5 from a dwelling-house ceased to be a capital offence. Lord Ellenborough, the Lord Chief Justice of his day, thought transportation as a punishment for stealing 5s. from a shop was quite inadequate substitute for the death penalty, and the Solicitor-General, Sir William Garrow, argued passionately that the Government could not exist without the protection of drawing and quartering".

England has replaced the gallows by prisons, and a macabre mix of retaliatory cruelty, a deterrent confinement defiles prison management. In many countries, long terms behind bars, harsh and humiliating regimen like solitary confinement and fetters all over, deprivations of basic needs to deepen the punitive thrust became the "zoological" penal policy embittering the culprit. Wincfred A. Elken writes: "At the turn of the century, a government committee was set up to investigate the work of the prisons. What impressed its members was not the deterrent value of imprisonment, but the extent to which the prisoners were brutalized and demoralised by their experience. The prisons were in fact breeding grounds of crime.

"The deterrent theory seems in fact to lead to an inevitable dilemma. Crime continues in spite of punishment and the logical answer is to make the punishments even more severe. Ultimately the point is reached when the demoralisation produced by these punishments becomes too glaringly obvious and the administrators of justice, and the public, become sickened by what the law demands. Experience has in fact shown that the purely repressive punishments are neither necessary nor effective".

The champions of severity of infliction, corporal or in-prison, as possessing a deterrent potential have lost the battle by now, because crimes have been increasing despite heavy penalties. A variety of reasons render impotent these draconian penal prescriptions, including the venality of investigative agencies, the judicial distance between the first charge and final guild and the easy purchase of acquittals or light sentences, through clever lawyering, and the non-performance of the criminal justice system which is creaking crumbling, credibility-lacking instrumentality. Even the barbarities in some of the middle-East countries become bearable, except in stray dramatic cruelties, because bribery and other pressures buy off where the law's claws otherwise tear into the flesh. Even the stern socialist societies and their penal pharmaceuticals suffer failure, at least in part. Reams can be written, hours can be spoken, to prove the point that terror and horror, as punitive armoury, only debase justice but do not deter the culprit except marginally. Of course, society must emphatically express public denunciation for some types of crime through punishment but brutal deterrence is fiendish folly. It frightens, never refines; it wounds, never heals; it embitters him, never binds him to others; it burns the skin, never awakens the soul. It works on the animal in man but neglects the spirit within. And penal torture hardens the criminal while our objective is to socialise and redeem the individual. Radical humanism and progressive penology must gravitate towards the therapeutic processes, which heal and humanise, restore and socialise, reconcile punishment with dignity of personhood.

ANIMAL CITIZEN

Copy of appeal made by Justice Shri V.R. Krishna Iyer, Vice-Chairman, Animal Welfare Board of India, to the Prime Minister of India, for banning export of frogs' legs.

Dear Prime Minister,

We wish to draw your compassionate consideration to an agonising issue which disturbs the conscience of all those who love living and have sensitive regard for our ahimsa heritage. The specific subject which we beseech you to examine is the ban on export of frogs' legs dismembered while the bleeding creature is alive and conscious.

The French have protected their frogs from extinction by law but India and Bangladesh supply frogs' legs. An estimated 70 million frogs a year are cut in twain and legs shipped abroad from India—in insufferable cruelty on a massive scale inflicted on innocent amphibians which, incidentally, are ecologically invaluable for our country's economy and national health.

Frogs are our friends as ecologists and sensitives of social health are aware. May we quote in support from famous humanist, Mr. Whiting:

> *"The large hungry frogs are really the best friends that the peasant farmers have, for they eat close on their own body-weight of insects and other crop pests each day, as well as carriers of waterborne diseases which afflict the farmers' cattle. They also control the insects that carry malaria and encephalitis now devastatingly on the increase".*

Annually Indian Business exports over 10,000 tons of live frogs:

> *"Ecologically these frogs would have eaten over 10,000 tonnes of crop pests PER DAY during the monsoon season, had they been left alive in the rice paddies and coconut gardens".*

The gains made by these cruel export tycoons are more than cancelled out by the vast health hazards to the common people. Writes Whites:

> *"At this time an agricultural research project led by Dr. A.G. Joshi of Bombay Natural History Society found that the spread of disease and damage to crops was increasingly due to the wholesale destruction of frogs. The £ $5^1/_2$ million in foreign exchange obtained from frogs' legs export was offset by a £ 13 million bill for imported pesticides to replace the frogs. Many of these broad spectrum insecticides are so dangerous to the operator and to the environment that their use in the Western World has been banned. The pesticides also affect the frogs' spawning grounds adversely. Frogs also control fresh-water fish parasites, thereby helping to maintain healthy fish stocks. Insect-borne diseases of cattle are on the increase.*
>
> *A frequent topic in the press is the alarming increase in deaths from malaria and encephalitis, both mosquito borne diseases".*

We humbly submit that the nation suffers more enormous, though invisible, losses than the heartless exporters seem to net. It is a fatal folly to permit this ecological disaster for the private profit of a few.

We may now briefly project the excruciating process in the words of White who is a great animal lover:

> *"The catchers – men and children – carry torches, the light from which dazzles the frogs so that they can be caught. Some are hunted with sticks. As they are caught, they are dropped into gunny sacks. Depending on their size, between 100 and 300 may be bundled into the gunny-bags before taken by bicycle or bus to the collecting centre. "20% may be dead when they arrive at the factory after having been humped and crushed for ten hours or more in the gunny sacks".*

Some are skinned alive, the leather being used for watchstraps and purses. The majority are *cut into two through their middles by being thrust against a fixed curving knife. The leg halves will be frozen, the writhing torsos tossed into a heap to die, minutes later.* Amphibians take longer to die than mammals:

> *"Apart from the cruelty, the lack of food hygiene causes concern. Flies settle thickly on the cut legs. Those that have died hours earlier are starting to putrify in the heat. The ice they are packed in is "local" water often unfit for drinking.*
>
> *In 1973 the USA temporarily banned the import of frogs' legs from India....."*
>
> *"The scenes show the frogs being taken from the gunny sacks the day following capture. Two or three attempts are made to cut through the lower abdomen. The operator stretches them horizontally in each hand and pushes them against a Datri, the traditional Indian cooking knife which has a curved blade fixed vertically to a plank held by a foot to the ground".*

The torso is tossed aside into a twitching bloody pile of moving limbs and gasping mouths to die painfully slowly.

> *"The dismembered legs have the long-webbed toes chopped off and are dropped into a bucket.* Later the now putrifying legs are transported in sacks of dirty ice to the factory".

Living frogs agonies in pain as they are cut in twain, their legs are dismembered and the webbed toes chopped off the legs and artless rural girls, for a bare living, do the skinning and packing. This unspeakable cruelty to speechless creature is a outrage on our *ahimsa* culture and an assassination of the spiritual remains of the Father of the Nation. In the name of humanism, we beg of you to ban this trade in torture and profit from vivisected limbs.

We plead with you, to respect the values of the Constitution and enforce the *fundamental duties Part IVA imposes on all Indians.* Dollar earnings by outraging the Constitution are illegal, immoral and unworthy of our national honour. In this connection, it may be apposite to read Article 51A:

> *"It shall be the duty of every citizen of India—*
>
> *(f) to value and preserve the rich heritage of our composite culture;*
>
> *(g) to protect and improve the natural environment and to have compassion for living creatures;*
>
> *(h) to develop humanism".*

To hack, in manner most foul, helpless millions of living creatures ecologically helpful to man and his healthful environs for a mess of business pottage stultifies the mandate of the Constitution to show compassion to living creatures, travesties the cultural testament from Buddha to Gandhi and involves the nation in health hazards by destroying Nature's balance and immunity system.

May we emphasize that the frog slaughter is a crime against Section 11(a) and (b) of the Prevention of Cruelty to Animals Act, 1960 and Part IVA of the Constitution? Compassionate people, in vast numbers, who are deeply moved by the spirit of Karuna towards all created beings are shocked and shamed by the vivisectionist violence and the pathological callousness behind the mass frogicide.

While cows and pigs rouse man's religious passion to butcher each other and Administrator's concern to extinguish such confrontations, there is another brutality of savage dimensions silently perpetrated in our fields and farms and factories, by a heartless brood of dollar-franc maniacs, on croaking creatures in excruciating pain. We urge you, well-meaning, quick-acting and uninhibited Primer Minister, to intervene and interdict this barbarity and defend humanistically a fundamental duty (Article 51A).

We close on a note of hope and speak for the voteless, voiceless, never-the-less, living amphibians.

A Plea for Universal Declaration of the rights of nature

An issue of fundamental significance and universal relevance needs to be brought into the consciousness of the World community. Ecology and environment, life in every form and evolution, have certain harmony and integrality that makes all creation kin. Spiritually speaking, the quintessence of the environmental movement, in its widest sweep, is that everything belongs to the Supreme Self and performs its *Karma* with a functional nexus. In practical terms, there is a purpose for everything in Nature too sacred to be destroyed. Eknath Easwaran has exquisitely expressed this idea which I may excerpt here:

> *"Nobody has any right to pollute the air, water, or seas, to cut down forests, or to wash away the topsoil. We do not own the earth. We are just transients who have been entrusted to leave the earth a little better than we found it. This is everybody's job; nobody is exempt from it and, in this sense, nobody is unemployed.*
>
> *"It follows that our environmental crisis demands that every one of us play a useful part, in our own way, to improve the environment wherever we live. If a person fails to do that, even if he makes a lot of money or if he wins a prestigious prize, the Buddha would say, "You haven't done what you have to do".*
>
> *"When you have done what you have to do, you will feel very secure, very fulfilled. As you discover the self in your own heart, you discover it simultaneously everywhere, in the people and creatures around you. You will feel very much at home in this universe. You don't need to take my word for it. Try it and see for yourself". ("Your Life is your message" by Eknath Easwaran, Nilgiri Press, USA - p. 92-93).*

Ahimsa of Gandhi or 'love thy neighbour' of Jesus proceed on the basic law of our being, the truth of our nature and our innate desire for peace, justice, order, freedom and personal dignity. This *advaidic* vision is the soul of our cultural heritage; and when we meditate with this unitive understanding, the mountains, the oceans, the forests and all living forms and inorganic things look divine. God (or call him by whatever name you like) sleeps in the mineral, wakes in the vegetable, walks in the animal, thinks in man and reaches realisation when the human ascent and the divine descent meet. If we are able to gain this *vistaramic* perspective, peace on earth becomes an easy essay to achieve. In the words of Adlai Stevenson, the human race is a family; men are brothers; all wars are civil wars. Such a holistic perception, makes the whole world kin and promotes a new world order alive with a sublime presence.

The U.N. Conference on Environment and Development and the Declaration made at Rio de Janeiro emanate from these spiritual depths. The order of Nature is itself a manifestation of this conceptual globalisation. The time has come for the nations and peoples everywhere to adopt the order of Nature as the cornerstone of the New World Human Order.

The philosophy of the Order may be tersely expressed thus:

Nature is made up of an inanimate terrestrial, aerial and aquatic ensemble, on the one hand and an animate vegetable, animal and human habitat, on the other hand.

'The human species must consider itself an element of the terrestrial habitat and must respect coexistence and symbiosis. Any failure to respect these is an attack on Nature, prejudicial to the whole ensemble of inanimate and animate beings.

'The actions to be rewarded concern, in particular, the safeguarding of the natural environment, the struggle against genocidal pollution, the safeguarding of the vegetable and animal species, animal protection, the teaching of the relations between humans and non-humans, the fight against speciesism and more generally, all actions tending to render efficient the Universal Declaration of the Rights of Animals, the Universal Declaration of the Rights of Plants and the Universal Declaration of the Rights of Nature which is drafted by Prof. Georges Heuse. The declarations and the Order of Nature will stimulate the perception of the cosmic integral Unity in human species.

There is no international nor national order comparable to the Order of Nature; the existing orders regard human beings as humans, and not as members of the community of Nature. The Order of Nature will be considered as the first supranational Order and the first planetary model.'

This Vedic vision of the Indian seers of ancient vintage is our proud heritage. The radiant light of this world of harmony and non-violence must persuade all humanity to adopt what Prof. Heuse, President of the World Foundation of Quality of Life, has called the Universal Declaration of the Rights of Nature. Animal Welfare, plant culture, organic and inorganic chemistry of existence find fulfilment only when everyone is conscientised into acceptance of the Universal Declaration of the Rights of Nature. The text of the Declaration is shown in the Annexure. This declaration was drafted by Prof. Georges Heuse (Belgium), President of the World Foundation for the Quality of Life (University of Ghent), author of the Universal Declaration of the Rights of Animals (1972) and proclaimed on 15th October, 1978 at UNESCO. I advocate the adoption of this declaration by Bharat of the Buddha and Gandhi and inspire humanity world-wide to attain harmony with everything everywhere.

Mobilise people's compassion to activise animal welfare legislation

The universality of divinity is a fundamental faith of Indian humanity rooted in the Rig Veda and manifest in the spiritual core of all religions. "The ancients have stated that God sleeps in the mineral, awakens in the vegetable, walks in the animal and thinks in man". The unity that runs thro' Creation is thus a basic truth. Nature has thus an integral relation with *animalia* and *homo sapiens* is an inseverable part of the evolutionary spiral, the highest peak of ecological ascent. The ecological and environmental preservation is vital for life to survive on earth. These great values are reflected in our Constitution, a rare good fortune and a binding recognition. The State and the citizen are duty bound to promote and preserve ecology and environment as mandated by Arts. 48A and 51A.

Justice to animal citizens is as basic to humanism as social justice is to an exploited people. You are no true Hindu, Buddhist, Jain, Parsi, Christian or Muslim if you do not accept the indivisible unity of Creation and the power of the invisible Creator. So it is that love of animals, in the widest connotation, is integral to the divine vision. Be you secular or spiritual, ecological fundamentals compel us to a compassionate relationship with our sub-human brethren. Here, indeed, is the starting point of the deeper awareness of the harmony of Nature, *Karuna* and *Ahimsa* as a part of our cultural heritage.

The philosophical perspective of Animal Welfare is thus part and parcel of our cultural heritage. Every time cruelty is practised on man or beast or bird or insect, we do violence to the Buddha and Mahavira. Every torture on an animal and every export of animals is a sin to the memory of the founders of Bharatiya Samskar.

Rukmini Devi, that gracious lady who symbolised kindness to animals in her person, moved Jawaharlal Nehru to pass a legislation and thus we have to-day the Prevention of Cruelty to Animals Act, 1960.

Laws are decorative pieces on the Statute Book unless there are powerful movements supportive of their provisions. The anatomy of the 1960 Act has powers and, functions and infrastructure and has the funding and control of the Government. Cruelty to animals is an offence and experimentation on animals is regulated but not abolished. Performing animals in circuses and otherwise for exhibition imply torture and so the Act has provisions for policing such performances and exhibitions with a view to prevent cruelty. With all this and one or two later amendments, cruel practices are continuing in the land where the cow is sacred, compassion is a constitutional duty but torturesome entertainment, bleeding, butchery, animal sacrifice and other forms of cruelty are still extant. Sans people's movement, cruelty to animals will never, cease.

Monkeys were exported for terribly cruel experimentation abroad but because of the agitation and propaganda led by Rukmini Devi, the Central Government banned this brutal export. I wonder whether, in the present hunger for acquisition of foreign exchange, the Government of our Republic, which casts a fundamental duty of compassion to all living creatures, may revive the despatch of frog and cattle meat and even monkeys, forgetting that the image of Indian culture depends not on the dollars earned by exports but by the values we cherish and the homage we pay to the Founding Fathers of Bharat's Samskar.

There are other ways of inflicting cruelties on animals, including non-vegetarian food and attractive dresses and other fancy goods. How true is the PETA appeal! The People for the Ethical Treatment of Animals (PETA), argues:

> *"If we want to help animals, the most important place to start is with our own lifestyles.*
>
> *What we eat, wear and use has a direct impact on the lives and deaths of animals. Every time we visit the grocery store, the pharmacy, or go shopping for sweaters or shoes, we vote with our consumer dollars for or against animal suffering.*
>
> *Here's how a few changes in our buying habits can help thousands of animals.*
>
> *The most direct contact most people have with animals is at mealtime—they eat them.*
>
> *No, we don't need animal products to live a healthy life."*

Leonardo Da Vinci is worth a quote:

> *"From an early age, I have abjured the use of meat, and the time will come when men will look upon the murder of animals as they look upon the murder of men".*

Now that the western winds are blowing and the consumerist craze is growing, there is a new peril to our animal brethren. For instance:

> *"The fur industry wages war on wildlife, the lucrative leather market bolsters the cattle industry, and wool comes from sheep who suffer unanaesthetized tooth grinding, tail cutting and unskilled shearing. Angora is made from the hair of rabbits bred for a fast-growing intensive confinement industry.*
>
> *By choosing products made with canvas, cotton, nylon, acrylic and other materials, we can clothe ourselves beautifully without endorsing cruelty.*
>
> *The more we realize that animals have real lives like our own, the more courage we have to inform others. Most people prefer not to be associated with animal suffering, but may not know the facts. Our silence must not contribute to their ignorance."*

Animals, said Henry Beston, an author-naturalist, are "other nations, caught with ourselves in the net of life and time". Like us they too fear pain and death. To torture them and derive delight by cruel sport, soft flesh and caging birds and lions is heartless imperialism and brutal exploitation. Animal's fur skin or flesh do not add to our inner joy but yet we like the feel, look and taste of these pieces of animals even though without these sordid additives, life can be healthier and lovelier.

A pamphlet titled: 'How Killing Them is Really Killing Us' instructively tells truths we should not hide.

> *"Public health and safety are jeopardized because researchers, encouraged by the multi-billion dollar animal supply industry, are reluctant to break away from old fashioned, unreliable and costly animal testing methods.*

Fifteen thousand children were born with severe deformities because Thalidomide, a sedative prescribed to pregnant women, was found "safe" after extensive animal testing. More sophisticated non-animal tests showed Thalidomide dangerous to the development of the fetus. Recently, E-Feral and Diethylstilbestrol have caused serious side effects and death in humans.

> *Many alternatives, such as highly developed computer and mathematical models, cell and tissue cultures, already exist. Emphasis must be placed on discovering and perfecting other alternatives."*

Tender calves are delicate meat. So too are dog's meat and snakes (skinned alive) and cockroaches and insects eaten in some odd countries practising crimson ideologies. To be carnivorous is to be cannibalistic, since man too is animal. But even in America, the exemplar for mundane pleasures, an awakening is discernible.

Meat is extremely high in saturated fats and in cholesterol, which accumulates in arterial walls and is a major factor in heart attacks.

Large amounts of antibiotics, growth stimulants and chemicals must be fed to meat animals now reared in crowded indoor environments. These chemicals are passed on to meat eaters, weakening human defenses against disease and rendering once helpful drugs useless.

The kidneys of a moderate meat eater must work three times harder than those of a vegetarian to deal with excess toxic wastes found in meat.

During World War II, Denmark and other Scandinavian countries were forced to switch to a non-meat diet due to the food blockade. Mortality rates for males dropped 34%, a world record. With the post-war return to meat eating the rate returned to "normal".

Current animal protection legislation merely protects animals from suffering and dying in public view and from becoming extinct. The differences between other species and ours do not justify prejudicial treatment, slavery and slaughter. The price of changing our habits is, at worst, inconvenience during adjustment. The benefits are to the other animals, our own health and vitality, world hunger and the whole ecosystem.

Truly, history will judge the worth of our "civilization" less by our technological accomplishments than by the way we treat our fellow beings."

'PETA' has a poignant poem on animals in labs which must move our heart if we have any.

"Unseen they suffer,
Unheard they cry,
In agony they linger,
In loneliness they die."

Animal experiments which are becoming more popular and more cruel are a source of severe suffering for innocent animals like mice, rabbits, guinea pigs and monkeys; and now a grave danger has arisen with patents being available in the U.S. for living species and genetic engineering becoming a source for scientific discoveries for mutations. Food, to look attractive and plentiful, draws on the liberal use of agro-chemicals; many of which are toxic, and their toxicity is assessed in laboratory animals. We must discourage the use of such products and encourage the need for safety by buying organically raised crops.

"By buying free range eggs, free range poultry, and meat from non-intensively reared livestock, we encourage the use of systems that are less dependent on animal-tested drugs and vaccines - as well as being more humane".

Likewise, we should avoid processed foods and those with artificial additives. Clothing and household fabrics, cosmetics and toiletries and other attractive consumer items involve, at some early stage, cruelty to animals in chemical experiments. Cruelty-free culture is safe, cheap, and dignified.

Drugs in various forms are being developed and tested in laboratory animals.

Ayurveda, Homeopathy, Unani, Siddha, Acupuncture, Naturopathy, Herbalism, Spiritual healing and other indigenous methods of cure do not involve animal experimentation. Therefore, it is a scientific superstition to insist on animal-experimented curatives. There are alternative therapies. There is a further factor to be remembered. What may work in an animal may not work in a human. More research in new organic foods, herbal cosmetics and other therapeutics can avoid cruelties to our sub-human species.

These days, killing of animals for food is accepted as an inevitable evil. This is not valid, but until people everywhere abjure meat and accept vegetarianism, slaughter houses will persist.

If there is no way of banning killing, abattoirs using minimum violence must be insisted on. Man, in his march towards higher culture and consciousness, has evolved agriculture as against hunting. The question is whether, so long as there is meat eating, we should reduce the pain of killing and make meat hygienic. But if the object is to build macro-size abattoirs to slaughter scientifically on a large scale, it may lead to the elimination of our cattle wealth, thus depleting a large animal resource for earning foreign exchange. This is a perversion of the spiritual essence of our culture and the "PCA Act of 1960". While we should fight animal sacrifice, we must conserve animal wealth in the spirit of Article 48 which casts an obligation on the State to organise agriculture and animal husbandry on modern and scientific lines and to preserve and improve the breeds and to prohibit the slaughter of cows and calves and other milch and drought cattle.

Abattoirs produce meat and meat-eating is prone to cause cancer and other diseases; and the traumatic terminal phase of the animal will add to the toxicity of the butchered beast or bird. The bacteria in raw or cooked meat eventually punish the eater. So it is that vegetarianism is becoming worldwide. Moreover, 16 kgs of foodgrains are needed for the animal body, to add 1 kg. of weight. So we deny grains for human food for boosting animal weight for heavier export and foreign exchange. However clean and well-kept the abattoir, the cattle dragged for slaughter knows by instinct its end, resists and runs and the gory agony and helpless curse in its pathetic eyes make the meat a medium of misery visited on the eater, innocent *tho' he be.*

Nor am I charmed by the cow protection groups who never spend a copper to feed neglected street cattle nor contribute to animal welfare but create religious tension and communal explosion. National interests and people's health are best promoted by habits of diet on organic-manured food and cultivation of aversion for meat for reasons of health, kindness and *satvic* development. Food and character interact.

Dairy products, so good for growth and health, necessitate preserving cattle wealth and improving their breed. We are reaching self-sufficiency in this field, thanks to Operation Flood and Dr. Kurien. Now to import milk powder or dairy products and kill our cows and buffaloes for export of meat is double dependency. Fresh milk, good for medicine, especially goat's milk, may tragically vanish under the globalisation dispensation! How myopic a policy of surrender to MNCs and petro-dollars!

> *"Among the ruminants, the goat in India has unique qualities like small size, clean habits, maintenance of low-grade ration, particularly roughages*

which are usually not used by other animals and converting such roughage into high-protein milk and meat absorbed from diverse ecological resources, with other advantages like early maturity, smaller gestation period, prolificacy (twins, triplets and even quadruplets are common), short interlactation interval and wide range of adaptability. Its milk being easily digestible is recommended for infants, the old and invalids.

It is an ideal animal for those with meagre resources like small and marginal farmers, especially those in the drought-prone areas, and even for the landless. It browses intermittently, quickly moves from shrub to shrub and never destroys the natural vegetation cover as some bigger animals like cattle and buffaloes do. This animal, which efficiently converts the natural vegetation into milk and meat is however wrongly conceived as an animal of denudation of forest cover leading to soil erosion and deforestation. On the other hand, it uses the minimum natural vegetation, without much wastage, to produce meat and milk with maximum protein. In India, as large portions of arable land are marginal in quality, having no irrigation facility, and marginal and small holders and landless are large in number, the goat has an ideal situation for survival and growth, where crop husbandry is not possible or uneconomic and where the masses of the poor have no alternative source of living, the goat supports the survival of the weaker sections of the population." (H.R. Kalia and A.R. Rajpurohit, 1985).

Another significant factor often treated with contempt, calling India as still in the bullock cart age, is the indifference to the drought force and power output of the varieties of draught animals available in the country like bullocks and buffaloes, donkeys and camels, mules and even elephants. If only we utilise the animal power of India, especially in the country side, studies show that fuel shortage and import of oil will disappear. Indeed, the West-biased attitude is the villain of the peace. Similarly, the use of bio-gas, compost and fertilisers, where cattle contribute much raw mass, is being overlooked. China did and does use bio-gas in a big way. Our energy crisis originates in power alienation from native resources.

There are many more uses of animalia, especially since India is blessed with animal abundance. What we need more than prevention of cruelty to animals, is promotion of utility through animals. The 'discovery of India' is never complete until we weave a lively fraternity between the human and animal species.

It is a profound and fascinating thought, in keeping with the new World Human Order, that we give life to a new Universal Animal Order which will be a symbiosis of living Creation with a cosmic dimension.

In a wider vision we must inaugurate a new movement for a Universal Declaration of the Rights of Animals.

All that I have spoken up to now relates to a new pluralism of human and animal mutuality. We have legislations and sacred texts, but the stark question is that in our materialist world with consumerist appetite the animal world and its happiness is drowned in the sadistic delights and dietary pleasures, compounding our savage past and our *asuric* present. To conquer these gargantuan vices and to restore the moral spiritual fibre of humanity we need mobilisation of popular opinion, conscientisation of human conduct and campaigns on a lofty scale harnessing social action groups and organising kindness clubs everywhere. High on the agenda of the nation must be the methodology of awakening and mobilising through mass action, sans which law will be dead letter and the Animal Welfare Board an apparatus without animation.

A tearing and raging campaign by NGOs is the only passionate alternative. We must reach schools, teach college students and publicise cruelty to animals as horrendous inhumanity through our media. Villagers may listen for a while but the winds of consumerist change are corrupting the minds of good people. So the task is hard, pamphleteering is necessary; exhibitions of animals in agony in cages and zoos, in circuses and pet-shops must brought luridly to the notice of civilized sections.

Governments must be pressurized to do the right thing lest India's image and cultural heritage suffer severe damage. Let us not betray the generations from the Buddha to Gandhi. Our tryst with destiny, made when India awoke to Independence, included an imperative that the nation will 'wipe every tear from every eye'. This applies to our animal brethren, parrots, doves and other birds with broken wings to be sold as pets or for delicate dish, lions and tigers cramped and doped in small cages and even elephants and bears brutally treated to perform impossible feats. Let us begin the crusade for compassion and we must win because our case is just.

The Spiritual Dimension of the Animal Citizen

Wrote William Blake:

> *"A dog starv'd at his master's gate*
> *Predicts the ruin of the State,*
> *A horse misus'd upon the road*
> *Calls to Heaven for human blood.*
> *Each outcry of the hunted hare*
> *A fibre from the brain does tear,*
> *A skylark wounded in the wing,*
> *A cherubim does cease to sing".*

Yes, elsewhere, Blake wrote an inspired piece on that creature 'The Lamb':

"Little Lamb, who made thee?
Dost thou know who made thee?
Gave thee life, and bid thee feed,
by the stream and o'er the mead;
Gave thee clothing of delight,
Softest clothing, woolly, bright;
Gave thee such a tender voice,
Making all the vales rejoice?

Poets have a sensitive soul and when we wish to soar to sublime heights let us turn to them. With a vision of all Creation, Walt Whitman poetized:

"I think I could turn and live with animals, they are so placid and self-contain'd,
I stand and look at them long and long.
They do not lie awake in the dark and weep for their sins,
They do not make me sick discussing their duty to God,
Not one is dissatisfied, not one is demented with the mania of owning things,
Not one kneels to another, nor to his kind that lived thousands of years ago,
Nor one is respectable or unhappy over the whole earth".

How glorious is bio-diversity in its range of versatile beauty, variegated wonder and unity in divinity! He who does not feel a togetherness in this dimension is deficient in higher culture or deeper religion.

Compassion for and fellowship with life, whatever its form, a feel for every spark of divinity whatever its form, a feel for every spark of divinity whatever its evolutionary gradation, makes the whole world kin. More explicitly, S.T. Coleridge told us of God and identity of all of us with that supreme, universal Being whom the sages called Brahman. I have often felt that all creation is the individualised manifestation of Cosmic Power, be it plant, beast or man. "The ancients have stated that God sleeps in the mineral, awakens in the vegetable, walks in the animal and thinks in man. [Psychic Exploration - A Challenge for Science - Edited by John White - Page 681]

The lines of Coleride are here:

"He prayeth well, who leveth well
Both man and bird and beast.
He prayeth best, who loveth best
All things both great and small;
For the dear God who loveth us,
He made and loveth all".

The beautiful divinisation and ecological integration gives meaning to our constitutional obligation (Article 51A) of compassion to all living creatures. To my mind, this expansion of consciousness is the spiritual foundation for animal welfare and the recognition of animal citizenship. Gandhiji, like St. Francis of Assisi, was able to see a brotherhood among Humans, Animals and Birds.

Profound is the thought, solace to the soul is the joy of life in all its forms. Such is the validation of all that we do to defend the Order of Nature as an inviolable creed.

The savage in man having lived a hunter's life in the past, dies hard and takes delight in flesh-food forgetting that some life has been killed to make for this carnivorous palate.

Smt. Indira Gandhi spoke sensitively when she warned that "the survival of man is dependant on the survival of animal and plant life". The dynamic unity of ecological species is best brought out by Dr. Yogesh Kumar Arora in an article written in 1987:

> *"Some years ago, the World Health Organisation took up a programme of DDT spraying on Borneo in an effort to control the mosquitoes. It proved very effective but destroyed wasps. These wasps preyed on caterpillars which ate the thatched roofs. So as a direct result of the mosquito control programmes, the hut roofs collapsed. Similarly, DDT spraying to kill house flies resulted in the death of small lizards - geckoes - which preyed on the former. The dead lizards were eaten by cats, which began to die. Eventually, this led to an enormous increase in the rat population, which not only began to invade the houses and consume the food but also spread plague. Finally cats were parachuted into remote Bornean villages to restore the ecological balance.*

In South Africa, a campaign was waged against hippopotamuses. The result was a rapid increase in a debilitating disease called Schistosomiasis, caused by a snail-carried parasite that attacks the human liver. Without the hippos, which served as natural bulldozers, the rivers silted up, the snails proliferated, and Schistosomiasis became a great health hazard.

Buffalo hunters and U.S. Army slaughtered the bull buffalo or bison herds so recklessly thereby 1900, the 60,000,000 bisons that once roamed the continent were almost wiped out. Finally, only few wild bisons were left in the entire United States. Cattle and sheep replaced bison for commercial reasons. But the ecology differed. The buffalos roamed freely allowing grasses to renew themselves but the new owners of the land fenced the pastures. The domestic animals stayed in one place eating the grasses and then the roots. The grasslands were thus destroyed".

The Hindu venerates Vishnu, Siva, Saraswati, Karthikeya and Krishna together with the Eagle (Garuda), the Bull (Nandi), the Swan, the Peacock and the Cow. Even trees are worshipped, not out of superstition, but because of supra-rational understanding. Today the grosser materialism which has possessed the five-star culinary culture is leading to wiping out of various species. A Report to former USA President Jimmy Carter says:

> *"Hundreds of thousands of species - perhaps as many as 20 per cent of all species on earth will be irretrievably lost as their habitats vanish".*

The cruelty towards living creatures, particularly the cattle, driven hundreds of miles, beaten as they walk, is insufferable and the slaughter produces unhealthy meat and stink and releases pathogenic microbes. Animal products are exported for foreign exchange, but the soul of Man is lost in the bargain. Another type of cruelty flourishes with none to protest.

> *"Approximately 10 million birds are taken from wild every year. Perhaps half die before they even reach their destination. Two of the biggest traders are Senegal and India. Between 1970 and 1980 India exported nearly 15 million birds.*

Many experts believe that if this process continues at its present rate the whole ecological balance could be affected".

Life, dear life, God's life deserves fraternal love. That is the spiritual foundation of material prosperity:

"The caterpillar on the leaf
Repeats to thee thy mother's grief.
Kill not the moth nor butterfly,
For the Last Judgment draweth nigh".

A song from *Narmada Bachao Andolan* moves our tears with compassion for creation

Whose are the forests and the land?
Ours, they are ours.
Whose the wood, the fuel?
Ours, they are ours.
Whose, the flowers and the grass?
Ours, they are ours.
Whose the cow, the cattle?
Ours, they are ours.
Whose are the bomboo groves?
Ours, they are ours.

The best ever said with acid pen is by Bernard Shaw:

Darwin taught us not that all men were monkeys once
But that some monkeys have no tails now.

HUMANITARIAN LAW – A HALTING HISTORY OF GLOBAL EVOLUTION

Introduction

Universal compassion is an inalienable component of ancient India's cultural vision in war and in peace. The Buddha renounced a princedom and spent a long life time in the ceaseless search for an end to human sorrow or *dukha*. Asoka, an Emperor who accepted Buddhism as his religion, renounced war as a means of conquest when he beheld the slaughter and ravages of a victorious war he waged. Even amidst the clash of arms *Dharma* shall govern. Such is the Hindu heritage of Manu vintage. The *Manu Smriti* says:

> *Let not the king strike with concealed weapons, nor weapons which are barbed, poisoned or the points of which are blazing with fire.*
>
> *He should not strike when he is on his chariot, one who is on the ground; he should not strike a person who is an eunuch, or who has surrendered or is fleeing from the battle-field or one who is sitting or accepts defeat.*
>
> *Nor one who is sleeping, nor one who has lost his armour, nor one who is naked, nor one who is only a spectator, nor one who is engaged in fighting with another.*
>
> *Nor one whose weapons are broken, nor one who is afflicted with sorrow, nor one who is grievously wounded, nor one who is in fear.*
>
> *These are the restrictions on an honourable warrior, which every soldier must remember during war.*
>
> *This is the declared law for warriors, which a Kshatriya must not transgress, if he were to remain unblemished, when he is fighting with his foes in the battle-field. He should fight only in accordance with Dharma, which is hence called Dharmayuddha.*

(Manu VII; 90-93 and 98; quoted by M. Rama Jois, Legal and Constitutional History of India; Vol. 1 pp.663-664)

Indeed, the Constitution of India, in keeping with this sublime cultural estate, has provided in article 51 an obligation on the State to promote international peace and security and foster respect for international law and treaty obligations in the dealings of organised peoples with one another. A fundamental duty has been cast on every citizen of India, to promote harmony among all the peoples of India, to have compassion for living creatures and to develop humanism and abjure violence. Thus the ethos of Indian humanity is in keeping with humanitarian legality whose logical culmination is a world of non-violence. The Delhi Declaration of Rajiv Gandhi and Gorbachev (1989) summons the finest spirit of India's composite cultural heritage when it advocates a war-free global humanity. The deeper springs of humanitarian law distinguish the people of India by the very fact that *Dharmayuddha* or the humanitarian regulation of warfare is in the very blood of Indian history.

Dynamic peace or *Shanti* in the Indian context, has a higher dimension and involved an inner spiritual conversion. Not mere cesssation of armed conflict by formal regulations governing warfare but by a spiritual urge and divine perspective manifested in the Indian ideology of *Shanti*. Not a utilitarian object of reducing suffering but a humanitarian goal of ensuring a necessary environment for the unfoldment of the personality of every individual or community. The emphasis is not on the materialistic values of managing combat to avoid bloodshed but a lofty outlook of reverence for life which is at the root of the Indian idea of humanism. Indeed, when the Bible speaks of "the peace of God which passeth all understanding", there is a deeper perception of divine impulse than a mere superficial suspension of armed conflicts.

The Growth and Development of IHL

Be that as it may, the world wove humanitarian jurisprudence over the centuries out of the sight of terrible suffering and the humane response to such savagery and inhumanity. Monographs, as early as the 14th century, and paragraphs in theological works of the Middle Ages, were moved by considerations of obviation unjust wars and farewell to macabre inflictions.

Humanitarian law appeared in Europe during the Age of Enlightenment. "They formulated a fundamentally humanitarian doctrine according to which war should be limited to combat between soldiers, without posing a threat either to the civilian population or non-military objects."

It was mostly in Geneva that humanitarian law was developed, eventually to spread over the western world and to acquire the name of the "Law of Geneva". The Red Cross also owed its origin to Henry Dunant, a citizen of Geneva, who was so horrified by the bleeding scenes of wounded soldiers abandoned on battle fields, that he made it his mission to find ways and means, in law and practice, to protect the victims of war. At the instance of the International Standing Committee for Aid to Wounded Soldiers (The Committee of Five), the Swiss Government convened a conference in Geneva, which resulted in the signing, on 22nd August, 1864, of the Convention for the Amelioration of the Condition of the Wounded in Armies in the Field.

To emphasize the Swiss origins of the movement, the decision was soon taken to adopt, as the distinctive sign of the protection granted to wounded soldiers, the inversed colours of the Swiss flag (a white cross on a red ground), that is to say, a red cross on a white ground. In 1880, the Committee of Five became the International Committee of the Red Cross (ICRC), a name it has kept to this day. One by one, numerous National Societies were created and they adopted the same emblem. At the request of certain Islamic countries, the Red Crescent was also admitted. The red lion and sun was used for a time by Iran, but was abandoned (in 1980) in favour of the red crescent.

(International Review of the Red Cross, July-August 1984.)

The penetrating spirituality and compassion which inspires the Indian view of humanitarianism is reflected in a way in the culture and constitution of the Indian people. Nevertheless, when we come to social terms and strengthening of a world human order, international law cannot twinkle as omnipotence in the sky nor shine futilely as the vanishing point of enforceable jurisprudence. So it is that a viable system of humanitarian laws, instrumentalities and operational strategies become necessary. Manu's *Yuddha Dharma* has practical value and ethical justification in this sense. World law, injecting humanist justice into brutal war victimisation, is still a slow soul-less process.

International jurists have distinguished between *human rights law* and *humanitarian law,* but the current trend is to view both through a compassionate lens to find overlapping areas, without being allergic to compartmentalisation of the two branches of jurisprudence. One of the effective means by which humanitarian processes in situations of armed conflicts operates is the use of the sublime instrument of the ICRC (International Committee of the Red Cross). In our world of ubiquitous belligerances and butcheries verging on genocide, the perennial presence of the Red Cross and the Red Crescent is a source of comfort to the conscience of peaceful peoples everywhere. The ICRC teams, in spite of risks, do a great job in areas of conflict intra-national and international. Some of the less known activities of the ICRC deserve to be disseminated. A.G. Noorani, in an article has brought out facts which citizens must know:

For instance, little is known about its services in tracing people separated from their families, known as the tracing activities. Throughout 1993 the ICRC's regional delegation based in New Delhi, which covers India, Bangladesh, Bhutan, Nepal and Myanmar, monitored the situation of some 1,75,000 refugees from Sri Lanka in some 130 camps in Tamil Nadu and, what is more, kept them informed of ICRC activities in their home country. The ICRC continued to provide tracing services for refugees who had been separated from their families and to issue travel documents to various refugees temporarily residing in India and accepted for permanent resettlement in third countries.

(A.G. Noorani, Economic and Political Weekly,
Vol. XXIX No. 30, p. 1897)

As the report makes clear, in law the work of the ICRC is based upon the Geneva Conventions and their Additional Protocols and the resolutions adopted by the International Conferences of the Red Cross and Red Crescent. Almost all states are bound by the famous Four Geneva Conventions of August 12, 1949, which in times of armed conflict, protect wounded, sick and shipwrecked members of the armed forces, prisoners of war and civilians. On June 8, 1977 two protocols were adopted. They reaffirm and amplify the humanitarian rules governing the conduct of hostilities (Protocol I) and to extend the body of humanitarian law applicable in armed conflict which is not of an international character. India has ratified the Geneva Conventions but it has not ratified the Additional Protocols. The Annual Report reveals that during his visit to New Delhi on March 9 and 10, 1993, the Delegate-General for Asia and Pacific of the ICRC raised with both—the home secretary and the foreign secretary "the question of India's possible ratification of the Additional Protocol as a support for a regime of international non-violence. Thou shall not betray article 51 of the Constitution.

Conscience and compassion in legal locomotion, through sad scenes of horror and cries of wounded soldiers left in pitiless neglect, pressured the International Committee of the Red Cross to sponsor the Geneva Conventions and the Additional Protocols. These international agreements establish the principle of disinterested aid to *all victims of war without discrimination* since they, through wounds, capture or shipwreck, are no longer enemies or capable agents of hostilities but merely suffering and helpless humans.

The Geneva Conventions

Humanitarian law, with its humble origin in Geneva, has become now a bulwark against the harshness, hardship and horror of war. The Humanitarian Conventions have been tuned to the current needs of a warring world with no holds barred and adapted to defend bleeding mankind victimised by victory through massacre. In between the two World Wars, the ICRC has laid the foundation for the establishment of a number of new Conventions like the Convention of the Treatment of Prisoners of War. Indeed, this was signed in the summer of 1929 and has protected millions of captured soldiers. With the end of World War II, the need to develop the humanitarian dimensions of International law gained momentum. Governments and National Red Cross Societies facilitated the progress of this process:

> *Three former Conventions had to be revised: the Geneva Convention of 1929 for the Relief of the Wounded and Sick in Armies in the Field, the Xth Hague Convention of 1907 for the adaptation to Maritime Warfare of the Principles of the Geneva Convention and the 1929 Convention on the Treatment of Prisoners of War. Furthermore, there was rugent need for a Convention for the protection of civilians, the absence of which had, during the world conflict, led to such grievous consequences.*
>
> (The Geneva Conventions of August 12, 1949; International Committee of the Red Cross; p.2.)

After careful scrutiny of the Draft Conventions, the matter came before the Conference held in Stockholm in August 1948. Considerable thought was bestowed on the various drafts and then emerged the 1949 Geneva Conventions.

The following four Conventions were the product of the fruitful debates:

I. *Geneva Convention for the Amelioration of the Condition of the Wounded and Sick in Armed Forces in the Field, of August 12, 1949.*

II. *Geneva Convention for the Amelioration of the Condition of Wounded, Sick and Shipwrecked Members of Armed Forces at Sea, of August 12, 1949.*

III. *Geneva Convention relative to the Treatment of Prisoners of War, of August 12, 1949.*

IV. *Geneva Convention relative to the Protection of Civilian Persons in Time of War, of August 12, 1949.*

After further Committee discussions, the Final Act was signed by a large number of countries. The general provisions of the Final Act deal with international conflicts, enemy occupation and civil war. They were followed by other special provisions which the Contracting Parties may conclude dealing with the inalienability of the right of protected persons, the duties of Protecting Powers, the activities of the International Committee of the Red Cross and Conciliation procedure between the Contracting Parties. Further refinements were made to the texts, one of the important contributions being the attempt to define "War Crimes" in International Law. However, the fact remains "War Crimes" eludes precise definition although its ghastliness does help identify, even without formal definition, that class of crimes.

The Geneva Conventions are now universally accepted, more or less. The first Geneva Convention deals with the *wounded and sick*, even as the Geneva second Convention (the Maritime Convention) is an extension of the first and applies to *maritime warfare*. The third Geneva Convention with its annexes deals with *prisoners of war* and vastly extends the Hague Convention on the same subject. Humane regulation of the conditions of those in captivity is an aspect of international law. The Prisoners of War Convention has helped numberless people involved in conflicts. Even so, it has been felt that agencies appointed to look after prisoners' interests and ensure that regulations concerning them are applied in full, should be as independent as possible of the political relations between the belligerents. This subject has been dealt with at length in the third Geneva Convention.

The fourth Geneva Convention (*civilians*) is a constructive contribution in the humanitarian dimension to international law. This new Convention is an elaboration which runs into several Articles and prohibits in particular:

(a) *Violence to life and person, in particular, torture, mutilations or cruel treatment.*

(b) *The taking hostages.*

(c) *Deportations*

(d) *Outrages upon personal dignity, in particular humiliating or degrading treatment, or adverse treatment founded on differences of race, colour nationality, religion, beliefs, sex, birth or social status.*

(e) *The passing of sentences and the carrying out of executions without previous judgment pronounced by a regularly constituted court affording all the judicial guarantees recognized as indispensable by civilized peoples.*

There is no need in this article to go into greater detail except to state that now we have a fairly comprehensive set of Geneva Conventions. Even so, to witness the brutal violations of the humanitarian spirit in the maddening passion of battles among brothers of yester years, with Big Power Megalomania and even the U.N. Peace-Keeping Forces, makes us realise 'the petty done and the undone vast' in the field of humanitarian jurisprudence. World War II was a macro-scale disaster with scenes of savagery no eye had seen before, no heart conceived ever and no human tongue could describe the desperate theatres of terror. This global holocaust had a seminal impact of awakening humankind to the urgency and adequacy of forbidding and punitively dealing with belligerent barbarity in the name of human dignity and peaceful progress of all peoples.

The March of Law after World War II

The League of Nations addressed but minimally the laws to humanize war, even as, prior to World War I, precious little was achieved by way of regulating the laws of war. The optimist view that the world would disarm itself after the holocaust proved illusory. And the irony of it is that the Conference convened in Geneva in 1925 to end the arms trade, produced a treaty on supervision but never entered into force due to lack of ratifications. The use of poison had been frowned upon by the Hague Regulations of 1899 and the Conference of 1925 strengthened it through the Protocol for the prohibition of the use in war of asphyxiating, poisonous and other gases and of bacteriological methods of warfare. The ban of 1925 has not won its humanitarian objective as is seen from the contemporary world struggling to extinguish sources of chemical warfare.

After the Second World War, the United Nations showed the same indifference as the League of Nations *vis-à-vis* armed conflicts and the law of the Hague. However, the principal progressive step taken was the adoption, through an International Conference held in 1954 at the Hague under the auspices of the UNESCO, of the Hague Convention for the Protection of Cultural Property in the Event of Armed Conflicts. Cultural property of perpetual value is a global asset which shall not be a prey to the ravages of war. The International Military Tribunal at Nuremberg was also a great step to validate and integrate the punitive jurisprudence against war criminals.

In 1949, the International Law Commission, an organ charged with codification of international law, it is unfortunate, did not place the law of armed conflicts on its agenda. However, the London agreement (August 1945) for the prosecution and punishment of the major war criminals was a positive step in the development of international law in this area:

> *The Charter defined the three categories of crimes coming within the jurisdiction of the Tribunal and for which there would be individual responsibility (crimes against peace, war crimes, and crimes against humanity). It also stated the principles of individual criminal liability, notably, the principle that the official position of defendants would 'not be considered as freeing them from responsibility or mitigating punishment', and the principle that an order would not free a defendant from responsibility but might be 'considered in mitigation of punishment if the Tribunal determines that justice so requires'.*
>
> *In 1946, the General Assembly of the United Nations in Resolution 95(1) reaffirmed these principles, as reformulated by the International Military Tribunal in its judgment (and therefore usually referred to since as the "Nuremberg principles") as generally valid principles of international law.*
>
> *(Frits Kalshoven, Constraints on the Waging of War, ICRC Publication, pp.18-19)*

The nuclear menace attracted the attention of the United Nations and the very first Resolution ever adopted by the General Assembly:

> *Provided for the establishment of an Atomic Energy Commission, charged inter alia with the task of formulating proposals designed to eliminate nuclear weapons from national armaments. In the ensuing years, the aspect of disarmament, apparent in these terms of reference (as opposed to the wartime use of the weapons at issue), largely dominated the debate, both in the Commission and its successors and in the General Assembly.*
>
> *On 24 November, 1961, however, the General Assembly, voted a Resolution focusing more particularly on the aspect of possible use of nuclear weapons. Resolution 1953 (XVI) declared that such use would be utterly unlawful on a number of grounds. The potential effect of this firm opening statement was considerably reduced, however, by part two of the Resolution which somewhat lamely requested the Secretary-General "to consult the governments of Member States to ascertain their views on the possibility of convening a special conference for signing a convention on the prohibition of the use of nuclear and thermonuclear weapons for war purposes", and to report on the results at the next session. (Needless to say, no such special conference was convened). The authority of the Resolution was reduced even further by the fact that quite a few States (with the United States, the United Kingdom and France, all three nuclear Powers, among them) voted against or abstained; the vote was 55 in favour, 20 against and 26 abstentions. Yet despite these defects, it is certainly permissible to see in the Resolution an expression of world opinion as represented in the General Assembly."*
>
> *(Resolution 1(1) of 24th January, 1946)*

1968, the Human Rights Year, twenty years after the birth of the U.N., found active interest being taken in the law of armed conflicts and at the Teheran Conference diverse aspects of human rights in such situations figured in the discussions. The Teheran principles gave better protection to civilians, prisoners of war, and upheld the prohibition of chemical warfare.

Skipping for a moment the momentous decision of the United Nations in favour of national liberation of colonies—an important chapter in World Law—, the General Assembly proceeded to impose restraints on certain mass weapons of destruction. The United Nations entered the area of law of war in the nineteen seventies and dealt with three aspects:

> *First and foremost, they contributed to cutting through the taboo resting on the subject. Secondly, they highlighted the idea of protection of human beings in their fundamental rights even in times of armed conflict. And thirdly, they made a valuable contribution to the debate on a number of specific questions, notably that of the position of guerrilla fighters in wars of national liberation.*

Thus the United Nations, in its sweeping concern for human rights, began to consider respect for human rights in armed conflicts. This lovely confluence between human rights and humanitarian justice is a beautiful blend of compassionate jurisprudence in its global and local applications recognised by the UN. In this context, the General Assembly Resolution 2444 (XXII) makes the first ever reference to the ICRC. Likewise, the ICRC, in its operations, began to be functional beyond the law of the Hague and took a new initiative by making a statement of fundamental principles governing the law of war, which no one would dare to deny. We may, at this stage, observe the happy process of two streams merging where the Hague and New York came together in one main flow. This close interaction between the UN and the ICRC is a strong foundation for the humanitarian law of armed conflicts in contemporary circumstances.

Many developments have taken place since and a whole new literature which deals with even nuclear weapons and protection of civilian populations and a host of other matters such as that "starvation of civilian as a method of warfare is prohibited", has done us proud as a civilised generation, ghastly praxis to the contrary notwithstanding. Frits Kalshoven rightly stresses:

> *The international humanitarian law of armed conflict, rather than being an end in itself, constitutes a means to an end: the preservation of humanity in the face of the reality of war. That reality confronts us every day; the means remains therefore necessary.*
>
> *The questions at issue in humanitarian law, no matter how varied and complicated, can be reduced to two fundamental problems: viz., the problem of balancing humanity against military necessity, and the obstacles posed by the sovereignty of States. Sovereignty and military necessity are the two evil spirits in our story—and evil spirits we will not be able to exercise soon. Although many, nowadays, regard State sovereignty as the main obstacle to a better society, it is cherished by the States themselves, both old and new, as their greatest asset and as an indispensable means to safeguard them against encroachments of their territorial integrity and political independence. Any ostensible interference with, or supervision of, their behaviour in time of armed conflict is interpreted all too quickly as an encroachment of this precious sovereignty.*

One outstanding but dreadful gap needs to be highlighted, despite the impressive edifice of law. Here again, Frits Kalshoven may be aptly quoted:

> *It should also be noted that none of the humanitarian treaties in force deals specifically with the use of nuclear weapons—quite irrespective of the expectations one might have of such a regulation. Another marked deficiency, and one that is far more directly noticeable in daily practice, arises from the absence of a set of special rules for guerrilla warfare, whether*

in the context of international or internal armed conflict. Warfare at sea was also largely disregarded during the recent conferences. Despite all this, the conclusion remains unaltered that much has been achieved in the sphere of international humanitarian law of armed conflict.

It should immediately be added that the adoption of treaty tests is a far cry from their application in practice. Observance of the Treaty obligations-restricting belligerent parties in their conduct of hostilities is rarely an automatic thing: more often than not, it has to be fought for step by step, so as to prevent an armed conflict from degenerating into the blind, meaningless death and destruction of total war. This battle for humanity is not always won. Yet, each partial success means that a prisoner will not have been tortured or put to death, a hand grenade not blindly lobbed into a crowd, a village not bombed into oblivion: that, in a word, man has not suffered unnecessarily from the scourge of war.

The gruesome agonies of war-torn people and the distress and destruction even in civil wars desiderate a dynamic law of life which is the humanist root of *Dharma*. The soul of the Red Cross is alleviation of suffering, internal or international. As Nocrani tersely sums up:

The legal bases of any action undertaken by the ICRC may be summed up as follows:

In the four Geneva Conventions of 1949 and Additional Protocol I, the international community gave the ICRC a mandate in the event of international armed conflict. In particular, the ICRC has the right to visit prisoners of war and civilian internees. The Conventions also confer on the ICRC a broad right of initiative.

In situations of armed conflict which are not international in character, the ICRC also has a right of initiative recognised by the States and enshrined in the four Geneva Conventions.

In the event of internal disturbances and tension, and in any other situation which warrants humanitarian action, the ICRC has a right of humanitarian initiative which is recognised in the Statutes of the International Red Cross and Red Crescent Movement and allows it to offer its services to governments without that offer constituting interference in the internal affairs of the State.

Article 3, common to all the Four Conventions provides for ICRC's role 'in the case of armed conflict not of an international character occurring in the territory of a signatory to the Convention.

Asoka's great rock edicts and Jesus Christ's Sermon on the Mount are the ceaseless springs of love, caring and sharing, which create humanitarian law and operate the Red Cross Movement.

One may conclude with the great thought of Grotius:

> *"I must retrace my steps, and must deprive those who wage war of nearly all the privileges which I seemed to grant, yet did not grant to them. For when I first set out to explain this part of the law of nations I bore witness that many things are said to be 'lawful' or 'permissible' for the reason that they are done with impunity, in part also because coactive tribunals lend to them their authority; things which nevertheless, either deviate from the rule of right (whether this has its basis in law strictly so called, or in the admonitions of other virtues), or at any rate may be omitted on higher grounds and with greater praise among good men."*

The right to life and righteousness in social conduct are together the foremost human right, be it in the domain of internal or international rule of law. Sans humanitarian law, between 'civilised' nations and savage tribes 'thin partition do their bounds divide'. The finest hour of Humanitarian Law and International Red Cross arrives when, in the field of human conflict or calamity, the sick and wounded, the innocent civilians and helpless victims of armed conflict, find a source of justice and a means of rescue and hope; and then history will proclaim that never in the field of human conflict or harrowing suffering was so much owed by so many to so few. That is the globalisation of compassion by law and deed.

HUMANITARIAN JURISPRUDENCE WITHIN THE PARAMETERS OF A GLOBAL DEMOCRATIC ORDER

Introduction

The crescendo and diminuendo of cultural history, the ebbs and tides of civilization and the rise and fall of compassion and humanism have their roots in the fluctuating evolution of *homo sapiens* from his animal ancestry. The human march through the ages is interesting study, but most impressive is the mental, kindlier eras of search for and consolidation of finer fellowships and happier relationships among peoples so as to weld a global order where what we may call the human soul (for want of a more expressive word) asserted itself against the brute in him to shape, albeit imperfectly, a glorious vision of a noble system recognising and respecting that great value, the diversity and dignity of the human being amidst wars and crimes and villanies and tortures. Such is the dark and dim but gradually more humane saga of humanitarian law and human rights which are ideological first cousins but identity-wise distinct. They belong to the same family of humanism as is evident from two statements, one of a great jurist Lauterpacht and the other of a famous statesman, Adlai Stevenson. The protection of human personality and of its fundamental rights is the ultimate purpose of all law, national and international, wrote Lauterpacht. Adlai Stevenson, once referring to the United Nations, said: "Human rights are at the core of everything we do or try to do". Among the purposes of the United Nations, the Charter of the United Nations highlights the following idea, revealing the proximity of humanitarian justice and respect for human rights:

> *To achieve international co-operation in solving international problems of an economic, social, cultural or humanitarian character, and in*

promoting and encouraging respect for human rights and for fundamental freedoms for all without distinction as to race, sex, language, or religion."

At the bottom is the concept that the peoples of the United Nations are determined "to reaffirm their faith in fundamental human rights, in the dignity and worth of the human person".

An Aside

Where personhood is in peril and injuries intimidate or afflict, human rights come into play and humanitarian justice in certain specialised situations operate. Prof. Hampson distinguishes the international law of armed conflicts and international human rights law. She argues:

"The starting point of the two bodies of rules is fundamentally different. Under the international law of armed conflicts, it is lawful to kill enemy combatants. Under international human rights law, an individual cannot be killed except in closely defined circumstances. This difference of focus is found throughout the respective spheres of the rules. So, for example, the international law of armed conflicts sees people in terms of groups, whereas human rights law generally sees them as individuals. It is less clear whether the philosophical origins of the rules diverge as much as this would suggest. That requires one to identify those origins.

In the international low of armed conflicts, States have accepted obligations with regard to their treatment of certain classes of people. With the incorporation of up-dated elements of the Hague Law in the 1977 Protocols, States have accepted obligations with regard to their conduct of military operations which consequentially affect a class of non-combatants civilians.

Whilst protocol I sets certain limits on operations in one's own territory and protocol II elaborates the previously rudimentary provision, common Article 3 of the Geneva Conventions, dealing with non-international armed conflicts, the bulk of the provisions deal with the treatment of the sick, injured and shipwrecked and prisoners of war. Human rights law, on the other hand, is most commonly invoked by nationals seeking to restrain the activities of their own State and its agents. This difference does not, of itself, establish that the two bodies of rules operate in different spheres. It is eloquent testimony to the fact that the situation which sovereign State are most reluctant to subject to the rule of law is that where the State itself is threatened by armed force within its frontiers. Even then, non-derogable human rights continue to apply and the international law of armed conflicts increasingly claims its reach into such situations.

It is submitted that it is unprofitable to emphasize the undeniably different cast of the two bodies of rules."

The learned author further points out that the Geneva Conventions and the Hague Law have received ratification from many States. Curiously enough the USA, UK, and France have not ratified the important Protocol I, although they are very vocal about human rights. Small wonder that the U.S. used methods in the Iraq War which are incompatible with humanitarian law. Use of unlawful weapons, intentional attack on civilians, torture and ill-treatment of prisoners are the guilt of some great power;

> *The States whose armed forces have been responsible for some of these breaches include the USA, USSR, France in Algeria and the UK in Northern Ireland. Those are all sophisticated, technologically developed forces. All took part in World War II. It was the experiences in that conflict which led to the formulation of the Geneva Conventions in 1949. All those States have ratified both the Geneva and the Hague Conventions. States which have breached the rules also include newly independent States, such as Sri Lanka and Nigeria and a newly created State, Israel. The record of Central and Latin American States in the conduct of internal armed conflicts is too well known to need detailing. In other words, the breaches of the international law of armed conflicts know no barriers of culture, level of development or technological sophistication. There are no enforcement of the rules. Whilst Commanders-in-Chief authorise blanket bombing of free fire zones which include civilian villages, Lieutenants and Captains are tried for the killing of civilians.*

We, thus, see that if human rights are to be a reality humanitarian law must bind and command respect from big powers. As Hampson points out:

> *Respect for the international law of armed conflicts has declined to such a point that it is actually counter-productive to elaborate new norms until the rehabilitation of the existing rules has been effected. To foster the myth of glorious apparel when the Emperor's clothes are in fact disintegrating could prove fatal. The health of the Emperor demands that he be given real clothes, however, dull and drab.*

Back to the main theme

The Universal Declaration of Human Rights accords recognition to the inherent dignity and inalienable rights of all members of the human family as the foundation of freedom, justice and peace in the world. The humanitarian context of the Bill of Human Rights is brought out in the Universal Declaration which condemns "disregard and contempt for human rights (which) have resulted in barbarous acts which have outraged the conscience of mankind." Thus the basic value is the dignity and worth of the human person which is defended by the twin branches of universal norms manifested in humanitarian law and human rights.

Indeed, as we study the international instruments, we perceive certain declarations and conventions against torture and other cruel, inhuman or degrading treatment or punishment. There is a great area where the two branches of the law overlap although more stress is laid on human rights than on humanitarian law. In one sense, humanitarian law, in its global sweeping semantic, will embrace large parts of human rights strictly so called. It is the manifesto of the human person that matters, whether in war or in peace.

This unifying feature of humanising jurisprudence may be illustrated in many ways. Let us take but one. The Convention against Torture and other Cruel, Inhuman or Degrading Treatment of Punishment is a clear example of how the Charter of United Nations recognises the equal and inalienable rights of all members of the human family as the foundation of freedom, justice and peace of the world. The quintessence of this Convention, indeed, its conscience, is that no one shall be subjected to torture or to cruel, inhuman or degrading treatment or punishment. The U.N. Declaration on the same point as early as 1975 discloses the determination of the U.N. to stamp out torture. Article 2(2) and (3) of the Convention mandate:

> *Article 2(1) ...*
>
> *Article 2(2) No exceptional circumstances whatsoever, whether a state of war or a threat of war, internal political instability or any other public emergency, may be invoked as a justification of torture.*
>
> *Article 2(3) An order from a superior officer or a public authority may not be invoked as a justification of torture.*

This command to States, covers not merely citizens of that State but also *'any person'*. Nor indeed can torture be a tool to extract evidence. A committee against torture is to be established under article 17, its members being elected by the States parties and so, its character is transnational. Article 22(1) declares the competence of the committee to receive and consider communications from and on behalf of individuals who claim to be victims of violation by a State party of the provisions of the Convention. Its findings shall be forwarded to the State party concerned and the individual. Thus it is apparent that cognizance is taken of violations by State by an international committee under the aegis of the U.N.

The International Covenant on Civil and Political Rights spreads out into a spectrum covering human rights and humanitarian law. Article 2 of the Covenant obligates each State party to respect and to ensure the benefits conferred thereby, regardless of national origin. Likewise every Member State undertakes to make legislative provision for the defence of these rights.

Very significantly, article 4 emphasises that even during times of public emergency, which threatens the life of the nation, the State parties shall not make any derogation from articles 6, 7, 8, 11, 15, 16 and 18. The right to life is thus protected even in war-like situations. Immunity from torture and slavery situations are equally prohibited. Nor shall freedom of thought and religion, conscience or belief be threatened. Article 20 applies in war and in peace and reads:

(1) *Any propaganda for war shall be prohibited by law.*

(2) *Any advocacy of national, racial or religious hatred that constitutes incitement to discrimination, hostility or violence shall be prohibited by law.*

There is no reason to think that the Human Rights Committee under the U.N. has no jurisdiction even where the violation is only of Humanitarian Law. In short, while autonomy, identity and the distinctive character of Humanitarian Law and Human Rights Law are discernible, the laws may overlap and even the agencies for enforcement may be the same.

In large part, international law is based on custom and convention constituting rules enforced upon States by international opinion or by the threat or fear of war. Salmond speaks of a kind of conventional law having its source in international agreements:

> *'to be binding, says Lord Cockburn 'the law must have received the assent of the nations who are to be bound by it. This assent may be express as by treaty or the acknowledged concurrence of Governments, or may be implied from established usage.'*
>
> *Because there is no supreme machinery to enforce international law, the proposition largely holds good even today that international law is the vanishing point of jurisprudence. However, world opinion as the sanction of global pressure on violating sovereigns, is a strong factor. Humanity, speaking in unison against outrageous inhumanity amounting to war crimes and the like, is also a potent force, supportive of humanitarian law. Suffice it to say that a common goal is the driving force of both humanitarian law and human rights law. The Second World War, which witnessed massacres and tortures on a macro-scale inflicted heartlessly, roused the conscience of mankind into action and catalysed the evolution of the two branches of law to the point of convergence in good measure. States but also covers rules governing the brutal treatment of some of their own nationals. When we speak of human rights in a larger sense, its focus is not limited to internal matters within the State, but gradually spreads to international spheres. For instance "while stressing that peace is the underlying condition for the full observance of human rights and war is their negation, the International Human Rights Conference of 1968 also*

proclaimed that even during the periods of armed conflict, humanitarian principles must prevail."

The adoption of the 1977 Protocols additional to the Geneva Conventions of 1949, containing rules that correspond to inalienable human rights, accentuated still further the convergence between the rules of humanitarian law and certain human rights rules. Moreover, by adopting Protocol II on the protection of victims of non-international armed conflicts, which supplements and defines Article 3 of the Geneva Conventions, and by stipulating in Article 75 of Protocol I and Article 4 of Protocol II respectively the fundamental guarantees concerning the treatment of persons affected by an international or non-international armed conflict, legislators achieved further progress in ensuring respect for human rights.

Around this "hard core", the mutual influence of human rights law and humanitarian law has emerged in resolutions adopted by the United Nations General Assembly and Security Council. For example, in the case of the conflict in the former Yugoslavia, and particularly with respect to Bosnia-Herzegovina, references to humanitarian law are particularly in evidence in number of resolutions adopted in 1992 by the U.N. Security Council and condemning violations of humanitarian law and human rights.

Similarly, recent practice by non-governmental organisations concerned with local conflicts, such as the International, is significant. There are many examples of recourse to both human rights law and humanitarian law provisions in conflict situations. Indeed, human rights violations in a non-international armed conflict are often simultaneously serious violations of the provisions contained in Article 3 or in Protocol II.

Humanity is indivisible and law, so long as it is meant to serve life, must have common features and applications nationally and internationally. Nevertheless there are specific characteristics of each in situations of armed conflicts:

Humanitarian law, which is an emergency law applicable in armed conflict, has aims which are more limited yet more clearly defined than are those of human rights law; its provisions are mandatory. Human rights law is applicable at all times, hence also in time of armed conflict, but its applicability is restricted by derogation clauses (except for the "hard core: rights) or by the manner in which it is interpreted by the bodies entrusted with its implementation.

Whereas the rules of international humanitarian law governing the protection of the individual in time of armed conflict are set forth in detail and adapted to circumstances, human rights law is more general and its provisions are not always applicable in practice to the various categories of persons affected by an armed conflict. Thus, the advantage of the former is that it covers violations both by governments and by armed opposition groups, whereas the latter deals primarily with the responsibilities of governments.

One fact stands out glaringly distinguishing the two branches of law. The monitoring and implementation of human rights law and humanitarian law are fundamentally different. For instance, the ICRC deals with humanitarian law while instrumentalities under the United Nations concern themselves with human rights law. The two branches are thus complementary but the victims to be protected in both cases are human beings. It is good to emphasise that the United Nations agencies and NGOs must support humanitarian law even if human rights law is a primary commitment. It may be sufficient to say that 'thin partition do their bounds divide.' They have their own autonomy and identity, separate institutions and systems. But their credal essence is common. It is that both swear by the individuals' right to life "and to physical and moral integrity; and security of person, which provides each individual with legal guarantees and stresses the prohibition of reprisals, collective punishment, hostage-taking and deportations."

The constituencies for humanitarian and human rights laws are sometimes different. Humanitarian law must control the armed forces, para-military groups and even the armed police. They must have specific structures and methods within States such as the International Red Cross and Red Crescent. While Human Rights regimes are widely known, humanitarian justice is less familiar and needs intensive campaigns to awaken the poignant depths of humanity's conscience. The thrust, however, of humanitarian law is to regulate hostilities, blend it with humanism and limit human hardships. Even amidst the clashes of arms the laws shall not be silent. Barbarity is not sanctioned even in war and brutalities against humanity are forbidden even under cover of warlike conditions. The terrible inflictions of the two World Wars costing unconscionable suffering for countless human beings, has left on mankind's mind indelible stains and incurable wounds. So it is that to save succeeding generations from the untold traumata of war and other ultra-national, yet shocking savageries that humanitarian law has emerged to alleviate the incalculable cruelties that follow upon civil war and international conflicts.

Humanitarian law is usually traced to the law of Geneva and the law of the Hague. But history records the spiritual beginnings of these legal principles even to ancient revulsions and moral compulsions. Together they constitute the heritage of humanist jurisprudence in its national and international dimensions. The law of Geneva consists of Four Conventions of 1949 and two Additional Protocols of 1977. The International Committee of the Red Cross, inspired the Geneva Corpus Juris and the Red Cross in times of conflicts seeks legal basis for its action of protection and assistance. The law of the Hague regulated hostilities and recognises military necessities and the preservation of the States. The Hague Conventions of 1899 revised in 1907 regulate the conduct of combatants and the protection of civilians. Geneva and The Hague shade off into each other. The protection of cultural property and restriction on the use of certain conventional weapons are part of humanitarian law. The First Geneva Convention which begins the statutory story of humanitarian law is of 1864 vintage even as the law of human rights springs from the Universal Declaration of 1948.

Early human societies governed by the law of the jungle used violence and inflicted unspeakable atrocities with no mercy. Savage tribes even in our own times behave with such bloody horror. Even so, some norms did prevail in the hoary past. Among the many instances of the laws of war, we may mention the *Mahabharata* war and the rules of Manu regulating conduct of warriors which read as fresh as modern guidelines:

> *Warriors are forbidden to kill enemies who are disabled and those who surrender; they must send the wounded back home after they are healed. Some provisions are amazingly similar to those in the Hague Regulations of 1907 on the laws and customs of war. Thus, for example, not all means of combat were permissible: all barbed or poisoned weapons were forbidden, along with flaming arrows; requisitions of enemy property were regulated, as were the conditions for detention of prisoners; it was forbidden to declare that no quarter would be granted.*

The *Dharma,* as a moral-jural concept, had its own dimension for the regulation of war. The noblest example of a victorious battle and the bleeding consequences sensitising the victor emperor into abandonment of war itself is that of Asoka who, in 225 B.C., invaded Kalinga but was disgusted by the horrors of war. So he declared in inscriptions that still exist that he would abjure war.

To him H.G. Wells pays the highest tribute thus:

> *Amidst the tens of thousands of names of monarchs that crowd the columns of history their majesties and graciousnesses and serenities and royal highnesses and the like, the names of Asoka shines and shines almost alone, a star. From the Volga to Japan his name is still honoured. China, Tibet and even India though it has left his doctrine, preserve the tradition of his greatness. More living men cherish his memory today than have ever heard the names of Constantine of Charleneague.*

This great epic Asoka chapter notwithstanding, a Hitler, notorious for the might of the long knives, wages a savage war in our macabre century. On the ashes of his monstrocities has been built the sound system of humanitarian law. It is tragic but true that the A.B.C. weapons (Atomic, Bacteriological and Chemical) still menace mankind. Other incendiary weapons including napalm and flame throwers, fragmentation weapons, such as cluster bombs, small calibre, high velocity projectiles which may have effects like those of dumdum bullets, and finally such perfidious weapons as delayed-action bombs which endanger relief efforts, land mines and booby traps intimidate humanity.

Even today deadly biological weapons with hostile potential stalk the earth. A ghastly picture, apart from the huge arsenal of atomic bombs America corners, is recently reported.

The Buddha and Zoraster notwithstanding, the world needs a strong regime of humanitarian law.

The dawn of the *Pax Romana* brought some sense of peace and respect for law and Marcus Aurelius representing a golden age. Jesus Christ, preaching love and compassion, elevated human consciousness into a divine principle. Likewise, there have been interludes.

Thinkers like Grotius laid a basis for the law of nations. Even he did not rule out war, but wrote, "In war, we must always have peace in mind". Subsequent history occasionally witnessed the humanisation of war and a world of violence was punctuated by treaties of friendship and peace. We must remember that even as early as 1785 the treaty reached by Frederick the Great and Benjamin Franklin stipulated that "in case of conflict the parties would abstain from blockades and that enemy civilians would be allowed to leave each country after a certain time. Prisoners of war would be fed and lodged in the same manner as the soldiers of the detaining power and a man of confidence would be allowed to visit them and provide them with relief".

Other similar documents formed the source of customary law which provided the following:

1. Hospitals shall be immunized and be barked by special flags, with identifying colours for each army.
2. The wounded and sick shall not be regarded as prisoners of war; they shall be cared for like the soldiers of the army which captured them and shall be returned to their own side.
3. Doctors and their assistants and chaplains shall not be taken as captives and shall be returned to their own side.
4. The lives of prisoners of war shall be protected and they shall be exchanged without ransom.
5. The peaceful civilian population shall not be molested.

Despite refined pages and pageants of history we come across Hiroshima and Nagasaki where so civilised a country like America bombed out human numbers in minutes creating scenes of woe, the like of which no eye had seen, no heart conceived and no human tongue can adequately tell. The Vietnam invasion was savageous writ large.

Parallel with these cruelties, we have positive ideas such as from the French Revolution and the American Declaration of Independence which have become the patrimony of the human race. Still we must mention Napolean who, as a conqueror, had hardly any concern for the wounded.

> *What he needed was new and healthy cannon fodder to feed his war machine. Mortality was therefore appallingly high in the army and the suffering of the wounded was frightful. One need only recall the horrors of the retreat from Russia, still memorable despite all that has happened since. The great dramas have their sordid aspects, and Austerlitz is quite properly described as a 'medical Waterloo'.*

The Birth of the Red Cross

An epic event with benign omen opened from the consciousness of the sensitized sector of the medical profession when some doctors were shaken up by the horrendous Napoleanic barbarity. Field hospitals were fired upon. Captured doctors were kept prisoners. Cold-blooded massacres were ordered on surrendered soldiers. These outrages found some famous doctors raise their voice in constructive protest. However, later military adventures like the Crimean War stabbed humanity's conscience, and then came Florence Nightingale (Lady of the Lamp) a young English woman who could not keep silent seeing the bleeding chaos in the war-torn cosmos. She successfully reduced the toll of death and misery and the British were impressed with her compassionate work. Other blood-curdling events followed with heavy loss of life and a young Swiss, Henry Dunant, organised a First Aid Movement in scenes of war. He wrote an impassioned book which ignited the sensitivity of society. He made two proposals: the first was to form a volunteer Relief Society in each country. Thus was midwifed the Red Cross Society. His second proposal was that nations meet in a Congress and adopt an inviolable international principle to provide a sound legal foundation for the protection of military hospitals and medical personnel. This merciful idea gave birth to the Geneva Convention. Later, a five-man committee met in February 1863 and formed itself into the founding body of the Red Cross and promoter of the Geneva Convention. In 1880 it adopted the name now globally recognised as the International Committee of the Red Cross (ICRC). Thus a humane wind of change conscientised mankind and repelled the charge that society deified money and forgot mankind. Humanitarian justice took concrete shape in some measure by this spirit of internationalism. The Red Cross is today the salutary symbol and kindly expression of the spirit of compassion in action and rescue operation in times of peace and war where unjust suffering is inflicted on innocent non-combatants, wounded soldiers, all others caught in military cross-fire and like predicaments or victimised by blockades and similar inhuman or treacherous measures during hostilities, civil wars and international conflicts. Red Cross is compassion in action, shelter, comfort and medical deliveries to alleviate agonies and response to the Gandhism summons, to wipe every tear from every eye where human life signals distress calls. It is institutionalised humanitarian justice as an oasis of succour in war-like situations. This international agency was founded by the Geneva Convention (1864) to assist those wounded or captured in war. All branches use the symbol of the Red Cross on a white ground, except Muslim branches which use the Red Crescent and Iran which used a Red Lion and Sun. Red Cross is now deeply established in humanity's consciousness as a lighted candle of love amidst the encircling gloom of terror and horror.

Humanitarian law is no longer Geneva and the Hague law but transcends these Conventions to reach cosmic stature and seek expression through the United Nations and other transnational instruments. This expanding horizon of humanitarian law is the vision unfolded at the International Conference of the Red-Cross in 1969 in Istanbul with the adoption of a declaration:

> *Proclaiming, among other things, that man has the right to enjoy lasting peace and live a full and satisfactory life founded on respect of his rights and his fundamental liberty. This goal can be achieved only if human rights, as set forth and defined in the Universal Declaration of Human Rights and the humanitarian conventions, are respected and observed.*
>
> *This message is as vital as ever today; it indicates the path to be followed if the "two crutches" that are humanitarian law and human rights are not to become the white canes of communities blinded by violence and barbarity.*

The gap between the "two crutches" slowly fades, since the spiritual urge behind humanitarian and human rights laws is the personhood and human dignity which inalienably inheres in every member of the world family. Right in the Universal Declaration of Human Rights in 1948, this trend of unity of concern in the duality of juristic expression is manifest. Indeed, the developments in both branches converge and diverge but the central concern is what I may call the *manifesto of the Person Everywhere.* This silent movement nourished by civilised people is the locomotive of humanitarian law which marches slowly from the depraved, deprived and desperate human sectors amidst mass hysteria and hell hostilities to hope, help and humanization. It is a spiritual adventure, a lofty project, a haven for those in distress offered by the collective goodness latent in each of us and gushing out at the right of unjust suffering and taking on jural forms with the support of community conscience. Illustratively, we find in the Declaration of St. Petersburg of 1868, provisions prohibiting the use of certain projectiles in times of war:

> *Considering that the progress of civilization should have the effect of alleviating as much as possible the calamities of war....*"; *1899 Hague Convention II with Respect to the Laws and Customs of War on Land: "Animated by the desire to serve.......the interests of humanity and the ever increasing requirements of civilisation.....*

Here is humanism restraining barbarism. That is the nidus of both branches of humane law. The inspiration for broadening the blended brew of humanist jurisprudence was enhanced by international non-governmental organisations and the United Nations in armed conflict situations. For instance, the International Commission of Jurists (ICJ) has relied on human rights and humanitarian law in some of their investigations. The ICJ study on the butchery of human rights in the Philippines illuminates the use of both branches of law. The Commission argues for article 3, common to the four Geneva Conventions and Additional Protocol II being applicable in conflict situations. The report observes that forced displacements of civilians are violations of human rights as well as of article 17 of Additional Protocol II.

Another example of NGOs fertilising this humane jurisprudence is the report of America's Watch and the Women's Right Projects with reference to Peru's armed conflicts and cruelties. There also article 3 is pressed into service. The findings are frightening:

> *There can be no doubt that the Shining Path violates with remarkable cruelty and abandon the prohibition of common article 3 against violence to life and person, murder and the passing of sentences and carrying out of executions without previous judgment by a regularly constituted court.*

Amnesty International (AI) while dealing with the abuse by non-governmental entities emphasised that the primary concern of AI is regarding State violations, but took the view that abuses by political non-governmental entities or armed opposition groups such as the 'Shining Path' in Peru should also come within the scope of AI's concerns. The taking of hostages, arbitrary killings, laying mines where civilian trains pass, throwing bombs in market places are also the concern of humanitarian law. This is an important imperative in a world of reckless terrorist indulging in human right abuses and brutal inhumanities. Addressing these concerns, AI first acknowledged that there is "a continuum of political non-governmental organizations which ranges from those which are very similar to governments to those organizations with little in common with governments". Given this fact, AI chose to focus its resources on "those entities having greater control over people, territory and the use of force". Additionally, the Council called for the development of criteria by which political non-governmental entities could be distinguished from groups falling outside AI's work, such as common criminal organizations. Second, recognizing that, "there are many unclear areas in armed conflict situations", AI decided to concentrate its attention on "patterns of abuse by non-governmental entities" which are contrary to principles of international humanitarian law. Third, the organisation expressly endorsed opposing the taking of hostages or deliberate and arbitrary killings by non-governmental entities whenever such opposition is practical "using any appropriate technique, including directly addressing the entity".

AI looked into the South African situation and conditions in Angola, Sudan and Liberia where human rights abuses by armed opposition movements bloodied peaceful life.

Even the United Nations has strengthened humanitarian law. The Security Council Resolutions relating to Bosnia-Herzegovina in 1922 illustrates U.N. reliance on humanitarian law. Security Council Resolution 764, 13th July, 1992 expressly affirmed justifying its action that "all parties are bound to comply with the obligations under international humanitarian law and in particular the Geneva Conventions of 12 August, 1949, and that persons who commit or order the commission of grave breaches of the Conventions are individually responsible in respect of such breaches".

In certain cases, "Humanitarian organisations and states are requested to compile information concerning breaches of humanitarian law, "including grave breaches of the Geneva Conventions", for submission to the Security Council. The Security Council expressly finds that "the Council will need to take further measures under the Charter" should the parties fail to comply with resolution 771.

We find other instances also of deep concern of the U.N. such as in former Yugoslavia:

> *Resolution 780 again expressed the Security Council's "grave alarm at continuing reports of widespread violations of international humanitarian law occurring within the territory of the former Yugoslavia" and reaffirmed the demand made in resolution 771 for all parties to cease and desist from all breaches of international humanitarian law.*

Thus, we have a progressive development in international law while the Universal and the International Covenant are supplemented by the Geneva Conventions of 1949 ratified by 185 countries. Humanitarian law applies to the military and the law enforcement officials and covers abuses by Governments and armed opposition groups while International Human Rights law ordinarily limits itself to the responsibilities of Government.

Of course, this is yet a grey area of law which must be strengthened by peoples consensus worldwide.

The Future of Humanitarian Jurisprudence

Human Rights have the sanction of U.N. Instruments and the Bangalore Principles (The ten point resolution of judges and jurists of the Commonwealth who met in Bangalore early in 1988) justify the assumption that fundamental rights and freedoms contained in international instruments constituting an impressive body of jurisprudence is of practical relevance and value to judges and lawyers generally. National courts may interpretatively use these international norms in deciding cases. Moreover many constitutions incorporate human rights which facilitate judicial enforcement. Adopting the same process there is bright prospect for judicial enforcement directly or indirectly of humanitarian laws as part of international obligations member states undertake. Article 51 of the Indian Constitution fosters respect for international law and undoubtedly humanitarian law commands such respect and can claim judicial acceptance. There is scope for jurists and judges to expand on this thesis, as part of the humanisation of legal systems, thereby developing a humanitarian legal culture applicable internally and internationally. It is apt to recapitulate the conclusion reached at the International Judicial Colloqium in Harare in 1989:

> *Fine statements in domestic laws or international and regional instruments are not enough. Rather it is essential to develop a culture of respect for internationally stated human rights norms which sees these norms applied in the domestic laws of all nations and given full effect. They must not be seen as alien to domestic law in national courts.*

Once we accept humanitarian justice as a vision and mission we can make an impact on the country by building up a cadre of humanitarian lawyers who will campaign to conscientise the community, the administrators and the judiciary about the great importance of this burgeoning branch of law. Indeed, the ICHLR and ICRC must find functional fulfillment in educating the student community, NGOs and other social activist not merely in the anatomy of humanitarian justice but also in the *locus standi* of social action groups to seek enforcement of this law. Exposure of law teachers to human justice in its humanitarian dimension and making available relevant literature to law schools are important and immediately feasible. Indeed, the Bar Councils and Bar Associations in the country should respond to the call of humanitarian law and promote its progress. Our governments should be converted to the view that humanitarian law justice are not hostile to governments and their policing functionaries. On the contrary it enhances the prestige of any administration which respects the ICRC and ICHLR and recognises that humanitarian justice only enhances the prestige of the State.

It is heartening to see that the European Community, the African and American Communities and other new movements and organizations are incorporating and enforcing human rights. Then why not humanitarian rights which have more critical relevance in our world of violence, terrorism and ubiquitous hostilities, while the State itself gets occasionally implicated, be barriered by international authority?

Conclusion

I appeal to the Indian State and society, to the NGOs with commitment to humanitarian law and to the States functionaries and echelons as well as the Bench and the Bar, with their professional power, to serve as beacon lights in the murky area where vast number of humans are victims of abuse of power. Let us salvage society from savagery and stand by Gandhi and humanity.

This spiritual dimension, this revolution in thinking is best stressed in that Magna Carta of our century's last chapter, *viz.*, the Delhi Declaration which is an address jointly made by Bharat and the (now dismembered and dead) Soviet Union to a world trundling violently, wickedly, to a fall and signed by Rajiv Gandhi and Gorbachev.

The Declaration set forth the following principles for building a nuclear-weapon-free and non-violent world:

1. Peaceful co-existence must become the universal norm of international relations:

   In the nuclear age it is necessary that international relations are restructures so that confrontation is replaced by cooperation, and conflict situations resolved through peaceful political means, not through military means.

2. Human life must be recognised as supreme:

   It is only man's creative genius that makes progress and development of civilization possible in a peaceful environment.

3. Non-violence should be the basis of community life:

   Philosophies and policies based on violence and intimidation, inequality and oppression, and discrimination on the basis of race, religion or colour, are immoral and impermissible. They spread intolerance, destroy man's noble aspirations and negate all human values.

Such is the concept, conscience and basic structure of humanitarian law and justice.

WOUNDED NATURE *vs.* HUMAN FUTURE

Divinity is manifestation of humanity and creative plurality. Jurisprudence 'in its cosmic dimension assumes its majesty and glows in its glory only when this magnificent subject from its micro to macro vision embraces the infinite aspects. It has been said most wisely. How comprehensive the rule of law is luminously expansive. If dharma in its parameters reaches out to creative wonder the subject of my lecture is vistaramic as explained above.

Having due regard to the several considerations involved, I chose a subject of current relevance and poignant portent ,"*Wounded Nature* v. *Human Future*". Nature is bleeding, amidst hi-tech glitter and profit-hungry adventures while our future is flickering and our survival somber, what with Man's torturous inhumanity to Nature and avaricious injury to culture.

Let me write a prefatory note before I begin the discussion. A holistic vision of Creation, which itself is the manifestation of the Absolute (taking in, as it does, the Unmanifest and the Manifest), is the spiritual legacy of ancient Indian vintage. So it is that the Constitution, in Article 51A, mandates compassion for all creation, promotion of humanism and harmony and protection of natural environment and ecology. This sublime ideology embraces all Nature, organic and inorganic matter and human and other species, each being a part of an integral whole. *Esa Vasyam idam sarvam* (God inhabits all creations) is the vedic wisdom,—a vision of the unity in divinity, diversity, and the happy synthesis of materialism and spiritual universality. Pluralism, in its phenomenal existentialism, is not negated but subsumed in the unitive perception of plurality as a play of the Supreme in its evolutionary spiral. In a broad perspective, Nature is the material manifestation of *Brahman*, and the human is the highest life form in this progressive process, the long march of the *Atman*, in human embodiment, towards the Infinite Absolute which is the celestial destination defined by different religions in divergent ways. Materialists, using dialectical tools, read through the contradictions in the Manifest, a struggle towards higher synthesis. But scientists and religionists agree that Nature is too sacred and inviolable to be traumatized by ecologically and environmentally hostile technology and hedonist thanatology. A finer harmony between nature and man is the basic condition of human survival and advance towards a better world. This is scientific sanity, unity in divinity and dynamic modus vivendi between development and human aspiration for happiness. The integral yoga of nature and man is thus fundamental to civilization and gross distortion of this beautiful balance will claim a painful price from humanity. This profound realization is the creedal essence of ecology, environment, conservation of nature and sustainable development. Such a revolutionary vision is the locomotive of human progress, this prolegomenon serves to explain the theme of my Lecture: "*Wounded Nature* v. *Human Future*".

The advocacy of wild life preservation, animal rights, vegetarianism and environmental protection have their roots in a new ethic of universal compassion inscribed long ago in the rock pillars of Emperor Asoka. The opposition to a host of insensitive operations such as sealing, whaling, wild life hunting, cattle slaughter, fur garments mid luxuries in diet and dress involving cruelty to creatures, animal experimentation for cosmetics and curative guinea pig methods can be traced to a vibrant humanism and green movements which transcend the coarse, unconscionable hungers of the savage stand in still lingering human personhood.

There is a spiritual connection between environmental and animal rights and harvesting of seals and other hunting operations carried to commercial excess. The following quote is typical of the ecology, economy and ideology connectivity that is gaining ground as part of the green campaign:

> *"A spiritual bond between Native hunter and animals is certainly implied in the invocations and allusions made by many environmentalists (see, for instance Udall 1962) to the deeper ecological understanding of native peoples. The best-known example of environmentalist – native kinship if found in the literature distributed by the Greenpeace.*
>
> *An ancient North American Indian legend predicts that when the Earth has been ravaged and the animals killed, a tribe of people from all races, creeds and colours would put their faith in deeds, not words, to make the land green again. They would be called 'The Warriors of the Rainbow', protectors of the environment".*[1]

---

1. George Wenzel, *Animal Rights Human Rights*, 1984, p. 134.

This higher perception of cosmic holism and social and moral interaction creates the reality of a single cognitive community and cultural identity that is the essence of egocentrism. Protest movements against commercial exploitation of seals and killing of other wild life are fuelled by a new awareness of justice for humbler sub-humans as the conscience of compassion for all living creatures—'regardless of whether it affects human beings, non-human beings or the Earth herself'. In sum, homosapiens, to be worthy of his spiritual - ethical status, must shed his carnivorous, morally callous appetite which is vulgar, vicious and too violent to be consistent with the values which mark the milestones of progress. In lines of penetrating, simplicity, Coleridge versified:

> *"He prayeth well, who loveth well*
>
> *Both man and bird and beast".*[2]

This is not a return to crude Nature worship nor primitive animistic pantheism but a refinement of the soul which resists the materialistic corrupt consumerist indulgence masked as pursuit of happiness. What is at risk is finer humanness, consonance with Nature and commitment to future generations which are the first charge on our power to use natural resources. Our glorious global future lies, not in a reversion to promitivism and asceticism and hands-off nature and its abundant bounties, but in a lovely, lively balance which sustains material development without ravishment of nature, pollution of environment and extermination of ecological excellence.

> *"We owe it to our ancestors to preserve entire those rights which they have delivered to our care: we owe it to our posterity not to suffer their dearest inheritance to be destroyed".*[3]

Our Constitution has mandated that, "The State shall endeavour to protect and improve the environment and to safeguard the forests and wild life of the country".[4]

Again, in another provision, writ in strong diction is the command:

> *"It shall be the duty of every citizen of India... to protect and improve the natural environment including forests, lakes, rivers and wild life, and to have compassion for living creatures".*[5]

The future is not a beggar eating what left-overs the present leaves on the table but the rightful heir to the bequeathment of the estate preserved prudently as trustee.

---

2. 'The Ancient Mariner', Part VII.
3. Junius, Letters: Public Advertiser, 1769-71.
4. The Constitution of India, Article 48A.
5. *Id.*, Article 51A(g).

The biosphere sustains us all. To preserve it is the path to progress. To pollute it is the route to ruin—may be today, may be tomorrow. Survival through suicide is the nostrum of those who wish us to wink at pollution as the necessary price of progress. Humanism and law must call the bluff. To muddle and bungle, to omit and abet, the rape of the earth is to dig the grave of humanity.

Justice to Nature is investment in life's unsullied joy:

"There is a pleasure in the pathless woods,
There is rapture on the lonely shore,
There is society where none intrudes,
By the deep sea, and music in its roar;
I love not Man the less, but Nature more,
From these our interviews".[6]

Man is nature's best promise and worst enemy. The ancients have stated that God sleeps in the mineral, awakens in the vegetable, walks in the animal and thinks in man. The sublime prospect that unfurls before civilization through the advances of science is darkened by the devastating misuse of technology to poison and pollute the biosphere and thereby to hold humanity in terrible peril of total liquidation of the life process. Man blinded by myopic profit-making, is matricidal towards Mother Earth and is rapidly making himself an endangered species. India, notwithstanding its primitive rurality and worship of cows, ice, eagles, peacocks, rivers, trees and plants, is violently violating ecological ethics. The compassion of the Buddha and the non-violence of Gandhi stand terribly travestied by the processes of pollution in India that is Bharat.

The unconscionable industrialization, the unpardonable deforestation and the inhuman extermination of living species betray an exploitative brutality and anti-social appetite for profit and pleasure incompatible with humanism and conservationism. The *Rig Veda* praises the beauty of the dawn (ushas) and worships Nature in all its glory. And yet today a bath in the *Yamuna* and *Ganga* is a sin against bodily health, not a salvation for the soul. So polluted and noxious are these 'Holy' waters now that the words of Rev. Martin Luther King Jr. that our scientific power has outrun our spiritual power and that we have guided missiles and misguided men.

Unsocial industrialism and socialist India

Opening wide ajar the doors into Indian industrial space to the multinationals and other corporates without a Code of Conduct,

6. Byron, "Childe Harold's Pilgrimage", C.I. Stanza 179.

environmental safeguards and social accountability and safety enforceable by law effectively is the gravest danger confronting the Nation today. Such a policy placatory corporate power, foreign or indigenous, is fraught with 'Union Carbide syndrome', fatal environmental pollution, lawless ecological injuries and yuppee-yankee cultural subversions, apart from deforestation and even defiance of Indian Justice whose arms may fail to reach corporate giants headquartered abroad. Human health is in peril because of noxious industrial operations of gargantuan MNCs. Even otherwise, the Central Government is somnolescent about environmental preservation, notwithstanding the Constitution. Two illustrations among hundreds I cite from that sensitive environmentalist Maneka Gandhi:

> *"I can give you a number of examples where the absence of proper vision has created very grave problems for the society. Take for instance the PVC fire in Delhi which was been proved to be carcinogenic. Every Delhiite runs a 50 per cent greater chance of cancer at the moment".*
>
> *"Take the case of aluminium foils. Aluminium comes from bauxite which is mined at tiger sanctuaries. Are encroached upon? Are we not going to create a situation where the species will get extinct?"*[7]

Do remember that given an absent and ineffective environmental disaster jurisprudence and forensic infrastructure, we are going to face many more tragic Bhopal assassinations. As Maneka Gandhi mentioned:

> *"Our government thinks that the unemployment problem in the country will get solved when these multinationals set up a number of industries here. The fact is, they are not going to set up labour-oriented industries in the first place to solve the unemployment problem. Secondly, they are not interested in setting up their factories in under-developed areas. The third and the most important danger is, they are coming out with those projects which are banned in their countries for environmental reasons. In effect, we are giving a red carpet welcome to those industries which have been banned in the developed countries. They will pollute the entire atmosphere and we will be compelled to drink polluted water and breathe polluted air. If these indiscriminate sanctions for environmentally hazardous industries continue, India will be doomed forever. We cannot allow that to happen".*[8]

Imagine the culpable governmental failure when we remember the Stockholm Conference and Resolutions.

The United Nations General Assembly passed a Resolution on December 15, 1972, emphasizing the need for active co-operation among the States in the field of human environment. The Resolution has designated June 5, as the World Environment day and has urged

7. Interview with Maneka Gandhi, Sunday Communicator dated 20-8-1995.
8. Interview with Maneka Gandhi, Sunday Communicator dated 20-8-1995.

Governments and Organizations in the United Nations system to undertake on that day every year world wide activities reaffirming their concern for the preservation and enhancement of the environment. On the same day another resolution was passed which provided for institutional and financial arrangements for international environmental co-operation. Among others, provisions were made for establishing a Governing Council for Environmental Programme, Environment Secretariat and Environment Fund.

Indira Gandhi, impressed by Stockholm sought to revolutionize legislatively the environmental safety of the Indian biosphere. Many laws were made, but when pitted against corporate power, laws failed to act and courts in their innocence acquit the guilty ignorantly. The situation is a deepening crisis even in America compounded by official secrecy. Ralph Nader in an old writing, observes about the US:

> *"A burgeoning technology is giving corporations more power than they choose to exercise responsibly. Witness, for example, the domestic chemical and biological warfare called, too charitably pollution. Concentration of economic power develops momentums of abuse in political, social, educational and union areas. Laws and antitrust and regulatory frameworks have been symbols rather than arms of democratic governing, while the corporate regulates control the public regulators".*[9]

Business depredators are too big for the law as the U.C.C. Bhopal tragedy proved. Violations are on the rapidly rising, scale of escalation. As for India, the best commentary on the impotency of anti-pollution Justice is the fact that the Supreme Court has recently directed, "The Central Pollution Control Board to serve notice on the 8378 noxious units, asking them to shift out of the National Capital Region".[10]

Harinder Singh writes in a renowned newspaper on 30th April, 1995:

> *"The first thing that strikes a first-comer to Delhi is the variety of pollution – a unique mix of noise and nose-shattering fumes hit him straight in the face, leaving him more than flabbergasted. For the Capital of India, said to be the third-most polluted city in the world (though some call it even worse than the Mexico City), is the earth's very own version of limbo, if not hell.*
>
> *It all began with Delhi attracting all kinds of petty traders from across the north India, leading, over a period of time, to the creation of a wholesale market, renowned as one-stop shop for all the cheap goods. As the next logical step, a host of very small industrial units sprung up in the city to cater to the needs of the wholesale market. And this put Delhi well on its way to acquiring the status of a polluted city.*

---

9. Introduction, Morton Mintz and Jerry S. Cohen, Amrica Inc. (1972), p. 14.
10. *M.C. Mehta* v. *Union of India*, 1995 (4) SCALE 789.

Along the way, every nook and corner of the city became 'infested' with such riches bringing manufacturing units. Even though the city administration tried to keep a step ahead of the proliferating units by setting up various industrial areas, it all proved futile: new units kept on springing up (literally) in non-conforming areas. Today the situation is such that these units contribute around 10 to 12 per cent to the total pollution.

Though the persons concerned – ministers, bureaucrats, etc.—made all the right kind of noises, it was not until M.C. Mehta, the renowned environmental lawyer, filed a public interest litigation (PIL) before the Supreme Court that the things began moving. Acting on it, the Apex Court, on March 24, directed the Central Pollution Control Board (CPCB) to serve notices on the 8.038 noxious units, asking them to shift out of the National Capital Region".[11]

Vehicular Pollution in Delhi with its 28 lakh automobiles pollute with black fumes the city's streets and nothing has yet been done to arrest this corrupt asphyxiation of the air. Delhi's denizens would soon have to work around with oxygen bags for sheer survival, all because pollution is profit and purity is a little expensive. Corporate power in Delhi, as in Washington D.C. can overpower. The reason is best given by a blunt statement by Woodrow Wilson long ago:

"The masters of the government of the United States are the combined capitalists and manufacturers of the United States... It is written over every intimate page of the record of Congress, it is written all through the history of Congress, it is written all through the history of conferences at the White House, that the suggestions of economic policy have come from one source, not from many sources... The government of the United States at present is a foster child of the special interests".[12]

We live in a world of depletion of natural resources, of desertification, of air pollution, of dangerous radiation, of chemical breakfasts, lunches and dinners more noxious than nutritious. Nature is 'in tears, while exploitation of resources is exasperating as our callous century advances, nature, wounded, retreats. This great contradiction is growing; and now, with CATTASTROPHE accompanied and the Uruguary, Round completed, MNCs have open sesame everywhere. Their rapacious activities have involved all of nature's sub-systems—the biosphere, atmosphere, hydrosphere and lithosphere—inflicting mortal wounds on 'homosphere' where humans live. Science will become the enemy of progress, the balance between man and nature, is shaken. Sustainable development, therefore, must restrain the terrorism of technology.

11. The Financial Express, 30th April, 1995.
12. The New Freedom, 1913, pp. 57-58.

Winston Churchill once warned, in a different context, of the insane consequences of excessive industrialization through homo-lethal, market-manic technology:

> *"The dark ages may return – the stone age may return on the gleaming wings of science; and what might now shower immeasurable material blessings upon mankind may even bring about its total destruction. Beware, I say! Time may be short".*[13]

The Third World is the worst victim, but the First World is also in peril. Ecology and environment, so necessary for human survival, are being wounded fatally leaving our human future in grave danger. A major culprit is capitalism's moneyocratic cannibalism. Even socialist States, with constitutional injunctions to protect nature, bring about disaster through callous industrialization and technological deprivation. The Third World with its poverty, air pollution by soot and rotting garbage fumes and filth, the absence of water supply systems and even toilets and shelter contribute to violation of nature, especially in the absence of ventilation in houses, over-crowding of human and animal co-existence in shocking rurality. While socialist States (none are now left!) have better aliveness to conservation of nature, capitalist countries are ecologically reckless and environmentally deleterious. President Theodore Roosevelt warned arrogant Americans:

> *"The natural resources of our country are in danger of exhaustion if we permit the old wasteful methods of exploiting them longer to continue... The time has come to inquire seriously what will happen when our forests are gone, when the coal, the iron, the oil, and the gas are exhausted, when the soils shall have been still further impoverished and washed into the streams, polluting the rivers, denuding the fields, and obstructing navigation. It is time for us now as a nation to exercise the same reasonable foresight in dealing with our great natural resources that would be shown by any prudent man in conserving and wisely using the property which contains the assurance of well-being for himself and his children".*[14]

In the late 1960s, Stewart Udall, the then Secretary of the Interior (America), sharply rebuked his countrymen:

> *"This nation leads the world in wealth and power, but also leads in the degradation of the human habitat. We have the most automobiles and the worst junkyards. We are the most mobile people on earth and we endure the worst congestion. We produce the most energy and have the foulest air. Our factories pour out more products and our rivers carry the heaviest loads of pollution".*[15]

---

13. As quoted in Krishna Iyer V.R., Environmental Protection and Legal Control, 1992, p. 13.
14. James Rathlesberger (Ed.), The Politics of Devastation, 1972, pp. 5, 7-8.
15. As quoted in Grigori Khozin, Big Business Against Nature, 1984, p. 18.

By the 1970s, an American moved to the Moon, but his launching pad lay, on a field of garbage. Ronald Reagan, then Governor of California told his electorate:

> *"There is no subject more on our minds than the preservation of our environment and the absolute necessity of waging an all-out war against the debauching of that environment".*[16]

Grigori Khozin, the Soviet Journalist quoted reports from the U.S. and said:

> *"In the early 1970s, as a result of a continuous deterioration in the quality of the working environment and of increased pollution at US factories, at least 1,00,000 people were dying every year and another 3,90,000 were being seriously disabled. In the Federal Republic of Germany, the number of people suffering from hearing defects due to factory noise in the 1960s rose 13.5 times compared with the previous decade; and the number of industrial workers suffering from skin diseases has been growing fast. In Sweden, an examination of workers employed in copper smelting works showed an increasing number of deaths due to cancer of the lungs, blood disease, cirrhosis of the liver and cardio-vascular disease. Medical men are alarmed at the continuous growth of hereditary diseases and even deformities among working-class children".*[17]

Many violations by *Corporations of the* laws concerning air and water pollution resulted in fines, but the ecological damage was not arrested. The West European countries also breached nature conservation. Grigori Khozin turns the lens on nature being reduced into a junkyard for all sorts of wastes. For instance:

> *"In the Reserve Mining Company alone has been daily pumping 67,000 tons of waste products containing dangerous elements into Lake Superior - one of the world's largest fresh water lakes (one-twelfth of all the reserves of clean fresh water on Earth). Special conferences convened by the public, court rulings, strict government orders, and even attempts to close down the plant have all failed to force the owners to abandon such 'commercial activity', which brings in an estimated daily profit of 14,000 - 24,000 dollars".*[18]

Pointing out that *many rivers in the West* are industrially polluted, Khozin takes the example of the Rhine and says:

> *"... every year waters of the Rhine pour into the North Sea 41 tons of mercury, 140 tons of arsenic, 1,700 tons of lead, 1,600 tons of copper, 13,100 tons of zinc, and 20 million tons of salts".*[19]

---

16. As quoted in Grigori Khozin, Big Business Against Nature, 1984, p. 19.
17. *Id.*, pp. 19, 20.
18. *Id.*, p. 20.
19. *Id.*, pp. 22, 23.

Limitless impurities have polluted most of the rivers and lakes of the US and, in the air, heavy toxic and other matter harmful to health threaten human life. US corporations experiment with chemical compounds geared to maximum and immediate profit and, in the bargain, spread toxic, carcinogenic and other harmful elements. Capitalism has no body to be burnt, nor soul to be damned. Industrialism even in socialist lands inflicts injury to environment and human life although to a lesser degree. The catalyst of capitalist industry is large profits, ecological havoc caused being of little consequence to its conscience. Agricultural production as an industrial operation, using chemical fertilizers and pesticides and consuming much power, has turned hostile to human health.

Forests are 'lungs' or oxygen factories which sustain life. But the great forests of all continents are vanishing at a dangerous pace and the deforestation-desertification syndrome is a terrible menace to human progress.[20]

Industrial wastes are often highly noxious and the 'advanced' countries corruptly transfer these sources of pollution to Third World countries. Developing nations are seduced into dismantling congenial plants and projects of appropriate technology and the politicians ad compradors of these weaker countries have a honeymoon with big corporations of the North. In the guise of covering the technological gap, corporations of capitalist countries build 'polluter' plants and consumer lollipops, imitative of the exotic Western lifestyle, in the territory of developing nations. When there is an outcry against these 'recolonisation' processes, propagandist unveracity on a big scale is used to take environmental and other evil fallouts as the inevitable price of 'progress'. Thus a fatalist acceptance is induced by drugging the people with false fairy tales about technological blessings. Affluent consumerism, hi-tech developmentalism and macroindebtedness are the troika which pushes Indian political economy 'into conquering Nature callous to consequences.

Today, with the collapse of Communist Kremlin and Crimson East Europe, and the ghastly, goofy thesis of exploitative market-friendliness, liberalization and globalization – Orwellian Newspeak – the South, including India, is jettisoning its Gandhi-Nehru heritage and, in simian fashion, adopting policies ruinous to the poor millions and narcotizing the creamy layers through imported hi-tech from outside. To interdict import of hazardous, environmentally obnoxious ad cost-wise and otherwise

---

20. As quoted in Grigori Khozin, Big Business Against Nature, 1984, p. 26. In the capitalist countries monopolies control the forest resources (in Sweden 75 per cent of the forests are privately owned, in Austria 74 per cent, in Great Britain 69 per cent, in the United States 68 per cent, in France 64 per cent, in Italy 61 per cent, in Japan 57 per cent and in West Germany 41 per cent, and they lay claim to the unlimited use of the forest resources of other countries as well, especially those of the developing nations.

objectionable plants, machines, collaborations and transfers is a hard job since MNCs have great clout with soft States and dubious rulers. They have Super-Power and G-7 pressure on their side to open up markets for foreign 'corporates' ignoring native capacities!

What the world does not know adequately is that big corporations are empires in themselves and can conquer the economies of lesser nations and can control the U.S. Presidency itself. Big business is private government, buys up mass media, manufactures news and views and conceals corporate crimes of robbery of nature, violation of the biosphere and adulteration of food and drink in secret making the consumer a victim. Misinformation about pollutive products apart, the power to prevent and punish giant producers from wounding Nature so as to defend the human future rests on the politicians who run the State apparatus. But the politician is an investment for Big Business and his voice is muted. Listen!

> *"The concentration of economic power, opinion power and political power creates a sort of closed loop. Politicians must raise money from corporations in order to pay the networks the enormous cost of television time. Corporate advertisers call the network tune. And the networks must curry favour with the successful politicians to assure their franchise. The open society seems to be closing - not by conspiracy, but by this mutual dependence".*[21]

The moneyocracy (Corporate Carnivores) contribute to legislators who, as *quid pro quo*, consent, sub rosa, never to use public power to protect public interest when large corporations pollute for profit and kill for more dividends. Open government and public accountability are myths wherever Big Business operates. This is a universal proposition best stated with poignant felicity by Alexander Solzhenitsyn in a letter to Russian Writers' union:

> *"Just the same, it is time to remember that the first thing we belong to is humanity. And humanity is separated from the animal world by thought and speech and they should naturally be free. If they are fettered, we go back to being animals. Publicity and openness, honest and complete – that is the prime condition for the health of every society, and ours, too. The man who does not want them in our country is indifferent to his fatherland and thinks only about his own gain. The man who does not want publicity and openness for his fatherland does not cleanse it of its diseases, but to drive them inside, so they may rot there".*[22]

---

21. Kingman Brewster, Jr. as quoted in America Inc., 1972, p. 195.
22. *Id.*, p. 107 (as quoted).

Open government and free information are the first casualty when corporate power operates against Nature in their felonious art of concealment and illicit control of political government. The pity of it is that in India (and the Third World) the foreign media and transnational companies let politicians fight over communal and other issues, while the Finance, Commerce, Agriculture and Power Ministries and ministers and millions go to sleep or go slow while Big Business, robs natural resources without protest noises and drug the public through buying up the empathies of opinion-makers, and media bosses. Whenever these corporate empires poison our biosphere to aggrandise themselves, they, in business interest, administer long sleeping doses to the Justice System so that litigative pyrotechnics may not create popular consternation. They divert legislators into internal quarrels and brickbats while MNCs cunningly colonise and carry away our natural wealth or cash in on our mines, bio-diversity and 'patent' their own prosperity contra-constitutionally, leaving judges and lawyers to worry about long-pending, never-ending Everest high docket arrears.

These long aberrations have intimate relevance to India too. The world is a village and poisonous proximity makes violence to Nature somewhere the victimization of people everywhere. And our natural resources and people's survival are in peril if we slumber over or admire the investmental infiltration and dark dacoity of billionaire businesses as victory, misled by 'official' versions and media marijuana. The great concern worldwide over conservation of Nature and the human future is grimly evident from the global deliberations in Ruo, Vienna and Copenhagen, in the felicitous diction of Dr. Singhvi, "A Tale of Three cities".[23]

Nature-friendly strategies of human advance are categorical imperatives. The responsibility for resource conservation lies mainly with the industry, not only because it is a major user of resources and a major polluter of the environment, but also because of its vast experience in producing useful products from natural materials, its ability for innovation, and its efficient organizational structure.

Nikita Moisseyev, a Soviet scientist writes, with wisdom and farsighted prospects, about our task to-day:

> *"The growing might of modern industrial civilisation increases not only man's power over nature but also nature's power over man – his dependence on the state of the biosphere. And man may easily cross the fatal threshold which marks the beginning of an unknown and unpredictable evolution of the natural environment in which there may be no place left for him. But the development of powerful technical capacities is accompanied by the development of science which opens up new vistas of progress, points*

23. The Rede Lecture 1993 in University of Cambridge.

out dangers and suggests ways of finding compromise solutions designed to avoid a catastrophe.

The first results obtained in this new line of research are already impressive, for they indicate new, alternative approaches to the present-day global situation and ways of civilisation's further development. Regrettably, these problems are being tackled today by small and separate groups of scientists whose work is almost unknown to the broad public, sometimes even to those on whom global decisions depend. It is necessary, therefore, to unite the efforts of scientists working in different fields.

When I say 'scientists' I do not mean only mathematicians, geophysicists, biologists and other 'natural scientists'. Our colleagues in the humanities can also play a big role. The fact is that natural scientists can indicate the limitations imposed by nature on human activity, but any restrictions or bans relating to human activity can only be put into practice by people. Here is where economists, sociologists and other scholars should take over and show how the spontaneous solution of contradictions must give way to institutions of accord. They should explain to people that the world today is quite different from what it was at the beginning and even in the middle of the 20th century. This means in effect that mankind faces the onset of an epoch that needs new ethics and new morals".[24]

What is advocated is not a primitive preservation of Nature by adopting a policy of strict 'birth control' over industry, preventing modernization altogether. The plea is for socially sensitive and sagacious production process where nature, like a mother, will help human advance, but will not tolerate stabbing her for sucking material blood instead of nutritious milk. After all, the biosphere is the environment of our life, it is the 'Nature' which surrounds us. The integral yoga of human survival and technological development assumes grave dimensions when we understand the implications of the contradiction between conservation, represented by the green movement, and hi-tech excesses promoted by MNCs with profit-oriented gold rush. It follows that to maintain a sustainable human order for India and the world, we must arrest irresponsible industrialization, lest the crucifixion of humanity be the penalty for Nature-callous adventurism. An aware statesmanship, *vis-a-vis* environment, ecology and nature friendliness, quote figures which are too moderate because more damage has been done since, you will do well to realize, that every year 16,000 million tones, of oxygen are burnt up and that 24,000 million tones of carbon dioxide are discharged into the atmosphere. The pollution of rivers, lakes, seas and oceans has reached a dangerous level, with about 50 per cent of all the pollution of the biosphere being caused by the United States, which has less than six per cent of the world's population. More macabre will be our future if we are

24. Man, Nature and the Future of Our Civilisation, 1987, pp. 92-93.

blind to the perils to the biosphere through unchecked pollution. But the picture is not all that bleak. Why? If there is social will and scientific talent, what is dismissed as waste may bless us as a resource.

The management of environmental pollution through creative strategies is a feasible prospect and we need not despair if sensitized statesmanship takes control of industrial growth and agricultural production. On an earlier occasion, when I had addressed the theme of "Waste into Wealth Operation" at a Conference organized by the Internationally renowned NEERI, I had advocated a positive approach to the issue:

> *"A constructive approach to pollution prevention and waste conversion pays dividends. Environment, and therefore, sustainable development must occupy a high place in the overall planning process. No system of production and consumption can sustain itself unless the residuals and wastes produced therefrom are assimilated through pragmatic management of the environment's carrying capacity, in keeping with the basic tenets of ecology. If pollution gets the better of the system, the victim will necessarily be society itself. Pollution prevention and resources conservation are two sides of the same coin".*[25]

One need not be an advocate of ascetic simplicity in the name of nature-friendly piety. Progress in science and technology can lead to rational and restrained regimes which will make life happy. The objection is to the immoral motto of maximum profit for corporate enterprises because the doomsday scenario will certainly visit the planet if science does not heed the need not to bleed nature. Toxic technology with terrorist thanatology is a grave danger to people's survival.

Humanitarian consideration must forbid undue exploitation of nature's resources and the democratic sense of distributive justice must halt the First World's money-manic enterprises from depredation of the natural resources of the Third World. Of course, under IMF indoctrination and MNC opiumisation, India and like countries happily believe the opposite of the real situation. The aggressive exploitation of our resource, despising the socialist complexion of our Republic and the caution of appropriate technology, which is the economic message we have adopted since freedom, may spell collapse of our structure.

Unfortunately, the glamorous glorification by the engineers of the New Economic Policy of the foreign investors in appropriate consumerist areas - the coke culture - successfully strangle people-oriented economic sanity, tighten thought control and shape opinion formation, the vast poor - the voiceless poor-being ignored and the unemployed numbers, swelling year after year, marginalised. What is the most important feature of India

25. Inaugural address on February 25, 1995, Conference on Appropriate Waste Management Technologies for Developing Countries, p. 7.

today is that there is no freedom of information of the operation of Government and of the foreign enterprises and no effective consultation when plants and factories, which adversely affect environment and ecology, are set up. Secrecy is becoming the rule of Indian official life. The CAG and Parliament having little time to probe into the darker sides of dubious contacts, the computerised process and the anti-human ascendancies of profit keeps down transparency. The social environment in a paper-logged Government makes the administration a dictatorship of files, keeping even the Ministers half-informed about what is actually taking place. Knowledge, so far as the public is concerned, is a forbidden fruit and even the courts are not informed about the truth. Small wonder the human future is bleak and a kind of Cassandra's curse makes competent foretellers of our fate receive tidings of dangers ahead with disbelief. We want progress, but without tears. We want freedom from permit raj and handcuffing regulations of the economy, but, conservation of Nature, when life faces the dilemma of "to be or not to be", should be the conscience of community good. For, Nature, under torture, may, in a rage of reprisal, rupture progress.

We, of the Third World, need more greening of our developmental projects, greening of our political perspectives, greening of our environment and greening of our people's consciousness before the red rage of people in pain rise and dethrone elite power at the polls. The Eco-greens seek to protect the natural world from toxic wastes, radiation, air pollution as well as promoting eco-friendly development, use of renewable-resource technology for energy and industry. We want ecological reformers whose holistic vision is radical, conservationist, furiously anti-pollutionist and pro-ecological and who regard the politics of macro-economic power, the real enemies of the New World Human Order. Commercial whaling, seal culling, dumping of toxic and radio-active wastes and manufacturing hazardous substances potentially harmful to health, contaminating environment and even doing genetic in tooth and claw will kill life in the long run if Big Business, with focus on the Almighty Dollar, ignore the conservation constitutionally mandated by Articles 48A[26] and 51A.[27] Grass-roots greens are growing in India, Sundarlal Bahaguna and Medha Patkar being conspicuous among masses of have-nots and handicapped, economic pariahs and the proletariat who have nothing to lose except their lives.

A little deviation, to drive home the Gandhian nexus with Nature and Development tuned to Third World ethos—and economic—demographic realities, Gandhi had the courage to warn against development based on industrial giantism and foreign technological domination. Modern

26. *Supra*, n. 5

27. *Supra*, n. 6.

machinery and technology had a tendency for concentration and centralization of wealth and power. The Constitution of India with its socialistic bias and orientation in regeneration of villages of destination conceptually accepted the Gandhian developmental model. The insatiable urge for amassing wealth takes the nation downhill in the path of progress.

If growth with justice is the path towards progress which is nature friendly we need a transformation in developmental thoughts with reverence for nature. Writes Paul Harrison, in what he calls a report from the battlefront in the war against poverty:

> *"One of the most distasteful aspects of the Western model of development has been its appalling arrogance, in the face both of nature and of traditional cultures. The rape of the earth has been central to the past progress of Western industrialism; the plunder and waste of irreplaceable resources, the poisoning or destruction of fragile ecosystems, the belief that man can mould nature with no need to take account of nature's reactions to such a violation. Disdain for traditional cultures and social system was a fundamental characteristic of all modern European empires, and this attitude spread to the new ruling elites who had adopted Western ways. As a result one development project after another triggered irreversible changes in local habitats. And the whole development process did not build on the foundations of traditional society but fell on it like a nuclear bomb and blew it apart.*
>
> *The concept of eco-development, or ecologically sound development, has been developed by the United Nations Environment Programme. Its basic principles are simple. Development should respect the local ecosystem. It should conserve resources, using renewable resources wherever possible. It should minimize waste and recycle as much as it can. And it should respect local, social and cultural patterns, by involving the local population in deciding on the style and pace of development".*[28]

Basically, development must be designed as a process of distributive justice when there is appalling poverty. A mad race to close the wealth gap with the West is as futile and foolish as the arms race. Social justice is nature-friendly while the hi-tech dehumanised race for more and more rapes the earth for pleasures and profits. If India is to obey the Gandhian-Nehruvian values of the Constitution, we have to re-think our New Economic Policy and tighten our belts determined not to surrender to the North. Here is the point of confluence between the Mahatma, Ambedkar, Nehru and the Green Movement, all of them being enveloped in the Supreme Buddha teaching of *ahimsa and antyodaya*.

Bigness has a seductive appeal. Why? Because inexorably economic power controls political power. The process fattens on itself and

28. The Third World Tomorrow, 1980, pp. 38-39.

demolishes democratic criticism by buying up the fourth estate. Those who own or control the mass media and macro industrial enterprises can work havoc with nature and environment safety and social justice rendering freedom of information a mirage. That is why Justice Douglas observed:

> *"Industrialized power should be decentralized. It should be scattered into many hands so that the fortune of the people will not be dependent on the whim or caprice, the political prejudice, the emotional stability of a few self-appointed men. The fact that they are not vicious men, but respectable and social-minded is irrelevant. That is the philosophy and command of the Sherman Act. It was founded on a theory of hostility to the concentration in private hands of power so great that only a government of the people should have it".*[29]

We owe it to our Founding Fathers to reject mammoth projects at once globalised and privatised and controlled by those who are beyond Indian Justice. The core creed is best expressed by E.M. Forster in his "Towards End":

> *"It is the vice of a vulgar mind to be thrilled by bigness, to think that a thousand square miles are a thousand times more wonderful than one square mile, and that a million square miles are almost the same as heaven".*[30]

The Indian greens may be ideologically economic iconoclasts in the eyes of the New Establishment. The Gandhians and Ambedkarites, Nehruites and greens, and many others, believe that the New Investment rush and technological passion are tomorrow's Frankenstein monster namely the MNCs recolonisation of India. Green economic thought for the Third World demands:

> *"...the development of appropriate, labour-intensive technologies, fundamental and reform, and a shift from industrialization and export-orientation towards increasing self-reliance. They also propose to establish a realistic, future-oriented price structure of nature resources that will give Third World countries the means for their own development, instead of forcing them to sell off their resources cheaply, merely to ensure their short-term survival. Finally, the Greens support South-South relationships, affirming that 'the people of the Third World themselves will find the solution to their problems'. The Green Economic Programme contains not only specific proposals for ecological, social, and economic measures, but also suggestions for financing these measures".*[31]

Recent industrial tragedies *like the Union Carbide catastrophe*, the Basle disaster, the Chernobyl Nuclear Power Plant collapse, the Three Mile

29. As quoted in America Inc., 1972, p. 447.
30. *Ibid.*
31. Charlene Spretnak and Fritj of Capra, Green Politics: The Global Promise, 1984, p. 97.

Island near-disaster, are among the other many unpublicised hazardous events, which are portents to send signals regarding grave risks to the good earth from adventurist industrializations. The World Bank has issued guidelines for identifying and controlling major hazard installations in developing countries and yet in our 'sound-proof' policy making rooms industrialization with a pachydermic disposition towards environment is considered by the economic planners as equivalent to development, making little distinction between technology and thanatology (science of death). Corporate interests invariably take precedence over the health and safety of workers and of the community.

The corporate tendency to down-play hazards is an art of misinformation. The Third World Governments, even after the UCC experience, have not insisted on a legally enforceable code of conduct for MNCs nor draft charter of rights for workers of denizens.

Agriculture itself is being industrialised under pressure from the North. World Hunger is, alas, Big Business.

Big Agri-business Corporations operate within Third World countries promise, green revolutions, manipulate seeds through genetic control, produce more grain to make their gains, but before long create an agricultural slavery. Pest management through pesticides which are dangerous and fertilizers sold at great price which in the long run destroy the soil cumulatively land up agriculturists in a chemical trap. A myth was created that corporate agri-business is good for the Third World. In truth fertilizers and pesticides dumped on the Third World enter the food chain, wind up in human tissue and produce grave health hazards. In short, using the scarcity scare, India and like countries are victims of the 'poison business' promoted by the US and G-7 countries under guise of greater benefits.

The new menace of the GATT (Gattastrophe) is patentisation by the advanced countries forcing India to abandon its nationally beneficial and rationally just law of patents and to adopt American prescriptions in this field of law. Products of bio-diversity abundant and essential for the life of the people are robbed by the West using the patent process. Neem for instance, is a herb of many uses for Indians, but the West is patentising neem products thereby preventing Indians from using India's natural wealth. Other instances of our bio-diversity becoming bio-scarcity are not available, but our Government is ready to jettison the life-saving and nationally inalienable genetic wealth to foreign firms thereby negotiating the people's right to life.

Degradation of Nature follows upon destruction of the plant world. How many species have been eliminated by Man by his rapacious operations! We are still left with a number of plants, invaluable for human health and happiness. Herbs and trees grant us fuel, food, wood, medicines, manures, fodder and even industrial raw material. We must worship the tree because we survive through their environmental contribution. If we wipe out forests, cut away herbal plants, fail to preserve herbariums, rare plant species and do research to discover their best uses and therapeutic advantages we are the losers in the long run. So we must have a cooperative culture where happy coexistence of minerals, plants, animals and humans is promoted. Environment and development has this dimension.

Useful tree species growing wild is capable of medicinal values, properly researched. For instance bael tree has many medicinal uses:

> *"Bael tree has many medicinal uses. The leaves, fruits and roots find medicinal applications. In eye diseases, the juice of the leaves is poured into the eyes and the paste of the leaves is applied over the eye lids. In Odema and chest pain, steam bath with the leaves is given. The juice of the leaves with black pepper is used in the treatment of jaundice. It is also prescribed in heart diseases. The juice of the leaves is given in cases of chest pain, cough and bronchitis. It is also effective in diabetes mellitus and in uterine inflammation.*
>
> *The unripe fruit is used in loss of appetite, diarrhoea etc. Mixed with sugar it is given in cases of bacillus dysentery and piles. The ripe fruit is also used for such purposes. The pulp of ripe fruit is aromatic and cooling. It is laxative and cures indigestion. It is a good source of vitamins, particularly riboflavin, minerals and carbohydrates. The root is commonly used in the treatment of rheumatic disease, mental disease and sleeplessness. It is also used to cure intermittent fever".*[32]

Oil palm development in India has great potential, provided you identify suitable areas for cultivation. Likewise coconut cultivation is extremely useful because of the anti-carcinogenic and anti-microbial qualities of coconut oil. There are many other uses of coconut oil which have come recently under close study. New methods of improving coconut farming such as conservation and use of organic sources may help reduce costs and increase productivity. Examples like these are many and this boon of a tree can be multiplied through strong extension systems. In short nature friendly farming has great promise in our country. But the facts are cruelly contrary. Take the instance of enlightened Kerala. The rich bio-reserve and scenic beauty of Periyar Wild Life Sanctuary is a matter of national pride.

One of the leading newspapers[33] reported the present malady of the bio-reserve:

> *"The picture of heads of wild elephants moving majestically along the lakeside in the background of lush green forest is so familiar to us through*

32. Tree World, a monthly newsletter, September, 1995.

33. The Hindu, 1st September, 1995.

the glossy posters of the tourism department, that it has become almost the visual symbol of Thekkady itself... The Kokkarakandam and Perakkad areas of the Thekkady range, which form parts of the sanctuary, had sandal forests just two years ago. But today there are hardly any sandal trees left. In May this year, nearly 100 trees were cut down and taken away. The poachers even cut trees from the roadside hardly 50 feet away from the Range Officer's residence. It was only then that the authorities noticed the felling...

The 'Vayana' trees which are valued for their bark used in large-scale agarbathy production are no longer to be seen in the forest. The illegal bark collectors strip the trees bare and they die. One person can debark one tree a day and usually a group of 15 is engaged for the work, says a shop owner at Thekkady. This means 15 trees were destroyed daily. The department officials plead their inability to book the culprits. They say there are not enough staff or vehicles. Also if a culprit is caught political pressure is brought on them to compound the case and let him free. There are a number of compounded cases in the range".

The human enemies of nature defy the law, because they are government-friendly. Are we, of this generation, safe trustees of the great estate of Nature? Rio notwithstanding, we are not.

The failure of the existing paradigm and the danger of opening up large economic space for corporate industry and agri-business is fraught with danger to nature and human life. Therefore, a new international legal regime is urgently called for if the people are to have their right to life assured against macro-accidents and ultra-hazardous activities. To begin with, the agenda of legal defense of human life must draft a code of international liability so that people's safety may gain priority. Special considerations for developing countries, with a new jurisdiction and jurisprudence, must be formulated. Transnational litigations must become simpler and easier of recourse. The Indian Supreme Court in *M.C. Mehta* v. *Union of India*,[34] adopted the principle of absolute liability for all activities which are "hazardous or inherently dangerous".[35] A 'negligence' theory of liability is no longer adequate to meet the challenges of transnational corporations. The foundation for a new international justice with easy access to enforcement force and ready recovery of compensation is a necessary concomitant of the new economic policy and the dangerous implications therein. One view presented by Ayesha Kadwani runs thus:

"When the risk of harm from an activity is transnational in character, major in degree and cannot be eliminated by the exercise of reasonable care, the state must be held strictly liable and originally responsible for

34. AIR 1987 SC 1086.

35. *Id.*, p. 1099.

consequent injury. The transnationally harzardous nature of a given activity may be determined by way of a contextual multiple factor analysis. It centers on ascertaining whether a significant risk of transnational damage exists, not in the sense of a high probability of minor damage but of severe damage associated even with very low probability. The hazardous nature may be further compounded by lack of State compliance with any incumbent duty of prior information and consultation. Transnational industrial accidents should therefore be treated as ultra hazardous activities justifying the application of a principle of absolute liability under national law. Such liability should attach jointly to the State and to the industrial enterprise in the facilities of which the accident has occurred.

A crucial element in allocating liability for transnational industrial accidents must be prevention. Such liability must be strict and indeed absolute. A strict liability standard will force industries and nations to weigh the benefit of a polluting activity against the injury caused by pollution. The main rationale for absolute international liability "should be to minimize the possibility of injurious consequences and to provide adequate redress where injurious consequences do occur" [Report of the International Law Commission, 35 U.N. GAOR, Supp. (No. 10), U.N. Doc. A/35/10 (1980), p. 365]. While States are increasingly willing to seek agreements about measures of prevention, they are generally unwilling to accept a direct linkage between preventing measures and liability for damage".[36]

Agriculture and Nature

One may briefly revisit the area of agri-business. Using organic manure for growing grains, India was raising its food supply in a self-reliant direction. The US popularised the use of pesticides tempting underdeveloped countries with export crop possibilities:

"An underdeveloped country, moreover, easily gets locked into producing more and more export crops, in part to earn foreign exchange to pay for more and more imported pesticides. Pesticides lead to an agricultural environment requiring more pesticides, as we will explain. The diminishing financial returns per acre that result often step up the pressure to devote even more land to export crops. The entire process bypasses the need of local people for food".

"Pesticides usage in underdeveloped countries is concentrated in little export-oriented enclaves that are functionally mere extensions of the agricultural systems of the industrial countries. In these enclaves pesticides are commonly applied so intensively that environmental scientists are given

36. Transnational Industrial Accident as Ultra Hazardous Activities in David Dembo et. A. (Eds.), Nothing to Lose But Our Lives, (1988), pp. 142-143.

the "opportunity" to study the effects of extreme chemical farming".[37]

The fact is that insecticides and other heavy pesticide doses did more harm than good. Plant-eating pests outnumbered their predators, the result being the defeat of pesticides despite expensive poison in the field. It must be remembered that half of the pesticides exported from the US is the Third World and often times people were getting sick because of pesticide use in agriculture. Litigation against the manufacturer for blurred vision, speech and memory blocks, nervous system disorders and the like have affected the American exporters:

> *"With low levels of literacy, meager extension services, and heavy company propaganda about the chemicals' benefits, farmers in the Third World cannot be expected to appreciate the hazards of an apparently innocuous white power".*[38]

Nevertheless, air-planes drop pesticides which are deadly sometimes. They enter into the food chains and windup in human tissues. This chemical drug has affected nature adversely and the food of the people fatally. The poison business despite life endangering hazards is continuing because of propaganda. In the *'Food First'*, the authors have completely exposed the bogus poison business for crops and gold courses and poison for beauty used for colouring fruits and vegetables to look attractive. The chemical companies put pressure to keep people ignorant about pesticidal dangers:

> *"The massive increase in pesticide use is not because of the pressure of hungry people's need for food... lack of pesticides is not what is keeping them hungry. The real threat is that pesticide technology is in the hands of few corporations that will profit only if they can continue to make farmers and "concerned" people everywhere believe that our very survival depends on the indiscriminate use of their products".*[39]

The truth is that the pesticide myth has the silent blessings of our Government which should have stopped their import long ago. Likewise, the ballyhoo about chemical fertilisers is fraudulent because organic manure available at home is far better than imported chemicals. In that, the author says:

> *"Chemical fertiliser must, therefore, never be thought of as a substitute for organic sources. First, all sources of organic matter should be mobilised and returned to the soil. Then, for countries like China and Algeria with petroleum available to produce chemical fertiliser, developing and using that*

37. Francis Moore Lappe and Joseph Collins, Food First, (1978), p. 61.
38. *Id.*, p. 65. A research term in Pakistan in 1974 reported that one customer, lacking a suitable container, unwrapped his turban, poured a granular pesticide therein, and replaced it on his head for transport.
39. *Id.*, p. 75.

potential can make sense. (Furthermore, even though China is making a big push to utilise its petroleum for fertiliser, 70 per cent of its fertiliser is still from organic sources, enough to guarantee sufficient food production)".[40]

The total dependence of Third World agriculture on First World monopolies must end, if nature and agriculture must come together. Indeed, the following observations are instructive when we consider local alternatives to imported chemicals:

> *"Take fertiliser. First of all we must keep in mind that shifting from monoculture to a variety of crops and instituting crop rotation will, as first steps, reduce the need for fertiliser. More important, however, the local potential for producing fertiliser from indigenous waste material is estimated to represent six to eight times the amount of nutrients in costly, largely imported, chemical fertilisers actually used by the underdeveloped countries. This energy and fertiliser potential can be tapped right at the village level, using materials that are often wasted.*
>
> *The fertiliser produced through the biogas technique is many times richer in nutrients than the waster products that went into it. By fermenting the village wastes of 500 human beings and 250 cattle, a biogas "plant" can supply the average cropped land of a typical Asian village with two and one half times the present nitrogen applied in the form of chemical fertilisers. Moreover, it can supply almost double the present daily energy needs of the village for cooking, water pumping, electricity, and industries".*[41]

Neem, earlier mentioned by me, as insecticide is available locally, and remember, it is an eco-friendly botanical pesticide. *Neem* is nature's bitter boon and if used widely defends agriculture batter from pests. Curious but true is the fact of conserving spiders to protect crops:

> *"Spiders are predators of pests like thrips, caterpillars, aphids, plant bugs, leaf hoppers, flies, etc. Their importance as pest control agents is not a recent discovery. On the contrary, their value has been acknowledged by farmers from time immemorial. Several ancient books on agriculture mention their importance. In China, even to the present day many elderly people in villages take the number of spiders in a field as a measure of its potential agricultural productivity. Fields abundant in spiders, prior to the introduction of chemical pesticide are now witnessing a change in the scenario. In addition to killing pests, these chemicals are also taking a heavy toll on useful insects. Preservation of spiders necessitates abandoning of these pesticides, or spot treatment and rational use of the same. Once pesticides are kept away from the fields, spiders invariably take shelter in the fields, feed on the pests and add to the productivity".*[42]

---

40. Francis Moore Lappe and Joseph Collins, Food First, (1978), p. 163.
41. *Id.*, pp. 482, 483.
42. Pesticide Post, Vol. 3, 3 May, 1995.

It is true that chemical fertilisers can increase yields but they cannot maintain or enhance the soil's organic matter which is the ultimate key to fertility. Organic matter maintains the porous soil structure, provides superior water holding capacity (critical during droughts) and allows oxygen to penetrate for use by soil organisms that break down manure, crop residues, and other organic matter. Seventy per cent. of China's fertilisers come from organic sources; why not India too? We should not be victimised by propaganda baloney of Fertiliser Corporations.

Yet another eco-friendly methodology has great potential. It is the way of transforming waste into wealth. India will belong to the world of waste if we do not recycle the accumulating waste. The wealth of waste will easily bless the country's industry if only political ignorance, social prejudice and sluggish industrialism give way to a new 'waste to wealth' operation, at once reducing pollution, re-enforcing conservation of nature and promoting eco-balance as an imperative. Garbage, if treated becomes power. Now, it produces plagues. Popular participation in making riches from rags is a measure we can and must utilise.

Environmental code and court

More than judge-made law and broad constitutional commands we need nature conservation—specific statutory outfits wherewith to confront environmental criminality and tort culpability. Of course, on-going programmes for judges from the trial to the Apex Court are very necessary to make for forensic nature-friendly adjudications.

A comprehensive legislation expressing the nation's stem determination to stamp our industrial pollution is a State obligation. Currently, the law is lame and the Bhopal tragedy has luridly revealed the shocking incompetence of our legal system and the shameful shortfalls in judicial jurisdiction and absence of 'disaster jurisprudence'. The Supreme Court of India, faced with this new terror, expanded on the Environment Protection Act, 1986, and insisted on a national policy and a code of ethics *vis-a-vis* industrial pollution. Moreover, we need mobile environmental courts since pollution is all over the rural and urban and on-the-spot justice is best.

I have no doubt, NEERI, party fills the bill in defending people's life from pollutive lethality. The new millennium, with all its boasts and all its hopes, can never really host humanity on the planet in the coming century, if expert institutions with commitment like NEERI, catalyse resistance to industrial wastes and contaminants and other developmentally deceptive but actually dangerous technologies. Sometime ago, I wrote what I think is here an apt quote:

> *"We need environment law societies, conservation organisations, informed intellectuals, independent scientists and mass mobilisation organs*

> *well informed on industrial pollution. A comprehensive code must provide for all these anti-pollution operations fighting Corporate Almighty. This is a vital policy position if the State is to take the danger of pollution by industry seriously".*[43]

The story of humanity is a perennial process with its advances and retreats, its triumphs and defeats. Now Life wins with achievements, but again, Death gains dark victories. What is puzzlesome is that in the small planet we eat each other in cannibalistic appetite, not by flesh being cooked *tandoori* fashion, as allegedly happened once in New Delhi, but by sucking people's economic blood to add riches and revel in sensual pleasure. Such a system besmirches our country because it betrays the cultural heritage Love which Jesus preached, the power of non-violence which Gandhiji permeated, every spiritual cell of his physical being, and all the vision and wisdom the sages and seers, prophets and revolutionaries lustrously gifted to our generation. Enlightenment is own inalienable, universal, millennial possession, with every human's partner in this precious treasure.

But where are we? Science marched forward, lightened our labours. Brightened our lovely lives. Dreams of prosperity and pleasure came true. But alongside came Satan challenging the divine in the human, using technology to conquer and kill, to corner wealth and sink in sex and drug and, in the bargain, the savage prevailed over the sage. The 'White Man' reappeared in history as Corporate Power and, backed by the Juggernaut of Super-Power, began to exploit all resources condemning all but the creamy layer to blood, toil, tears and sweat. The maxim of this immoral, incorporated, Power (Private) Limited was and is Business as Usual.

The intoxication of material advance, drugged by desire for more and armed with modern technology, began to torture Nature reckless of consequences, polluted environment to profiteer, mindless of the boomerang effect, exterminated ecology and bruised bio-diversity with gluttonous intent. Then came the criminal challenge to Nature and its indispensable role in human welfare. You may rush to the moor but shall not be a loon in your self-hypnotised selfishness! And yet, it is Private Multinationals Incorporated which ravish Nature in search of rapist pleasure; but the sentence of death, for their crime, is visited on humanity unlimited and generations unborn. So, the dialectic of Mother Earth under technological siege and heady, hedonist lust with Epicurean urge, is that our fish will perish, our water will no longer be potable, our air dangerous to breathe, our food chemically poisoned, our eyes and ears become dysfunctional, our body invite AID syndrome and cancer from skin to soul and our dear earth forbidden for habitation, having eaten the forbidden fruit of technological induced thanatos.

---

43. V.R. Krishna Iyer, Environment Protection and Legal Defence, (1993), p. 139.

> *Our minerals, animals and humankind have a unity in divinity and each has a* dharma *to discard which is to deserve future shock.*

The universality of the calamity of intoxicated macro-pollutive projects, industrial and agricultural, is well brought out by Cheen Yoke Ling in a recent article titled "Economic Boom takes a heavy toll in Environment". They ring a bell for every sensitive Indian and so I quote excerpts from it:

> *"Protest against a dam to be built on prime farm land led to the killing of four villagers on the island of Madura, off Eastern Java. More than one million farmers in North-East Thailand were faced with massive displacement to make way for large-scale tree plantations to supply pulp for the global paper industry. Defence of ancestral lands against logging in Sarawak, Malaysia saw more than 400 indigenous villagers arrested since 1987. Indigenous women who decry toxic pesticide poisoning in the Philippines were threatened with a lawsuit by Hoechst, one of the world's biggest chemical transnational corporations".*
>
> *"The changes have been traumatic for the environment and local populations. Structural shifts in resource use and perceptions of nature, and escalating materialism among a growing urban middle class are driving to the surface fundamental clashes between those who benefit from economic success and those who are victimised. A familiar lament of farmers and indigenous peoples is "Our land, our forest are more than what you see. They are our life, our spirit. We are only guardians". The equally familiar reaction is "These selfish and ignorant people are obstacles to development". In that confrontation, Non-Governmental Organisations and peoples' movements (those of farmers, fishermen, indigenous peoples) have emerged. Their roles range from mediators to protagonists".*
>
> *"Sadly, the lessons are not learnt, and we find that the same short-term exploitation continues in Malaysia and Indonesia. Consequently, water shortage and water pollution caused by industrial/urban growth are on the rise. NGOs and even some officials in the region anticipate deeper water crisis in the next decade.*
>
> *In the farming communities, time-tested traditional systems of agriculture have been largely displaced by the promised technological miracle of the Green Revolution. The result is a wiping out of seeds diversity from farms, a growing dependence on chemicals which do not work but instead injure and even kill farmers and agricultural workers, soil made infertile by the use of chemicals and machinery, and huge irrigation and drainage systems which are failing".*[44]

What we need is to conquer this pest of "Progress", this menace to human advance is for the NGOs to fight the vice and sensitive scientists join together to launch a campaign of enlightened opposition to the insanity of neo development engineered by MNCs:

---

44. Indian Communicator, 5th October, 1995.

"Environmentalists argue, with strong documented evidence, that megadams have an unmitigated record of problems. Local populations refuse to be displaced. The Pak Moon dam in Thailand, the Nipah dam on Madura island and the revived Bakum dam in Sarawak are but some hot spots of contention.

Where agriculture is promoted, it is inevitably export-looking, too. Monoculture crops (oil palm, cocoa, trees for pulp), horticulture, exotic fruit and vegetable production as well as aquaculture open up environmentally sensitive areas such as forests and wetlands. These projects also threaten local food production and marginalise small farmers and fishermen.

In Malaysia, the clearing of forest in a watershed in the Kinta Highlands for growing temperate flowers for export, and the clear cutting of 5,000 acres of inact pert swamp forest in Pahang for the world's largest eel farm owned by a Taiwanese company, hit the national news in 1993. Local fishermen and NGOs in Southern Thailand have been fighting for the last few years against large-scale shrimp culture which is leaving in its wake environmental disasters and impoverished coastal communities".[45]

Even golf as earlier mentioned by me is a game that goes against common people:

"The latest area of conflict is golf course and resort development. Rapid industrialisation in South-East Asia inevitably brings with it recreational facilities which are an obsession with the Japanese investors who are major players in the region's growth. Golf courses and related tourism development have created land conflicts with local rural people, destruction of forests, coral reefs and other sensitive environments as well as water contamination from sewage and the massive amounts of toxic chemicals used for greens. These projects also promote an elitist lifestyle at the expense of the needs of poor people and the environment, and as more business deals are struck on golf courses than in boardrooms, the rising elite of South-East Asia is fast adopting a similar lifestyle.

This trend is the subject of growing protest. In Singapore, plans to build a golf course in a reservoir catchment area were dropped. Public protest following complaints of safety hazards by pilots in Malaysia resulted in the halting of night golfing near the Subang International Airport. The Department of Environment is, for the first time, taking to court a golf course developer who did not conduct an environmental impact assessment before bulldozing forest in Fraser's Hill, causing tremendous soil erosion.

In Indonesia, a coalition of NGOs is working with affected communities to prevent golf course construction on farmlands and environmentally sensitive areas. New regulations were enacted in Java in May 1993, but

45. Indian Communicator, 5th October, 1995.

construction of approved projects continued. Protest by farmers, human rights activists and lawyers were met with arrests and harassment".[46]

It is thus apparent that humanity is being victimised in its ecological and environmental dimensions by a creamy layer of humanity, corrupted by the passion for pleasure and the fashion for high life.

At this point, I turn to a lecture—delectable, elegantly worded and pregnant with grave portent—delivered by Dr. L.M. Singhvi titled, with characteristic flavour, "A Tale of Three Cities", which has touched a poignant chord in me reminding me of the contrast in Indian's human categories.[47]

Of course there are 'White' Indians, – a fifty of our population who claim that we are in the best of times and there are dark Indians—over five hundred million in number—who sorrowingly say it is the worst of times. Some put faith in the new era of the MNC entry. The poor are shocked to see prices of essentials rise sky-high. Inevitable, I am fascinated by the aptness of a Charles Dickens' quote, from *A Tale of Two Cities*. To my mind, the passage applies to the white Indian - dark Indian contradiction. Here is the delectably worded Dickensian dialectic. Although he said it about London and Paris, about 1775, I repeat it for India, 1995:

> *"It was the best of times, it was the worst of times, it was the age of wisdom, it was the age of foolishness, it was the epoch of belief, it was the epoch of incredulity, it was the season of light, it was the season of darkness, it was the spring of hope, it was the winter of despair, we had everything before us, we had nothing before us, we were all going direct to Heaven, we were all going direct the other way".*

When scientists with concern for the human future, statesmen with far sight for the next generation and sage thinkers with commitment for the ages ahead ponder beyond myopic political midgets, they will discover that the Stockholm Conference of the Seventies had stressed Nature but the greed of the rich countries paid no heed to the needs of preserving Nature, judged by the deeds and projects by which 'advanced' technology is tearing up the earth and the biosphere. The United Nations, by several instruments, has prescribed and proscribed various measures hoping that planetary patriotism would control corporate terrorism against nature. Nevertheless, the erosion of environmental values has to be arrested if the world process is to hold out a happy promise. Dr. Singhvi, in his felicitous speech, polished his presentation on this point:

> *"The tale of the first of my three cities did not really begin in Rio. Nor did it begin with the UN Conference on Environment and Development also*

46. Indian Communicator, 5th October, 1995.

47. *Supra.* n. 23

known as Earth Summit in June 1992. It had begun ever since and each time human beings perceived their shared tenancy of Planet Earth, their membership of the human family and their future. And it is an endless tale. In a sense it began in 1972 in Stockholm which was quite unlike Rio. The seeds for the harvest in Rio were sown in Stockholm. In twenty years, propitious and somewhat modest beginning made in Stockholm had become a mighty movement enlivened by a new found sense of the oneness of our world, and its common future".[48]

The ancient Upanishads had told us of human unity, of all Creation enjoying a holistic indivisibility and of a total togetherness in mutual reverence if the Earth were to be our home. The West violated this wisdom until scientists and statesmen beheld the grave threat. This hereafter of humanity, when futurologists got scared, forced the nations to convene, under the auspices of the United Nations, the Earth Summit at Rio de Janerio.

With a sense of sublime patriotism, with vibrant universalism, we may look at the ancient wisdom manifest in reverence for all of Nature's Creation. Hinduism, if I may venture in all humility has emphasised the communion with the Earth and has taught us in its panentheistic (as distinct from pantheistic) world view, the sacramentalism of St. Francis of Assisi as well as the echo philosophy of Western thinkers.

Contrary to the carmalism of current times in the stirring opening of Ishopanishad. *G. Naganathan, a theosophist quotes and remarks:*

"The entire universe and everything in it, animate and inanimate, is His. Let us not cover anything. Let us treat everything around us reverently, as custodians. We have no charter for dominion. All wealth is commonwealth. Let us enjoy but neither hoard nor kill. The humble frog has as much right to live as we.

Following the Hindu's reverential approach to every aspect of life is the creation of a phalanx of minor and major divinities, or deities or Devatas, though no other religion has been more forthright and clear on the ultimate nature of the one and only Reality. Each deity presides over a certain function, has a certain consort, uses a particular vehicle, giving them a concrete aspect that appeals to less spiritually sophisticated lay people. All these insignia have a deep philosophical symbolism. What might interest us presently is that all these vehicles are mostly drawn from the world of animals, birds, and even reptiles. For example, Brahma has a swan, Vishnu has a garuda, a type of eagle, Siva rides a bull, Ganesh a mouse, Subrahmanya a peacock, and so on. The idea is only to emphasise the kinship with animals. Trees have the divinity Vanadevata. War is presided over by the Goddess Chamundi riding a lion. Sound has a divinity, the

48. *Supra*, n. 23. p. 7.

Nadabrahmam. The Goddess Saraswathi presides over music and arts. Lakshmi sitting on a lotus deals with wealth. Parvathi, the consort of Siva, rules the entire Nature. All these divinities serve to consecrate every aspect of daily life. The whole pantheon serves to emphasise the one ultimate Reality".[49]

The Brihad-aranyaka lifts ecology to sublime dignity in one of its early stanzas:

> *"He who dwells in all beings and is within all beings, whom all beings do not know, whose body all beings are, who controls all beings from within—He is thy Self, the controller within, the immortal".*

One may conclude this noble thought with a vedic prayer which pleads for total concord with the Universe:

> *"Peace of sky, peace of mid-region, peace of earth,*
>
> *Peace of water, peace of plants, peace of trees,*
>
> *Peace of all Gods, peace of Brahman,*
>
> *Peace of the Universe,*
>
> *Peace of peace; May that peace come to me". – Yajur Veda.*

When history was boasting of the pinnacle of civilised opulence in our times, the scientists realised mankind was precipitously perched on the brink of disaster, devastation, destruction and dark annihilation. And so, the agenda of the Earth Summit discussed the subject, "Wounded Nature Human Future", if I may put it that way. Dr. Singhvi, with lawyerly advocacy and brilliant study, presented the crisis of humanity in his Rede Lecture:

> *"The Report of the World Commission on Environment and Development titled, "Our Common Future" had pointed out in 1987 lapses of environmental neglect and degradation and the perils of developmental failures. It pointed out that in terms of absolute numbers there were more hungry people in the world than ever before; their numbers were increasing even though global production had increased faster than the population growth. It pointed out that the number of those who lacked fuel to cook and warm themselves were increasing and the gap between the rich and poor nations was widening. It also pointed out that each year some six million hectares of productive dryland was turning into worthless desert and more than 11 million hectares of forest were destroyed. During the 1970s, twice as many people suffered each year from natural disasters as during the 1960s. In the 1960s, some 18.5 million people were affected annually by drought and 5.2 million by floods; in 1970s correspondingly 24.4 million by floods; in 1970s correspondingly 24.4 million and 15.4 million people were*

49. Animal Welfare and Nature: Hindu scriptual Perspectives, 1989, p. 2.

> *affected annually. Numbers of victims of cyclones and earthquakes also increased considerably. Worse still we have persisted in a profligate use of Earth's finite resources and have continued to precipitate global warming and climate change by excessive burning of fossil fuels, denude the forest cover of the Earth, cause desertification and extreme scarcity of water, necessitate shifting of agricultural areas, raise sea levels, flood coastal cities, submerge low-lying islands and disrupt national economies. Pollution is rampant. There is a criminal dumping of industrial waste. The plantet's protective ozone shield is on the brink of depletion. Toxic substances poison the human food chain and the underground water tables. The world's bio-diversity is being progressively destroyed. We have already transgressed the tolerance limits of benign Nature and the dangers are clear and present. As the UN Commission had concluded, the environmental crisis, the development crisis and the energy crisis are all one and the crisis is global. The crisis can no longer be contained in national compartments or labelled leisurely under neat traditional classifications".*[50]

The urgent case for a dynamic harmony among human beings, North and South, and Nature, from the earth to outer space, is grimly obvious, and so, the new concept of sustainable development, a creative *modus vivendi* and a new equity, flexibility and spirit of unity, became the empasis and main thrust of the Rio Declaration and Agenda 21 adopted at that city.

Nikhil Chakravartty, elder statesman among Indian journalists, observed about the Rio finale:

> *"What is the message that has come from Rio? The massive gathering at the Earth Summit with the unprecedented turnout of various denominations of activists from all parts of the world, gave it a truly global character which no other international gathering of the past could claim".*[51]

Rio leaves mankind with a macabre prospect and clear mandate, even as Stockholm marks a conscientising event and epochal message. Today, the problem of environment is universally accepted as central to the survival of living Earth.

This grave concern accompanied by a great commitment is a positive achievement at the end of 12 days of oral skirmishes, play of forces, and voices of peoples, commencing from 3rd June, 1992. This Summit, *vis-a-vis* environmental challenges, was constructive in many dimensions. The balance-sheet of this marathon meet where as many as 115 Heads of States and Governments and a while lot of other nations took part, organising conferences, and crystalising, through instruments and documentations, clearer perspectives and firmer objectives with supportive action plans is

50. *Supra*, n. 23, pp. 8-9.
51. Mainstream, Hube 27, 1992, p. 7.

in mankind's favour. UNCED was, after all, a tremendous triumph, whatever its shortcomings. Rome was not built in a day. But 'the undone vast' makes our future vulnerable.

The 27-point Rio Declaration claimed general consensus. Even the former US President Bush felt compelled to present himself at Rio and offer his views on the three tough issues of forestry, funding and convention on biological diversity. The countries of the G-77 group, which has stalwarts like Prime Minister Hamathir Mohammed, took strong stances on issues like cutting down of emission of carbon monoxide and other pollutants by the US and other industrial countries. Fortunately, the pressure built up at the Summit imparted a new vision even to the nations of the north like Germany, Japan, France and Britain, unmindful of the hostile attitude of hegemonist US so as to sign the Convention on biological diversity. There was tension on the issue of forests. The Americans wanted to globalise the forest wealth of the South while the American woodlands like in Texas were sought to be kept out of the purview of the treaty. The Third World fought back and Kamal Nath, the Indian environment minister, saw through the game as his observations reveal: "The US finds it more profitable to have forests in India than Texas". Finally, the principles on forestry were adopted unanimously. The North was the main polluter and must atone for the guilt by paying for the clean-up. Trees, it was recognised, were more than a giver of oxygen, but were a multi-purpose blessing. India worships since our ancients were wiser than our West-polluted generation. But our barons of the woods are timber-felling our Future.

Two basic principles emerge from Rio. Firstly, the human beings are the centre of sustainable development and secondly, that an interdependence and indivisibility with global expansiveness is a must when we speak of development and environment. The song of Rio is the reality of harmony, justly based on universal compassion and fundamental fraternity. A series of accords were signed proving, "we are the world; we are the children" – a song sung at the same time by the young in all the Nations to save the hungry in Africa. The Rio Summit is a new manifesto for mankind.

Among the lessons of the Earth Summit Conference what the world must learn are the following:

1. The North, comprising 20 per cent of the world's population and consuming 80 per cent of its reserves (the US consumes the lion's share), is reluctant to take any initiative to save humanity from environmental degradation and the adversities of under-development. Have the 'haves' ever in history shared with the 'have-nots' a holistic strategy to make all humanity a global brotherhood in development, environment and ecology, save under

the sole force of cosmic collective conscience which is the locomotive of history?

2. Victory comes once the South stands together and awareness dawns on the North that the Earth is environmentally indivisible.
3. The prognosis is bright if the nations, weak and strong, present a united front against eco-imperialism.
4. Finally, as the Brazilian President underscored on the eve of the Rio Summit: "You can't have an environmentally healthy planet in a world that is socially unjust".
5. Have the nations any recipe for success? Such a viable proposal is what Mahathir Mohammed made:

   A global fund, financed by national contributions assessed on the basis of population and carbon dioxide emissions, would be created to assure the success of this vast effort at reforestation and new forestation. Such a project would not only solve, at least partially, one of the world's most important environmental problems, it would also exemplify an approach to saving the Earth through cooperative efforts that are fair and just for all, not merely for the North.

A new global order must build a justice-informed society.

Environment, ecology, population, poverty and life in luxury, all have an impact on the escalating global disorder. In this context, we must remember the World Population Day (July 10th) because it is a day to celebrate humanity, to look back and consider human achievements, and also to look forward to the new kind of world our children will inherit.

True we have made a mammoth step forward on paper. What is guaranteed against G-7 treachery and criminal abetment by Third World politicians who look for the next election and not the next generation? I must conclude with a sad note from Robert Frost:[52]

"The woods are lovely, dark, and deep,
But I have promises to keep,
And miles to go before I sleep,
And miles to go before I sleep".

52. "Stopping by Woods on a Snowy Evening" in C.T. Thomas (Ed.), Twentieth Century Verse: An Anglo-American Anthology, 1986, p. 110-111.

PLACHIMADA PATRIOTISM—TOXICOLA TERRORISM

The right to life is a foremost human right sans which societal survival ceases to exist. Air, water, outer space and everything without which generations of Creation cannot exist is universal asset, indefeasible wealth of the world.

Humanity needs water for a hundred reasons and so civilized progress is inconceivable without potable aqua. Indeed, the need for water world-wide and for ages, is ever so necessary that it is no exaggeration to consider the vision of the future of the human species as too fundamental to be diminished even a wee bit in importance.

The habitable countries, globally spread, struggle for sources of water, air and what not today, that the dire need for collecting and preserving every ounce of potable water and breathable air is humanity's highest priority. Under such circumstances every drop of rain has to be harvested, every well of water has to be conserved and every pool or pond has to be preserved as humanity's universal reservoir without unjust reservation.

Water is never a private asset and ever a universal property. Every person born on the planet has thus an imperative claim to a just quantum of people's share of social uses of water. Every village, every town, every rural corner belongs to the world; and no monopoly, no cornering, no profiteering, no racketeering is permissible since homo sapiens cannot live without that gift of nature called water in as pure a form as what keeps life a human process. *The right to life is integral to the Universal Declaration of Human Rights. This is ancient non-negotiable jurisprudence.*

In this context, it is planetary patriotism, humanist nationalism, universal desideratum to insist on physical-moral, civilization equity, and non-negotiable imperative to demand and grant Nature's gift of water. Every village in India, every use of social water, has a human claim, a moral mandate, an equitable samaritarianism. This is *Gramswaraj*, village self-sufficiency and habitat humanism. Viewed in this social justice perspective and humanitarian *wettanschuung (vision of life)*, greedy globalisation of water as cornered wealth by Gargantuan corporates and planet-wide rapacious processes have to be subjected to social justice, humanitarian control of water resources and fair sharing of basic needs like water. Cadaverous corporates of the world's water resources by tactics of thanatonic terrorism is gross inhumanity. Parch our rivers, dry our underground storage, wipe out our global ecology and inhibit green environment of flowing water and collective dams to make money, and you are guilty of carnage and massive monstrosity.

Water is infinite power and humanity is its owner. 'I came, I saw and I was conquered' said Franklin D Roosevelt as he inaugurated the Hoover Dam (30 Sep., 1935)

A universal vision of water in infinite quantum is a human wonder sans which mankind survival has serious limitation. It is appropriate to begin with what great visionaries have looked at with worldwide prospects. Let me quote from a classic work:

> *I Came, I saw and I was conquered.*
>
> *President Franklin D. Roosevelt at Hoover Dam inauguration ceremony, 30 September, 1935*
>
> *Hoover Dam, an astonishingly graceful curve of concrete pushing back the Colorado River to fill its deep canyon on the Arizona-Nevada border, unleashed the big dam era. Wallace Stegner, the great novelist and essayist of the US West, was overawed when he visited the 221-metre-high dam in 1946, a decade after its completion:*
>
> *It is certainly one of the world's wonders, that sweeping cliff of concrete, those impetuous elevators, the labyrinth of tunnels, the huge power stations. Everything about the dam is marked by the immense smooth efficient beauty that seems peculiarly American.*

To many other writers, leaders, engineers, bureaucrats, nationalist and revolutionaries of the subsequent six decades, big dams have been potent symbols of both patriotic pride and the conquest of nature by human ingenuity. Providers of electric power, water and food; tamers of floods; greeners of the desert; guarantors of national independence—for most of our century, dams, the largest single structures built by humanity, have symbolized progress, whether that amorphous concept be the creation of capitalist wealth, the spreading of the fruits of socialism, or the great march of communism.

At the opening of the Nangal Canal in the Punjab in 1954, Pandit Jawaharlal Nehru, the first Prime Minister of India, described his 'strange exhilaration and excitement' at seeing the canal and the construction site of the Bhakra Dam. Nehru expressed his awe through nationalism mixed with religious reverence:

> *What a stupendous, magnificent work—a work which only that nation can take up which has faith and boldness! .... it has become symbol of a nation's will to march forward with strength, determination and courage..... as I walked around the (dam) site I thought that these days the biggest temple and mosque and gurdwara is the place where man works for the good of mankind. Which place can be greater than this, Bhakra-Nagal, where thousands and lakhs (Hundreds of thousands) of men have worked, have shed their blood and sweat and laid down their lives as well? Where can be a greater and holier place than this, which we can regard as higher?*

Massive dams are much more than simply machines to generate electricity and store water. They are concrete, rock and earth expressions of the dominant ideology of the technological age: icons of economic development and scientific progress to match nuclear bombs and motor cars. The builders of Hoover were advised by an architect to strip the dam of planned ornamentation in order to accentuate the visual power of its colossal concrete face.

The ecology and politics of large dams can gain practical dimension and dialectical directions only by humanitarian jurisprudence.

(Silenced Rivers by Patrick Mc Cully, Page 1-3)

The rule of law runs close to the rule of life and the Indian Constitution, in its humanist vision, has made environmental-ecological preservation a fundamental value. Rivers which are the source of potable and well water, sands that sustain riverbeds, river banks, greenery, bridges, coastal beaches which contain rare minerals and offshore sea beds which protect the littoral stretches, are a precious natural resource indispensable for human survival. Coastal seabeds if dredged for sand by builders may be deleterious to fishing wealth on which the fishing communities depend for livelihood. It follows that rivers, sands and coastal water have communal uses too cardinal to be neglected and too fundamental to be commercialized. Indeed, the higher jurisprudence of Article 21 of the Constitution (right to life) embraces the protection and preservation of Nature's gift without which life ceases to be viable and human rights become a *simulacrum*.

> *The Stockholm Declaration of United Nations on Human Environment evidences this seminal proposition:*
>
> *16. The natural resources of the earth, including the air, water, land, flora and fauna and especially representative samples of natural system, must be safeguarded for the benefit of present and future generations through careful planning or management, as appropriate. .... Nature*

conservation including wildlife must therefore receive importance in planning for economic development.

17. In *State of Tamil Nadu* v. *Hind Stone,* AIR 1981 SC 711 it has been observed as follows:

"Rivers, forests, minerals and such other resources constitute a nation's natural wealth. These resources are not to be frittered away and exhausted by any one generation. Every generation owes a duty to all succeeding generations to develop and conserve the natural resources of the nation in the best possible way. It is in the interest of mankind. It is in the interest of the nation."

18. During the Summit in Rio de Janeiro, UNESCO offered the following vision of the future.

"Every generation should leave water, air and soil resources as pure and unpolluted as when it came to earth. Each generation should leave undiminished all the species of minerals it found existing on earth."

Therefore if our rivers are raped by nocturnal extortion, if our sea sands are dredged mindless to fish culture and rare minerals, the havoc that will follow will be irretrievable and clandestine pillage will inflict permanent harm. The Madras High Court dealing with sand mining to slaughter point vividly described the horrendous calamity flowing from what may be described as mafia mining.

20. Sand mining has an adverse and destructive impact. Its disastrous effect is unimaginable. It has "crippled the riverine ecology and depleted the ground water table resulting in a nascent desertification process". It has affected the stability of riverbanks leading to loss of whole chunks of land making large areas flood prone. Drain channels to lakes, ponds, tanks and irrigation are blocked since there is no more water. The river bed goes down far below the receive canals. It has been identified as the main reason for the water crisis. The potable nature of available drinking water is affected as the sweet water acquifers (recharger and purifier) are destroyed by quarrying. It has increased the base flow of ground water to the rivers. It also causes sea water intrusion further than usual upstream through back water and river mouths. As enough sand does not reach the river mouths to make natural barriers along the coast, sea water and sand enter the back waters and rivers. This ultimately leads to saline intrusion into ground water. It has also seriously affected the structural stability of several bridges. River bridges and railway tracks are severely damaged by sand mining in violation of rules and lease deeds. Flooding of agricultural lands due to break in linkage between discharge/channels and river basins. There is destruction of Agriculture/Mangrove Eco System. Houses and buildings collapse due to erosion. The groundwater table goes down in all the river basins affecting agriculture severely. The sand mining permitted in private lands adjacent to riverbeds enables private owners to encroach the river bed illegally. Public roads are also seriously damaged. Drinking water has turned saline. Accidents occur due to heavy lorry traffic. The noise and dust thrown up by the lorries carrying quarried sand affect the people's health.

21. It takes millions of years for natural denudation of hard rock into sand. The current rate of extraction is far more than what nature is capable of replenishing. Alternative materials have to be found to replace river sand in construction activities. Excessive deepening of the river bed due to sand removal also accentuates soil erosion. Reduction in sediment supply from the rivers due to indiscriminate extraction will deplete the quantum of beach sand which in turn contributes to increased erosion along the coast line. (Paras 20 and 21 of the Judgment) (Contempt Application 561 of 2001)

The sand-depletion terrorism practiced on Nature by lawless looters inflicts an unconstitutional blow on the survival of the species. Articles 48A and 51A furnish the principles of jurisprudence which are fundamental to our governance under the Rule of Law. Section 3 of the Environment (Protection) Act, 1986 is geared to the great goal of preserving nature's bounty sans which societal survival will eventually be a mirage.

Water is a primary human need to deprive which is to deny the right to life. Indeed, the world may go to war on the struggle to control water. States dispute violently on the claim to water. People in cities and towns suffer desperately for want of drinking water. This gift of nature has to be equitably distributed for every human being to keep life going. But the water mafiosi which strangle sources of supply corruptly and make the right to life a misery. The State has a great duty vis-a-vis distribution of drinking water. Our rivers are sacred; so too our lakes and dams which serve several social uses. Aqua robbery by corporates is becoming common but is dereliction of State duty. One alleged instance in Kerala may be given illustratively although this crime against the community is multiplying:

The Hindustan Coca-Cola Beverages Pvt. Ltd established this unit in 1998-99 in approximately 40 acre plot (previously multi-cropped paddy lands) at Plachimada of Perumatty Panchayat in Chittur Taluk of Palakkad District, Kerala. About 70 permanent workers and 150 casual labourers are employed in the factory. On an average about 85 lorry loads of beverage production (Mirinda, Thums up, Coca Cola besides Kinley Mineral Water), each loads containing 550-600 cases and each case containing 24 300ml bottles leave the factory premises every day.

More than 60 borewells (beside 2 open wells) are sunk in the factory compound extracting some 15,00,000 liters of water. The site is located a few meters away from the main irrigation canal from the Moolathara barrage. The site is located about 3 kms away from the Meenkara dam reservoir, a few hundred meters west of Kambalathara and Vengalakkayam storage reservoirs and 2 kms away from the main Chitturpuzha (river).

Processing activities as purification of water, preparation of the bottled drinks, cleaning of bottles etc. generates a large quantum of contaminated waters and chemical waste besides plastic, paper, metallic and other solid waste.

The core principle of public law is: The State is a trustee of all natural resources and is under a legal duty to protect them. These rare resources are meant for public use and cannot be converted into private ownership. The *locus classicus* on this point is blazed in *M.C. Mehta* v. *Kamal Nath.* The relevant head note relating to environmental degradation runs thus:

The notion that public has a right to expect certain lands and natural areas to retain their natural characteristic is finding its way into the law of the land. The ancient Roman Empire developed a legal theory known as the "Doctrine of the Public Trust". The Public Trust Doctrine primarily rests on the principle that certain resources like air, water, sea and the forests have such a great importance to the people as a whole that it would be wholly unjustified to make them a subject of private ownership. *The said resources being a gift of nature, they should be made freely available to everyone irrespective of the status in life. The doctrine enjoins upon the Government to protect the resources for the enjoyment of the general public rather than to permit their use for private ownership or commercial purposes. Though the public trust doctrine under the English common law extended only to certain traditional uses such as navigation, commerce and fishing, the American Courts in recent cases expanded the concept of the public trust doctrine. The observations of the Supreme Court of California in Mono Lake case clearly show the judicial concern in protecting all ecologically important lands, for example fresh water, wetlands or riparian forests. The observation therein to the effect that the protection of ecological values is among the purposes of public trust, may give rise to an argument that the ecology and the environment protection is a relevant factor to determine which lands, waters or airs are protected by the public trust doctrine. The Courts in United States are finally beginning to adopt this reasoning and are expanding the public trust to encompass new types of lands and waters. There is no reason why the public trust doctrine should not be expanded to include all ecosystems operating in our natural resources. Our legal system—based on English common law—includes the public trust doctrine as part of its jurisprudence.* The State is the trustee of all natural resources which are by nature meant for public use and enjoyment. Public at large is the beneficiary of the sea-shore, running waters, airs, forests and ecologically fragile lands. *The State as a trustee is under a legal duty to protect the natural resources. These resources meant for public use cannot be converted into private ownership. Thus the Public Trust doctrine is a part of the land. (1997) 1 SCC P-338/339.*

A sound sum-up of the law by a California Court sets it out with striking brevity:

> *Thus, the public trust is more than an affirmation of State power to use public property for public purposes.* It is an affirmation of the duty of the State to protect the people's common heritage of streams, lakes, marshlands and tidelands, *surrendering that right of protection only in rare cases when the abandonment of that right is consistent with the purposes of the trust..........*

(1997) 1 SCC P-411/412.

In an exploitative society the struggle between members of the public for whom rivers and sands are their life breath and those who belong to the aqua-sand mafia the court has to use judge power to defend the people and the Constitution. The Supreme Court, in the Cricket Association of Bengal case, referred to *Airways as public property* to be utilized to the greatest public good without being allowed to be monopolised or hijacked by a few privileged persons of group. Waterways also attract the trustee doctrine. In the *M.I. Builder's* case (1999 SCC Page 464) the Court stressed the validity of the trustee doctrine. It is therefore settled law that the public have a paramount right to priority of use of river waters, sand beds and other ecologically fragile assets. The objective of the public trust has evolved in tandem with the changing public perception of the integral dependence of humanity and ecology.

The reverence of divine water in great leaps, and the glory of the Ganga in vast resources are wonders which are the world's celestial sources. What can be loftier and holier places than these waters from little wells to larger dams from small streams to broad canals?

Now we come to the menace of multinational corporations like the Colas consuming all the water, converting all the perennial springs, depriving the poor and the hungry, the mother and the child of water without which life becomes extinct! Plachimada, with its deep sources of water, other rivers of earth which supply us our basic needs and our snows melting to replenish our rivers—these are unusual phenomena—the cosmic wealth entire! If law of life to be sustained, corporates cannot deny every human life, every drop of water. Be you ever so large a corporate power, the law of life is above you. Man, woman and child *come first* and no corporate might, no technologic power, no economic cabal nor military arsenal can supersede people's rights. Plachimad, symbolic of man's right to pure water, which the bowles of Earth make available to mankind, is World Power for the well-being of mankind. If Peoples' waters are plundered, polluted, profiteered and converted into market, leaving the helpless to die of thirst the earth becomes a desert. Peoples everywhere must win. If *We the people of India*, one billion strong, claim Bharat's water resources properly planned, there never shall be global multinational Big Business in food and water. What we need today therefore is to arise and awake, make rivers speak, wells rise in levels, share what belongs to all through social justice. Let us unite, agitate and demand our right to water. No deep bore-well shall bully the poor, no Cola shall die water-less.

Journalists must stand united because the Fourth Estate has power over humanity's mind voice in our democratic order. Each according to his need, is the rule of water Corporate exploitation, denying human water and conquering market is the Cola cult. The Struggle to demand water which belongs to us all cannot wait any longer. Unite for water, all humanity, we shall change the world!

There is one thing stronger than all the armies in the world; and that is an idea whose time has come. (VICTOR HUGO).

RABINDRANATH TAGORE—THE ASSESSMENT OF A VISIONARY[1]

May I pay my homage to the rare sage whom advanced age cultural holism made world's guru dev and whose name gained global fame as the winner in 1913 of the first Nobel Prize for Asia and as a spiritual torch for mankind and held aloft the celestial wisdom for which ancient Bharat has been noted for millennia. This indefinable, indelible, ever illuminating personality—Rabindranath—is beyond materialist grasp and inarticulate by sensory faculties. Sublime philosopher, profound thinker, noetic paradigm, foremost among the eclectic literati and world's glorious visionaries, he excelled in every branch of letters. Rabindranath was too great for words, too creative for music and painting, love of Nature and aesthetic beauty. He is an omni-presence so long as Bharat belights civilization. Of him one may exquisitely apply the divine verses of Taittriya Upanishad:

Yato vacho nivartente
aprapya manasa saha
Anandam brahmano vidwan
na bibheti kadachana

(*Taittriya Upanishad. II Valli, IV Anuvaka*)

Wherefrom words turn back,

Together with the mind, not having attained
The bliss of Brahma, he who knows,
Fears not anytime at all.

(*Robert Ermest Hume, Oxford University Press, 1998*)

What statesmanly marvel of a man was he? What divinity in Incarnation? What spiritual-temporal riddle, what majesty and mystery

1. Reproduced from the convocation address at the Rabindra Bharati University delivered on 7th May, 2004.

de profundis was he? In the noblest semantic sense, I would call this versatile miracle 'a riddle, wrapped in a mystery inside an enigma'.

He wrote his first verse in the eighth year and the last on his last birthday (7th May 1941). The poet, even on the tragic day of surgery (July 30) dictated a few lethal lines:

> *The first day's sun*
> had asked
> at the manifestation of new being,
> who are you?
> He gets no answer.
> Year after year went by
> the last sun of the day
> the last question utters
> on the western seashore
> in the silent evening—
> who are you?
> *He gets no answer.*[2]

PART-II

Rabindranath Tagore is a message of the Infinite to a narrow world, a glorious gesture of ceaseless Creation amidst a contradictory note of destruction, a voice of harmony, humanity and realism beguiled by illusion nescience and ignorance. The very first stanza in the Gitanjali reveals the vision and unfolds the mission of the poet who is in search of truth too vast to be grasped by words and songs and colours of flowers. Let me quote:-

> *Thou hast made me endless, such is thy pleasure. This frail vessel thou emptiest again and again, and fillest it ever with fresh life.*
>
> *This little flute of a reed thou hast carried over hills and dales, and hast breathed through it melodies eternally new.*
>
> *At the immortal touch of thy hands my little heart loses its limits in joy and gives birth to utterance ineffable.*
>
> *Thy infinite gifts come to me only on these very small hands of mine. Ages pass, and still thou pourest, and still there is room to fill.*

That life and death are not opposite phenomena but a process, holistic and perennial. Look at the loveliest and most innocent expression of this grand idea:

> *I was not aware of the moment when I first crossed the threshold of this life.*
>
> *What was the power that made me open out into this vast mystery like a bud in the forest at midnight!*

2. Life of Tagore by Probhat Kumar Mukherji p-202.

When in the morning I looked upon the light I felt in a moment that I was no stranger in this world, that the inscrutable without name and form had taken me in its arms in the form of my own mother.

Even so, in death the same unknown will appear as ever known to me. And because I love this life, I know I shall love death as well.

The child cried out when from the right breast the mother takes it away, in the very next moment to find in the left one its consolation[3].

The transience of life is often lost on mundane humanity and myopic leaders are terribly afraid of death or loss of power. Death-bound littleness is not all that we are. This larger vision of Tagore is the poet's sense of the Absolute. To gain the meaning of his philosophy, to dive to the depths of his oceanic thought one must realize the spiritual urge expressed by W.B. Yeats, who, in its Introduction to the Gitanjali says: 'I read Rabindranath every day, read one line of his is to forget all the troubles of the world'. Tagore, like the Indian civilization, itself has been content to discover the soul and surrender himself to its spontaneity. All his great literature and grand poetry, his insightful stories and lofty novels are not only flowing from the deepest sources of ancient Indian culture but are marked by a beauty unexcelled by Chaucer and Shakespeare and Wordsworth. Writes W.B. Yeats:

An innocence, a simplicity that one does not find elsewhere in literature makes the birds and the leaves seem as near to him as they are near to children, and the changes of the seasons great events as before our thoughts had arisen between them and us. At times I wonder if he has it from the literature of Bengal or from religion, and at other times, remembering the birds alighting on his brother's hands, I find pleasure in thinking it hereditary, a mystery that was growing through the centuries like the courtesy of a Tristan or a Pelanore.[4]

All that I have said is the noblest product of the world's Himalayan mind. A whole universe of meaning is unfurled in lovely lines and magnificent prose through the matchless wisdom of his writings and lectures too inspirational to compare with contemporary literate.

PART-III

Rabindranath Tagore was a universal man, the humanist whose heart had no boundaries, the soul whose sensitivity touched every creature. The world today is so engrossed in materialism that the values we inherited from ancient Indian days have withered. Man, as man, does not exist and the beast in him survives. Charles Darwin has remarked:

---

3. Gitanjali XCV P-62.
4. Gitanjali – p-xvi.

We must, however, acknowledge, as it seems to me, that man with all his noble qualities,....still bears in his bodily frame the indelible stamp of his lowly origin.[5]

Gandhiji, the advocate of ahimsa rejected the idea of 'development' as a creation of material wealth or the satisfaction of insatiable, endlessly multiplied needs. 'In so far as we have made the modern materialistic craze our goal, so far are we going downhill in the path of progress'. Rabindranath, in his poems and passionate prose writings, warned the world against this vulgarity and violence, war, hatred and the consequent danger to humanity. The Buddha and Christ and the compassion they embodied were part of the teachings of Tagore.

In poem No. 88 addressed to Buddha, Tagore says:

The world today is wild with the
delirium of hatred,
the conflicts are cruel and unceasing in
anguish,
crooked are its paths, tangled its bonds
of greed.
....
Countries far and wide flaunt on their
foreheads
the blood-red mark of hatred.
Touch them with thy right hand,
make them one in spirit,
bring rhythm of beauty.

O Serene, O Free,
in thine immeasurable mercy and goodness
wipe away all dark stains from the heart
of this earth.

('Poems' published by Visva-Bharati, 2nd edition, pp. 123-125, reprinted 1946)

In this poem Tagore thinks of the sufferings not of his own country but of the whole world. He has an international outlook on life. A strong historical consciousness of things and events in the world is a special characteristic of his poetic creations during the period. This is evident in his poem No. 102 in which he denounces the subjugation of Africa by the white races:

5. Oxford Dictionary of Quotations – P-171/24.

The savage greed of the civilized stripped
naked its unashamed inhumanity.
You wept and your cry was smothered,
your forest traits became muddy with
tears and blood,
while the nailed boots of the robbers
left their indelible prints
along the history of your indignity.[6]

('Poems' (Visva-Bharati) 2nd edition, p. 159.)

Those who claim that globalisation, liberalization, privatization and marketisation are a progressive step must read and re-read the great poet and feel the horror of inhumanity our civilization has in its nadir reached.

Hypocrisy of rituals and pretentiousness of piety which hide modern man's miasmatic corruption find Tagore condemn cosmetic religion and concealed malignancy. There is magnificent poetry, there is lofty spirituality in Tagore's castigation of devotees of gods with no sympathy for humans:

> *Leave this chanting and singing and telling of beads! Whom dost thou worship in this lonely dark corner of a temple with doors all shut? Open thine eyes and see thy God is not before thee!*
>
> *He is there where the tiller is tilling the hard ground and where the pathmaker is breaking stones. He is with them in sun and in shower, and his garment is covered with dust. Put off thy holy mantle and even like him come down on the dusty soil!*
>
> *Deliverance? Where is this deliverance to be found? Our master himself has joyfully taken upon him the bonds of creation; he is bound with us all forever.*
>
> *Come out of thy meditations and leave aside thy flowers and incense! What harm is there if thy clothes become tattered and stained? Meet him and stand by him in toil and in sweat of they brow.*[7]

Those who go to church or ring the bells in temples or buy god by offerings must open their minds, feel the presence of God in everyone and hate torture and nuclear arsenals in the name of patriotism and peace and exploitation. Rabindranath is so poignantly relevant today where massacres and terrorisms make butchery the rule of life and human liberation alien to culture. Indeed, the great poet is a spiritual pacifist of such deep import that the writings, especially the Gitanjali, must be compulsory education for modern students and politicians. Says W.B. Yeats:

---

6. Realism and Humanism—An Assessment by Rabindranath Tagore, p-288/289.
7. Gitanjali – Stanza XI – P-6/7).

We write long books where no page perhaps has any quality to make writing a pleasure, being confident in some general design, just as we fight and make money and fill our heads with politics—all dull things in the doing—while Mr. Tagore, like the Indian civilization itself, has been content to discover the soul and surrender himself to its spontaneity.[8]

What a sinister syndrome of diabolic illusion deadens and darkens the soul of polished but violent civilization today! Material accumulations, himalayan fortunes, conquest of nations and seizure of power, hold riches and greed as achievements. Napoleon Bonaparte once said:

There is only one thing in this world, and that is to keep acquiring money and more money, power and more power. All the rest is meaningless.[9]

The truth is that wealth and avarice are prison, not glory, slavery, not liberty. I have not ever read so powerful a stanza as these lines in Gitanjali:

Prisoner, tell me, who was it that bound you?

'It was my master,' said the prisoner. 'I thought I could outdo everybody in the world in wealth and power, and I amassed in my own treasure-house the money due to my king. When sleep overcame me I lay upon the bed that was for my lord, and on waking up I found I was a prisoner in my own treasure-house.'

'Prisoner, tell me, who was it that wrought this unbreakable chain?'

'It was I,' said the prisoner, 'who forged this chain very carefully. I thought my invincible power would hold the world captive leaving me in a freedom undisturbed. Thus night and day I worked at the chain with huge fires and cruel hard strokes. When at last the work was done and the links were complete and unbreakable, I found that it held me in its grip.[10]

A world of the rich few are builders of prisons. If modern man is to abolish slavery and liberate his life from moral bondage he has to imbibe the quintessence of the profound values we see in the quoted verses. Iron bars are misunderstood as huge bank balance and gold unlimited. What a folly that moral bankrupts and felonious cupidity are confused with riches and captivity of cash accumulation. The mass majority is in hunger and the proprietarian is rolling in a restless soul. John Pilger writes:

As labour is cheapened and cast aside; as social legislation is eliminated and whole countries are transformed into one big plantation, one big mining camp, one big 'free trade' zone stripped of rights, sovereignty and wealth; as the rise of technology exacerbates class differences rather than abolishing them, increasing the vulnerability and tempo of work; as the guardians of

---

8. Gitanjali - Stanza III – P-xvi.
9. Hidden Agendas P-445.
10. Gitanjali – Stanza XXX1 p-18.

this faith reduce 'free speech' to esoteric jargon, the warnings now come from within the new orthodoxy itself.[11]

The world is changing for the worse. Rabindranath in his globophobic vision is pleading for a world order where humanity will survive, with the right to life in dignity, preserve as a human right of every human member. Tagore, a world teacher far ahead of his time had told us truths, the leaders and philosophers have yet to understand in their cosmic significance.

PART IV

Tagore was a poetic ambassador from heaven to humanity with a mandate for deliverance from craze for money, from appetite for acquisition. His priority was for Nature and man was part thereof. Not that man was secondary but humanity was an integral part of Creation. A conversation with Gandhiji and Tagore is revelatory of the revolutionary difference in emphasis which may perhaps be misleading. The truth is that for Rabindranath Universe has wholeness and, like Walt Whitman, could identify itself with all creatures on an equal basis. Let me site the exchange between the two great persons—Gandhiji and Gurudev.

> *"Once Gurudev Rabindranath Tagore asked Gandhiji, "Gandhiji are you so unromantic? When in the early dawn, the morning sun rises, does it not fill your heart with joy to see its reddish glow? When the birds sing does not your heart thrill with its divine music? When the rose opens its petals and blooms in the garden does its sight not bring cheer to your heart?"*
>
> *The Mahatma replied "Gurudev, I am not dumb or insensitive, as not to be moved by the beauty of the rose or the morning rays of the sun or the divine music of the birds. But what can I do? My one desire, my one anxiety, my one ambition is when shall I see the red tint of the rose on the cheeks of hungry naked millions of my people? When shall I hear the sweet and melodious song of the birds in place of their agonizing sights? When will such music come out of their soul and when will that day come when the light of the morning sun will illumine the heart of the common man in India? When will I see its luster and brightness on his face?"*

For Tagore divinity everywhere and compassion fraternal to all creatures. I recollect a small incident on this occasion. My wife and I travelled to Hungary long ago where, near the shores of the Boden Sea we beheld a tree. Close to it, Tagore had written a few lines which we read with great interest:

When I am no longer on this earth, my tree,
Let the ever-renewed leaves of thy spring
Murmur to the wayfarers,
The poet did love while he lived.

---

11. Hidden Agendas, P-609/610.

My visit was in the early 80's and I reproduce this poem in a local journal since I was so touched by the arboreal beauty which attracted the poet. Today, the wonder of a tree, the fragrance of a flower and the joy of the sky have no appeal to our mechanical man. Nature has to inscribe itself on the human soul. Tagore tried to rehumanize man. Look at Whitman who reminds us of this sweet sense of identity:

I believe a leaf of grass is no less than the
journey-work of the stars.
And the pismire is equally perfect, and a grain of
Sand, and the egg of the wren,
And the tree toad is a chef-d' oeuvre for the highest,
And the running blackberry would adorn the parlors of heaven.[12]

In the faces of men and women I see God, and in my
own face in the glass,
I find letters from God dropt in the street, and every
one is sign'd by God's name,
And I leave them where they are for I know that
wheresoe'er I go.
Others will punctually come for ever and ever.[13]

We have lost our innocence as humans but must recapture the world of Tagore and his sense of humanism. Not that man does not matter but like our ancients a dynamic divinity in every creature has to inform our consciousness. Let me quote Dr. Bhattacharya to drive home my point. Ancient India worshipped man and sub-human fellow-beings and Rabindranath Tagore was part of this cultural heritage.

Our epics like the Mahabharata and Ramayana divinised even animals. However, Tagore did give high place to the human avatar:

In innumerable songs he has expressed his deep love for Man, Nature and their affectionate touch and has even lamented how he would miss them after his death. He writes,

"I have loved the world
And jave wrapped it within my heart in numberless folds.
The light and shadow of night and morn
Have flooded my consciousness,
Till my life and my world have become one.
I have loved the light of the world,
Therefore I love this life.
Yet I know,
I shall have to take leave of it one day.
My voice will no more blossom in this air,

12. Oxford Quotations, P-570:21.

13. Oxford Quotations, P-571:4.

Nor my eyes bathe in this light.
My heart will not rush forth to greet the early dawn,
Nor will the starry night whisper her secrets
Into my ears." (A Flight of Swans—p.39) [14]

Tagore on Religion of Man is a lesson for the current corrupted soul and vulgarised mind of the human being who has ceased to be human and has surrendered to worldly pleasures and violent pressures. Our poet loved universal man and so, in his famous poem "Africa", he greeted the dawn of a new civilization, the spirit inculcating courage and determination to build up a new society where freedom reigns supreme. The cultural cohesion and global unification were Tagore's great contribution. Alas, every religion is fighting every other today. Schematic bigotry and divisive butcheries bleeding nations make the world a lunatic asylum 'red in tooth and claw' where God is the first casualty. In Religion of Man, Tagore puts his thought emphatically:

Man must triumph in his search for eternal truth. And what is that truth? That is pure human love. So, man must know another man. Man must love another man. This world must be one global family.

The developing nations have a new message of hope and aspiration from the poet.

Tagore addresses the young developing nations with a special message. He writes.

"Through the troubled history of man
comes sweeping a blind fury of
destruction
and the towers of civilization topple
down to dust.
In the chaos of moral nihilism
are trampled underfoot by marauders
the best treasures of Man heroically won
by the martyrs for ages.
Come, young nations,
proclaim the fight for freedom,
raise up the banner of invincible faith.
Build bridges with your life across the
gaping earth blasted by hatred,
and march forward."[15]

The dignity and divinity of man and the presence of its value in every human being makes humanity one and the global family unitive. Indeed, for Tagore the animate and inanimate are all part of the Universal Power. For him God sleeps in the mineral, wakes in the vegetable, walks in the animal and thinks in man. Only this vision can save the peoples of the world from felonious fragmentation and social disruption. The western

14. Relevance of Tagore, P-21.
15. Relevance of Tagore, P-25.

civilization has imposed the monoculture of the mind on all the peoples of the earth with an imperious and imperial authority which makes nations 'neo-slaves'. Therefore, we need an insurrection of subjugated knowledge against the devourment of capitalism. If democratic pluralism and lovely humanism are the richness of our great heritage, to preserve this treasure is universal patriotism. Before I conclude we must read for you, Tagore's message to his fellow beings:

Man must triumph in his search for eternal truth.
And what is that truth? That is pure human love.
So, man must know another man. Man must love another man. This world must be one global family.
The developing nations have a new message of hope and aspiration from the poet.
Tagore addressed the young developing nations with a special message. He writes:
Through the troubled history of man
comes sweeping a blind fury of destruction
and the towers of civilization topple
down to dust.
In the chaos of moral nihilism
are tramled underfoot by marauders
he best treasures of Man heroically won
by the martyrs for ages.
Come, young nations,
proclaim the fight for freedom
raise up the banner of invincible faith.
Build bridges with your life across the
gaping earth blasted by hatred,
and march forward.[16]

Rabindranath Tagore has burning relevance to homo sapiens for this mad millennium and decadent culture. Here is one of the greatest poets of the contemporary world to save humanity from the crisis of civilization.

Was he a poet of the people? He was. Indeed, he was a creative power who saw through his spiritual eyes the civilizations of ages to discover the world was temporal and spiritual, and had a unique focus a new dawn, a great awakening a dynamic dialectic, a humanity whose divinity gave validity to joy which is the birthright of existence. Rabindranath was a personality in whom divine descent and human ascent had confluence.

Blood and tears mar nations and peace is the first desideratum for survival of human kind. Can there be a more anguished call than Tagore's poem?

16. Relevance of Tagore, P-25.

"The war drums are sounded
..
They pray for success;
or they must raise weeping wailing
in their wake, sever ties of love,
plant flags on the ashes of desolated
homes,
devastate the centers of culture
and shrines of beauty,
mark red with blood their trail
across green meadows and populous
markets..

They will punctuate each thousand of
te maimed and killed
wth the trumpeting of their triumph,
arouse demon's mirth at the sight
of the limbs torn bleeding from women
and children; ....
and therefore they march to the temple
of Buddha, the compassionate,
to claim his blessings,
while loud beats the drum rat-a-tat
and earth trembles.[17]

The finest lines of literature of the noblest thoughts expressive human rights and the most sublime ideas which not all the armies in the world can destroy are found in the Gitanjali which is Tagore's testament to humanity:

Where the mind is without fear and the head is held high;
Where knowledge is free;
Where the world has not been broken up into fragments by narrow domestic walls;
Where words come out from the depth of truth;
Where tireless striving stretches its arms towards perfection;
Where the clear stream of reason has not lost its way into the dreary desert sand of dead habit;
Where the mind is led forward by thee into ever-widening
thought and action—
Into that heaven of freedom, my Father, let my country awake.[18]

Rabindranath Tagore, among the world's greatest poet in whom East and West met millennia merged in the modern centuries left for us in boundless verses the manifesto of humanity which will ever remain the hope of the world emanating from Rabindra Bharati the nidus of glorious Indian wisdom.

17. Realism and Humanism—An Assessment, P-290/291.

18. Gitanjali—Stanza, XXXV: P-20.